Back in You with Lean and Green Diet

3 Books in 1 | Healthy Guide for Young People with Easy to Prepare Budget Friendly Recipes to improve Your Performance and Weight Loss Quickly

By Lorely McAdams

Table of Contents

Lean and Green Diet Cookbook for Men

Lean and Green Diet Cookbook for Athletes

Lean and Green Diet Cookbook On a Budget

Lean and Green Diet Cookbook for Men

Dr. McAdams Strong Diet Plan | A New Way to Sculpt Your Body and Lose Weight with Delicious, Affordable and Easy-to-Prepare Recipes

By Lorely McAdams

Chapter 1 - Introduction

The lean and green diet has quickly gained popularity, mainly because it is a healthy diet that allows you to quickly lose weight, but these are just some of its benefits. Here is a description of the lean and green diet and its benefits for men's health.

Basically, the lean and green diet consists of a high protein intake and a moderate carbohydrate intake, avoiding the intake of trans fats and sugars. Focusing on lean protein and good carbohydrates.

In fact, did you know that a high protein intake is related to an increase in libido, this is due to two factors, on the one hand it gives you the necessary energy without exceeding the caloric intake and on the other hand proteins help you to improve the production of testosterone, which can also increase your libido and improve the quality of sperm, increasing fertility and increasing muscle mass.

So, you will be able to develop your muscles and your libido at the same time, it is the perfect combination.

Main benefits for men.

The lean and green diet brings great benefits for everyone, especially for men, for example:
- *As mentioned in the previous section, it increases your libido and your fertility since it is proven that proteins improve sperm quality.*
- *Auxiliary for the development of muscles, it is ideal for thin men because it will make you have muscle mass and if you are a thick man it will allow you to shape your muscles, for which it is important to accompany it with an exercise routine and you will see better results.*
- *It is an excellent aid in weight loss with short term results, because it reduces calorie and carbohydrate intake through a proven meal plan and allows for portion-controlled snacks.*
- *Improves blood pressure because with this diet you have a low sodium intake (2,300 mg of sodium per day approximately).*
- *Prevents diabetes, as it is a balanced diet that promotes protein intake and avoids the consumption of sugars. Did you know that men are more prone to develop diabetes, according to the Centers for Disease Control and Prevention (CDC) 745 thousand men in the USA suffer from diabetes (according to a report published in 2020).*

As you will see there are many benefits, and the best of all is easy to follow, so take the step and improve your life

Chapter 2 -   Breakfast Recipes

1) Tomato and Avocado Omelet

Preparation Time: 5 Minutes   **Cooking Time: 5 Minutes**   **Servings: 1**

Ingredients:

- 2 Eggs
- ¼ avocado, diced
- 4 Cherry tomatoes, halved
- 1 tablespoon cilantro, chopped
- Squeezed lime juice
- Pinch of salt

Directions:

⇒ Put together the avocado, tomatoes, cilantro, lime juice, and salt in a small bowl, then mix well and set aside.

⇒ Warm a medium non-stick skillet on medium heat, whisk the eggs until frothy and add to the pan. Move the eggs around gently with a rubber spatula until they begin to set.

⇒ Scatter the avocado mixture over half of the omelet. Remove from heat, and slide the omelet onto a plate as you fold it in half.

⇒ Serve immediately.

Nutrition: Calories: 433 kcal Protein: 25.55g Fat: 32.75g Carbohydrates: 10.06g

2) Vegan-Friendly Banana Bread

Preparation Time: 15 Minutes   **Cooking Time: 40 Minutes**   **Servings: 4-6**

Ingredients:

- 2 Ripe bananas, mashed
- 1/3 Cup brewed coffee
- 3 Tbsp. Chia seeds
- 6 Tbsp. Water
- ½ Cup soft vegan butter
- ½ Cup maple syrup
- 2 Cups flour
- 2 Tsp. Baking powder
- 1 Tsp. Cinnamon powder
- 1 Tsp. Allspice
- ½ Tsp. Salt

Directions:

⇒ Set the oven at 350°F.

⇒ Bring the chia seeds in a small bowl, then soak them with 6 Tbsp. of water. Stir well and set aside.

⇒ In a mixing bowl, mix using a hand mixer the vegan butter and maple syrup until it turns fluffy. Add the chia seeds along with the mashed bananas.

⇒ Mix well, and then add the coffee.

⇒ Meanwhile, sift all the dry ingredients (flour, baking powder, cinnamon powder, allspice, and salt) and then gradually add into the bowl with the wet ingredients.

⇒ Combine the ingredients well, and then pour over a baking pan lined with parchment paper.

⇒ Place in the oven to bake for at least 30-40 minutes or until the toothpick comes out clean after inserting in the bread.

⇒ Allow the bread to cool before serving.

Nutrition: Calories: 371 kcal Protein: 5.59g Fat: 16.81g Carbohydrates: 49.98g

3) Cinnamon Pancakes With Coconut

Preparation Time: 5 Minutes   **Cooking Time: 18 Minutes**   **Servings:2**

Ingredients:

- 2 Organic eggs
- 1 Tbsp. Almond flour
- 2 oz. Cream cheese
- ¼ Cup shredded coconut and more for garnishing
- ½ Tbsp. Erythritol

- 1/8 Tsp. Salt
- 1 Tsp. Cinnamon
- 4 Tbsp. Stevia
- ½ Tbsp. Olive oil

Directions:

⇒ Crack eggs in a bowl, beat until fluffy and then beat in flour and cream cheese until smooth.

⇒ Add remaining ingredients and then stir until well combined.

⇒ Take a frying pan, place it over medium heat, grease it with oil, then pour in half of the batter and cook for 3 to 4 minutes per side until the pancake has cooked and nicely golden brown.

⇒ Transfer pancake to a plate and cook another pancake in the same manner by using the remaining batter.

⇒ Sprinkle coconut on top of cooked pancakes and serve.

Nutrition: Calories: 575 Total Fat: 51g Total Carbs: 3.5g Protein: 19g

4) Huevos Rancheros

Preparation Time: 5 Minutes   **Cooking Time: 5 Minutes**   **Servings:2**

Ingredients:

- (2) 8-inch Whole-wheat tortillas
- 2 Hard-boiled eggs, sliced
- 2 Slices of Canadian bacon or ham

- 1-ounce Slices of cheddar cheese
- 2 Tbsp. Salsa

Directions:

⇒ Prepare the hard-boiled eggs.

⇒ Put one tortilla on a plate, top with a slice of Canadian bacon or ham, the sliced egg, and a slice of cheddar cheese. Roll the tortilla up

⇒ Repeat with the remaining ingredients to prepare the second burrito.

⇒ Serve immediately with 1 Tbsp. Salsa.

Nutrition: Calories: 741 kcal Protein: 36.12g Fat: 30.75g Carbohydrates: 79.37g

5) Flaxseed Porridge With Cinnamon

Preparation Time: 10 Minutes   **Cooking Time: 5 Minutes**   **Servings:4**

Ingredients:

- 1 sp. Cinnamon
- 1½ Tsp. Stevia
- 1 Tbsp. Unsalted butter
- 2 Tbsp. Flaxseed meal

- 2 Tbsp. Flaxseed oatmeal
- ½ Cup shredded coconut
- 1 Cup heavy cream
- 2 Cups of water

Directions:

⇒ Take a medium pot, place it over low heat, add all the ingredients in it, stir until mixed and bring the mixture to boil.

⇒ When the mixture has boiled, remove the pot from heat, stir it well and divide it evenly between four bowls.

⇒ Let porridge rest for 10 minutes until slightly thicken, and then serve.

Nutrition: Calories: 171 Total Fat: 16g Total Carbs: 6g Protein: 2g

6) Pumpkin & Banana Waffles

Preparation Time: 15 Minutes   **Cooking Time: 5 Minutes**   **Servings:4**

Ingredients:

- ½ Cup almond flour
- ½ Cup coconut flour
- 1 Tsp. baking soda
- 1½ Teaspoons ground cinnamon
- ¾ Teaspoons ground ginger
- ½ Teaspoon ground cloves
- ½ Teaspoon ground nutmeg

- Salt, to taste
- 2 Tablespoons olive oil
- 5 Large organic eggs
- ¾ Cup almond milk
- ½ Cup pumpkin puree
- 2 Medium bananas, peeled and sliced

Directions:

⇒ Preheat the waffle iron, and after that, grease it.

⇒ In a sizable bowl, mix together flours, baking soda, and spices.

⇒ In a blender, put the remaining ingredients and pulse till smooth.

⇒ Add the flour mixture and pulse till

⇒ In the preheated waffle iron, add the required quantity of mixture.

⇒ Cook approximately 4-5 minutes.

⇒ Repeat using the remaining mixture.

Nutrition: Calories: 357.2 Fat: 28.5g Carbohydrates: 19.7g Fiber: 4g Protein: 14g

7) Banana Cashew Toast

Preparation Time: 10 minutes   **Cooking Time: 0 minutes**   **Servings:3**

Ingredients:

- 1 Cup roasted cashews (unsalted)
- 4 Pieces of oat bread
- 2 Ripe medium-sized bananas
- Dash of salt
- Pinch of cinnamon
- 2 Tsp. Flax meals
- 2 Tsp. Honey

Directions:

⇒ Peel and slice the bananas into ½-inch pieces. Toast the bread. In a food processor, puree the salt and cashews until they are smooth. Use the puree as a spread on the toasts.

⇒ On top of the spread, arrange a layer of bananas. Add flax meals and a dash of cinnamon on top of the bananas. Top the toast with honey.

Nutrition: Calories: 634 kcal Protein: 13.42g Fat: 47.6g Carbohydrates: 48.02g

8) Apple Oatmeal

Preparation Time: 10 Minutes   **Cooking Time: 5 Minutes**   **Servings:2**

Ingredients:

- 2/3 Cups rolled oats
- 1 Cup water
- 1 Teaspoon ground cinnamon
- 1 Cup of any non-fat milk, coconut milk, or almond milk (optional)
- ¼ Cup fresh apple juice
- 1 Chopped apple (unpeeled or peeled)

Directions:

⇒ Place the water, juice, and apple in a deep pot. Bring to boil over medium heat.

⇒ Add the oats and cinnamon. Bring to another boil.

⇒ Lower the heat temperature and let it simmer for 3 minutes or until it is thick.

⇒ Divide the serving into two and serve with milk.

Nutrition: Calories: 277 kcal Protein: 12.69g Fat: 7.69g Carbohydrates: 52.71g

9) Strawberry-Oat-Chocolate Chip Muffins

Preparation Time: 10 Minutes   **Cooking Time: 23 Minutes**   **Servings: 12**

Ingredients:

- 1¼ C. Whole wheat pastry flour
- 1 C. Rolled oats
- ¾ Tsp. Baking soda
- ½ Tsp. Baking powder
- ¼ Tsp. Salt
- 1 Heaping cup bananas (about 2 to 3 large very ripe bananas)
- 1 Tbsp. Extra virgin olive oil
- 1 Tbsp. Honey or agave nectar

- 1 Tsp. Vanilla
- 1 Egg
- 1 Egg white
- 1/3 C. Nonfat plain Greek yogurt
- ½ C. Unsweetened vanilla almond milk
- 1/3 C. mini chocolate chips
- 2/3 C. Diced strawberries
- 12 Thin slices of strawberries (about 3-4 strawberries) for garnish, if desired

Directions:

⇒ Set the oven to 350°F and lightly grease a standard 12-cup muffin pan or grease with paper liners. In a large-sized mixing bowl, combine flour, oats, baking powder, baking soda, chips, and salt. Stir to blend. Set aside the two tablespoons of the mixture.

⇒ In a separate huge mixing bowl, combine together the mashed banana, olive oil, honey, and vanilla. Next, beat in the egg and egg white and beat until combined. Now add in Greek yogurt and almond milk and beat with an electric mixer on low until smooth.

⇒ Gradually put wet ingredients to dry ingredients and blend until just combined, but don't over mix the batter as it will make the muffins firm.

⇒ Fill each muffin cup 2/3 full of batter. Gently tap the pan on the counter to even out the batter. Place a thin slice of strawberry onto each muffin, if desired. Put the pan in the oven, then cook for 18 to 23 minutes, place a toothpick in the middle of the muffins, and check if it comes out clean. Take off from the oven and let sit for 5 to 10 minutes in the pan before placing on a cooling rack.

Nutrition: Calories: 91 kcal Protein: 4.02g Fat: 2.63g Carbohydrates: 16.31g

10) Oatmeal-Applesauce Muffins

Preparation Time: 15 Minutes   **Cooking Time: 25 Minutes**   **Servings: 12**

Ingredients:

Topping:

- 1/4 Cup rolled oats
- 1 Tbsp. brown sugar
- 1/8 Tsp. cinnamon
- 1 Tbsp. unsalted butter, melted

Muffins:

- 1 C. Old fashioned rolled oats (not instant)
- 1 C. Non-fat milk
- 1 C. Whole wheat flour
- ½ C. Brown sugar

- ½ C. Unsweetened applesauce
- 2 egg Whites
- 1 tsp. Baking powder
- ½ tsp. Baking soda
- ½ Tsp. Salt
- ½ Tsp. Cinnamon
- ½ Tsp. Sugar
- Raisins or nuts (opt.)

Directions:

⇒ To begin, first, presoak the oats in milk for 1 hour.

⇒ Set the oven to 400°F, then grease a standard 12-cup muffin pan with cooking spray or use paper liners.

⇒ In a mixing bowl, combine oat-milk mixture, applesauce, and egg whites. Blend well and set aside.

⇒ In a separate bowl, put together the whole wheat flour, brown sugar, baking powder, baking soda, salt, sugar, and cinnamon, then mix.

⇒ Gradually put wet ingredients to dry ingredients and blend until just combined, but don't over mix the batter as it will make the muffins firm. Add raisins or nuts (opt.).

⇒ Prepare to top, in a small bowl, whisk together the oats, brown sugar, and cinnamon. Add in melted butter and toss gently with a fork to coat ingredients.

⇒ Fill each muffin cup 2/3 full of batter. Sprinkle topping on the top of each batter-filled muffin cup. Tap the pan gently on the counter to even out the batter. Place the muffin pan in the oven and cook for 20 to 25 minutes or until a toothpick put in the middle of one of the muffins comes out clean. Take off from the oven and let sit for 5 minutes before serving.

Nutrition: Calories: 115 kcal Protein: 5.06g Fat: 2.57g Carbohydrates: 22.33g

11) Barley Breakfast Bowl With Lemon Yogurt Sauce

Preparation Time: 10 Minutes   **Cooking Time: 0 Minutes**   **Servings:2**

Ingredients:

- 1½ C. Cooked barley, keep warm
- 1 C. Mung bean sprouts (or preferred variety)
- 1/3 C. Cotija cheese or queso fresco, crumbled
- ¼ C. Sliced almonds, toasted
- ¼ Tsp. Kosher salt
- 1 Small avocado, peeled/pitted, and flesh diced or sliced
- ½ Tsp. Sea salt
- ¼ Tsp. Fresh ground black pepper

- Lemon Yogurt Sauce
- 1 C. Greek plain yogurt
- 1 Tsp. Lemon zest, finely grated
- 1 Tsp. Fresh lemon juice
- ¼ C. Fresh mint or parsley, chopped
- Sea salt, to taste
- Fresh ground black pepper, to taste

Directions:

⇒ First, prepare the Lemon Yogurt Sauce. Combine the plain yogurt, lemon zest and juice, fresh mint or parsley, and salt & pepper in a bowl and stir to blend well. Cover and refrigerate until ready to serve.

⇒ Next, prepare the barley bowl. In a small mixing bowl, combine the barley, bean sprouts, cheese, almonds, and salt. Stir to mix well.

⇒ Divide the barley mixture into two serving bowls. Top each barley bowl with two tablespoons of Lemon yogurt sauce and avocado. Put a pinch of salt and pepper to taste, serve, and enjoy!

Nutrition: Calories: 432 kcal Protein: 13.6g Fat: 23.37g Carbohydrates: 47.62g

12) Blueberry-Bran Breakfast Sundae

Preparation Time: 10 Minutes   **Cooking Time: 0 Minutes**   **Servings:2**

Ingredients:

- 2 Cups Vanilla or lemon-flavored low-fat yogurt (preferably Greek yogurt) or flavor of choice.
- 2 Cups Bran flakes
- 1/4 Cup Fresh blueberries

- 2 Tbsp. Sliced almonds (or nuts of choice)
- 2 Tbsp. Chopped pecans (or nuts of choice)
- 2 Tbsp. Dried cranberries (or dried or fresh fruit of choice)

Directions:

⇒ In a bowl, place 1 cup of yogurt and one cup of bran flakes.

⇒ Top with 1/8 cup of fresh blueberries, followed by one tablespoon each of sliced almonds, chopped pecans, and dried cranberries.

⇒ Repeat using the remaining ingredients to make a second serving. Serve immediately.

Nutrition: Calories: 420 kcal Protein: 21.12g Fat: 13.58g Carbohydrates: 59.8g

13) Banana-Oatmeal Vegan Pancakes

Preparation Time: 5 Minutes   **Cooking Time: 5 Minutes**   **Servings: 12**

Ingredients:

- 1¼ C. Old fashioned oats
- ½ C. Organic whole wheat flour
- 2 Tsp. Baking powder
- ½ Tsp. Sea salt
- 1½ C. Soymilk
- 2 Ripe bananas

Directions:

⇒ To begin, heat griddle or skillet over medium heat.

⇒ Next, place all ingredients, except for the banana, into a blender and process until smooth. Add the bananas to the blender and blend until smooth.

⇒ Lightly grease the griddle with olive or coconut oil, then pour ¼ c. of batter onto griddle and cook for at least 2 to 3 minutes, then flip and cook for about 2 minutes or up when the pancake is golden brown and cooked through.

⇒ Repeat the process with the remaining batter.

Nutrition: Calories: 59 kcal Protein: 3.49g Fat: 1.48g Carbohydrates: 11.52g

14) Omelette à la Margherita

Preparation Time: 10 Minutes   **Cooking Time: 20 Minutes**   **Servings: 2**

Ingredients:

- 3 Eggs
- 50g of Parmesan cheese
- 2 Tbsp. heavy cream
- 1 Tbsp. olive oil
- 1 Teaspoon oregano
- Nutmeg
- Salt
- Pepper

For covering:

- 3 - 4 Stalks of basil
- 1 Tomato
- 100g of Grated mozzarella

Directions:

⇒ Mix the cream and eggs in a medium bowl.

⇒ Add the grated parmesan, nutmeg, oregano, pepper, salt, and stir everything.

⇒ Heat the oil in a pan.

⇒ Add ½ of the egg and cream to the pan.

⇒ Let the omelet set over medium heat, turn it, and then remove it.

⇒ Repeat with the second half of the egg mixture.

⇒ Cut the tomatoes into slices and place them on top of the omelets.

⇒ Scatter the mozzarella over the tomatoes.

⇒ Place the omelets on a baking sheet.

⇒ Cook at 180 degrees for 5 to 10 minutes.

⇒ Then take the omelets out and decorate them with the basil leaves.

Nutrition: Kcal: 402 Carbohydrates: 7g Protein: 21g Fat: 34g

15) Peanut Butter-Banana Muffins

Preparation Time: 15 Minutes   **Cooking Time: 25 Minutes**   **Servings: 12**

Ingredients:

- 1½ C. All-purpose flour
- 1 C. Old-fashioned oats
- 1 Tsp. Baking powder
- ½ Tsp. Baking soda
- ½ Tsp. Salt
- 2 Tbsp. Applesauce

- ¾ C. Light brown sugar
- 2 Large eggs
- 1 C. Mashed banana (about 3 bananas)
- 6 Tbsp. Creamy peanut butter
- 1 C. Low-fat buttermilk

Directions:

⇒ Bring a small non-stick skillet on medium heat and spray lightly with cooking spray. Add in the bell pepper and onion and sauté for 1 to 2 minutes, or until both are tender and the onion translucent.

⇒ In a small bowl, crack in eggs and whisk. Add in milk; whisk until well-blended. Pour eggs into the pan and cook, frequently stirring until eggs are scrambled to your liking.

⇒ To serve, spoon half the egg mixture into each tortilla, wrap, and serve. Try serving with a side of fresh fruit for a complete meal.

Nutrition: Calories: 187 kcal Protein: 8.12g Fat: 6.25g Carbohydrates: 27.82g

Chapter 3 -   Side Recipes

16) Tuna Spinach Casserole

Preparation Time: 30 Minutes   **Cooking Time: 25 Minutes**   **Servings: 8**

Ingredients:

- 18 Ounces mushroom soup, creamy
- ½ Cup milk
- 12 Ounces white tuna, solid, in water, drained
- 8 Ounces crescent dinner rolls, refrigerated
- 8 Ounces egg noodles, wide, uncooked
- 8 Ounces cheddar cheese, shredded
- 9 Ounces spinach, chopped, frozen, thawed, drained
- 2 Teaspoons lemon peel grated

Directions:

⇒ Preheat the oven to 350 degrees Fahrenheit.

⇒ Put cooking spray onto a glass baking dish (11x7-inch).

⇒ Follow package directions in cooking and draining the noodles.

⇒ Stir the cheese (1 ½ cups) and soup together in a skillet heated on medium. Once cheese melts, stir in your noodles, milk, spinach, tuna, and lemon peel. Once bubbling, pour into the prepped dish.

⇒ Unroll the dough and sprinkle with remaining cheese (½ cup). Roll up dough and pinch at the edges to seal. Slice into eight portions and place over the tuna mixture.

⇒ Put all in the Air-fry mode for twenty to twenty-five minutes.

Nutrition: Calories: 400 Fat: 10g Protein: 20g Carbohydrates: 30g

17) Lean and Green Chicken Pesto Pasta

Preparation Time: 5 Minutes   **Cooking Time: 15 Minutes**   **Servings: 1**

Ingredients:

- 3 Cups of raw kale leaves
- 2 Tbsp. of olive oil
- 2 Cups of fresh basil
- 1/4 teaspoon salt
- 3 Tbsp. Lemon juice
- Three garlic cloves
- 2 Cups of cooked chicken breast
- 1 Cup of baby spinach
- 6 Ounces of uncooked chicken pasta
- 3 Ounces of diced fresh mozzarella
- Basil leaves or red pepper flakes to garnish

Directions:

⇒ Start by making the pesto; add the kale, lemon juice, basil, garlic cloves, olive oil, and salt to a blender and blend until smooth.

⇒ Add salt and pepper to taste.

⇒ Cook the pasta and strain off the water. Reserve 1/4 cup of the liquid.

⇒ Get a bowl and mix everything, the cooked pasta, pesto, diced chicken, spinach, mozzarella, and the reserved pasta liquid.

⇒ Sprinkle the mixture with additional chopped basil or red paper flakes (optional).

⇒ Now your salad is ready. You may serve it warm or chilled. Also, it can be taken as a salad mix-ins or as a side dish. Leftovers should be stored in the refrigerator inside an air-tight container for 3-5 days.

Nutrition: Calories: 244 Protein: 20.5g Carbohydrates: 22.5g Fats: 10g

18) Open-Face Egg Sandwiches With Cilantro-Jalapeño Spread

Preparation Time: 20 Minutes   **Cooking Time: 10 Minutes**   **Servings: 2**

Ingredients:

For the cilantro and jalapeño spread:

- 1 Cup filled up fresh cilantro leaves and stems (about a bunch)
- 1 Jalapeño pepper, seeded and roughly chopped
- ½ Cup extra-virgin olive oil
- ¼ Cup pepitas (hulled pumpkin seeds), raw or roasted
- 2 Garlic cloves, thinly sliced
- 1 Tablespoon freshly squeezed lime juice
- 1 Teaspoon kosher salt

For the eggs:

- 4 Large eggs
- ¼ Cup milk
- ¼ to ½ Teaspoon Kosher Salt
- 2 Tablespoons butter

For the sandwich:

- 2 Bread slices
- 1 Tablespoon butter
- 1 Avocado, halved, pitted, and divided into slices
- Microgreens or sprouts for garnish

Directions:

⇒ To make the cilantro and jalapeño spread:

⇒ In a food processor, combine the cilantro, jalapeño, oil, pepitas, garlic, lime juice, and salt. Whirl until smooth. Refrigerate it if preparing in advance; otherwise, set it aside.

⇒ To make the eggs:

⇒ In a medium bowl, whisk the eggs, milk, and salt.

⇒ Dissolve the butter in a skillet over low heat, swirling to coat the bottom of the pan. Pour in the whisked eggs.

⇒ Cook until they begin to set, using a heatproof spatula, push them to the sides, allowing the uncooked portions to run into the bottom of the skillet.

⇒ Continue until the eggs are set.

⇒ To assemble the sandwiches:

⇒ Toast the bread and spread it with butter.

⇒ Spread a spoonful of the cilantro-jalapeño spread on each piece of toast. Top each with scrambled eggs.

⇒ Arrange avocado over each sandwich and garnish with microgreens.

Nutrition: Calories: 711 Total fat: 4g Cholesterol: 54mg Fiber: 12g Protein: 12g Sodium: 327mg

19) Lemony Parmesan Salmon

Preparation Time: 10 Minutes   **Cooking Time: 25 Minutes**   **Servings: 4**

Ingredients:

- 2 Tablespoons butter, melted
- 2 Tablespoons green onions, sliced thinly
- 3/4 Cups breadcrumbs, white, fresh
- 1/4 Teaspoon thyme leaves, dried

- 1 Piece salmon fillet, 1 ¼-pound
- 1/4 Teaspoon salt
- 1/4 Cup parmesan cheese, grated
- 2 Teaspoons lemon peel, grated

Directions:

⇒ Preheat the oven to 350 degrees Fahrenheit.

⇒ Mist cooking spray onto a baking pan (shallow). Fill with pat-dried salmon—brush salmon with butter (1 tablespoon) before sprinkling with salt.

⇒ Combine the breadcrumbs with onions, thyme, lemon peel, cheese, and remaining butter (1 tablespoon).

⇒ Cover salmon with the breadcrumb mixture. Air-fry for fifteen to twenty-five minutes.

Nutrition: Calories: 290 Fat: 10g Protein: 30g Carbohydrates: 0g

20) Chicken Omelet

Preparation Time: 5 Minutes   **Cooking Time: 15 Minutes**   **Servings: 1**

Ingredients:

- 2 Bacon slices; cooked and crumbled
- 2 Eggs
- 1 Tablespoon homemade mayonnaise
- 1 Tomato; chopped.
- 1-Ounce rotisserie chicken; shredded

- 1 Teaspoon mustard
- 1 Small avocado; pitted, peeled, and chopped.
- Salt and black pepper, to the taste.

Directions:

⇒ In a bowl, mix eggs with some salt and pepper and whisk gently.

⇒ Heat up a pan over medium heat; spray with some cooking oil, add eggs and cook your omelet for 5 minutes

⇒ Add chicken, avocado, tomato, bacon, mayo, and mustard on one half of the omelet.

⇒ Fold omelet, cover the pan and cook for 5 minutes more

⇒ Transfer to a plate and serve

Nutrition: Calories: 400 Fat: 32 Fiber: 6 Carbs: 4 Protein: 25

21) Pepper Pesto Lamb

Preparation Time: 15 Minutes   **Cooking Time: 1 Hour 15 Minutes**   **Servings: 12**

Ingredients:

For the Pesto:

- 1/4 Cup rosemary leaves, fresh
- 3 Pieces garlic cloves
- 3/4 Cups parsley, fresh, packed firmly
- 1/4 Cup mint leaves, fresh
- 2 Tablespoons olive oil

Lamb:

- 7 ½ Ounces red bell peppers, roasted, drained
- 5 Pounds leg of lamb, boneless, rolled
- 2 Teaspoons seasoning, lemon pepper

Directions:

⇒ Preheat the oven to 325 degrees Fahrenheit.

⇒ Mix the pesto ingredients in the food processor.

⇒ Unroll the lamb and cover the cut side with pesto. Top with roasted peppers before rolling up the lamb and tying with kitchen twine.

⇒ Coat lamb with seasoning (lemon pepper) and air-fry for one hour.

Nutrition: Calories: 310 Fat: 10g Protein: 40.0g Carbohydrates: 0g

22) Tasty WW Pancakes

Preparation Time: 12 Minutes   **Cooking Time: 3 Minutes**   **Servings:4**

Ingredients:

- 2 Ounces cream cheese
- 1 Teaspoon stevia
- ½ Teaspoon cinnamon; ground
- 2 Eggs
- Cooking spray

Directions:

⇒ Mix the eggs with the cream cheese, stevia, and cinnamon in a blender, and mix well.

⇒ Heat a pan with cooking spray over medium-high heat, add 1/4 of the batter, spread well, cook 2 minutes, invert and cook 1 minute more

⇒ Move to a plate and repeat with the rest of the dough.

⇒ Serve them right away.

Nutrition: Calories: 344 Fat: 23 Fiber: 12 Carbs: 3 Protein: 16

23) Greek Style Mini Burger Pies

Preparation Time: 15 Minutes   **Cooking Time: 40 Minutes**   **Servings:6**

Ingredients:

Burger mixture:

- 1 Piece onion, large, chopped
- ½ Cup red bell peppers, roasted, diced
- 1 Pound ground lamb, 80% lean
- 1/4 Teaspoon red pepper flakes
- 2 Ounces feta cheese, crumbled

Baking mixture:

- Milk (½ cup)
- Biscuit mix, classic (½ cup)
- Eggs (2 pieces)

Directions:

⇒ Preheat oven to 350 degrees Fahrenheit.

⇒ Grease 12 muffin cups using cooking spray.

⇒ Cook the onion and lamb in a skillet heated on medium-high. Once the lamb is browned and cooked through, drain and let cool for five minutes, stir together with feta cheese, roasted red peppers, and red pepper flakes.

⇒ Whisk the baking mixture ingredients together. Fill each muffin cup with the baking mixture (1 tablespoon).

⇒ Air-fry the dish for twenty-five to thirty minutes. Let cool before serving.

Nutrition: Calories: 270 Fat: 10g Protein: 10g Carbohydrates: 10g

24) Family Fun Pizza

Preparation Time: 30 Minutes   **Cooking Time: 25 Minutes**   **Servings: 16**

Ingredients:

For the Pizza crust:

- 1 Cup water, warm
- ½ Teaspoon salt
- 1 Cup flour, whole wheat
- 2 Tablespoons olive oil
- 1 Package dry yeast, quick active
- 1 ½ Cups flour, all-purpose
- Cornmeal
- Olive Oil

Filling:

- 1 Cup onion, chopped
- 4 Ounces mushrooms, sliced, drained
- 2 Garlic cloves, chopped finely
- 1/4 Cup parmesan cheese, grated
- 1 Pound ground lamb, 80% lean
- 1 Teaspoon Italian seasoning
- 8 Ounces pizza sauce
- 2 Cups Mozzarella Cheese, Shredded

Directions:

⇒ Mix yeast with warm water. Combine with the flours, oil (2 tablespoons), and salt by stirring and then beating vigorously for half a minute. Let the dough sit for twenty minutes.

⇒ Preheat oven to 350 degrees Fahrenheit.

⇒ Prep 2 square pans (8-inch) by greasing with oil before sprinkling with cornmeal.

⇒ Cut the rested dough in half; place each half inside each pan.

⇒ Set aside, covered, for thirty to forty-five minutes. Cook in the air fryer for twenty to twenty-two minutes.

⇒ Sauté the onion, lamb, garlic, and Italian seasoning until beef is completely cooked. Drain and set aside.

⇒ Cover the air-fried crusts with pizza sauce before topping with beef mixture, cheeses, and mushrooms.

⇒ Return to oven and cook for twenty minutes.

Nutrition: Calories: 215 Fat: 0g Protein: 10g Carbohydrates: 20.0g

25) Mouth-watering Pie

Preparation Time: 15 Minutes   **Cooking Time: 45 Minutes**   **Servings: 8**

Ingredients:

- 3/4-Pound beef; ground
- ½ Onion; chopped.
- 1 Pie crust
- 3 Tablespoons taco seasoning
- 1 Teaspoon baking soda
- Mango salsa for serving

- ½ Red bell pepper; chopped.
- A handful of cilantro; chopped.
- 8 Eggs
- 1 Teaspoon coconut oil
- Salt and black pepper to the taste.

Directions:

⇒ Heat up a pan, add oil, beef, cook until it browns, and mix it with salt, pepper, and taco seasoning.

⇒ Stir again, transfer to a bowl and leave aside for now.

⇒ Heat up the pan again over medium heat with cooking juices from the meat, add onion and pepper, stir, and cook for 4 minutes.

⇒ Add eggs, baking soda, and some salt and stir well.

⇒ Add cilantro; stir again, and take off the heat.

⇒ Spread beef mix in the pie crust, add veggies mix and spread over the meat, heat the oven at 350 degrees F, and bake for 45 minutes.

⇒ Leave the pie to cool down a bit, slice, divide between plates and serve with mango salsa on top.

Nutrition: Calories: 198 Fat: 11 Fiber: 1 Carbs: 12 Protein: 12

26) Bacon Wings

Preparation Time: 15 Minutes   **Cooking Time: 1 Hour 15 Minutes**   **Servings: 12**

Ingredients:

- 12 Pieces bacon strips
- 1 Teaspoon paprika
- 1 Tablespoon black pepper
- 1 Teaspoon oregano
- 12 Pieces chicken wings

- 1 Tablespoon kosher salt
- 1 Tablespoon brown sugar
- 1 Teaspoon chili powder
- Celery sticks
- Blue cheese dressing

Directions:

⇒ Preheat the air fryer at 325 degrees Fahrenheit.

⇒ Mix sugar, salt, chili powder, oregano, pepper, and paprika. Coat chicken wings with this dry rub.

⇒ Wrap a bacon strip around each wing. Arrange wrapped wings in the air fryer basket.

⇒ Cook for thirty minutes on each side in the air fryer. Let cool for five minutes.

⇒ Serve and enjoy with celery and blue cheese.

Nutrition: Calories: 100 Fat: 0g Protein: 0g Carbohydrates: 0g

27) Almond Pancakes

Preparation Time: 10 Minutes   **Cooking Time: 13 Minutes**   **Servings: 12**

Ingredients:

- 6 Eggs
- 1/4 Cup almonds; toasted
- 2 Ounces cocoa chocolate
- 1 Teaspoon almond extract
- 1/3 Cup coconut; shredded
- ½ Teaspoon baking powder

- 1/4 Cup coconut oil
- ½ Cup coconut flour
- 1/4 Cup stevia
- 1 Cup almond milk
- Cooking spray
- A pinch of salt

Directions:

⇒ Mix coconut flour with stevia, baking powder, salt, and coconut and stir.

⇒ Add coconut oil, eggs, almond milk, and the almond extract and stir well again.

⇒ Add chocolate and almonds and whisk well again.

⇒ Heat up a pan and add cooking spray; add two tablespoons batter, spread into a circle, cook until golden, flip, cook again until it's done, and transfer to a pan.

⇒ Do the same for the rest of the batter, and serve your pancakes right away.

Nutrition: Calories: 266 Fat: 13 Fiber: 8 Carbs: 10 Protein: 11

Chapter 4 - Salads Recipes

28) Barley and Lentil Salad

Preparation Time: 5 Minutes   **Cooking Time: 0 Minutes**   **Servings:2**

Ingredients:

- 1 Head romaine lettuce
- ¾ Cup cooked barley
- 2 Cups cooked lentils
- 1 Diced carrot
- ¼ Chopped red onion

- ¼ Cup olives
- ½ Chopped cucumber
- 3 Tablespoons olive oil
- 2 Tablespoons fresh lemon juice

Directions:

⇒ Mix all ingredients together. Add kosher salt and black pepper to taste.

Nutrition: Calories: 213 Protein: 21g Carbohydrate: 6g Fat: 9g

29) Blueberry Cantaloupe Avocado Salad

Preparation Time: 5 Minutes   **Cooking Time: 0 Minutes**   **Servings:2**

Ingredients:

- 1 Diced cantaloupe
- 2–3 Chopped avocados
- 1 Package of blueberries

- ¼ Cup olive oil
- 1/8 Cup balsamic vinegar

Directions:

⇒ Mix all ingredients.

Nutrition: Calories: 406 Protein: 9g Carbohydrate: 32g Fat: 5g

30) Wild Rice Prawn Salad

Preparation Time: 5 Minutes   **Cooking Time: 35 Minutes**   **Servings:6**

Ingredients:

- ¾ Cup wild rice
- 1¾ Cups chicken stock
- 1 Pound prawns
- Salt and pepper to taste

- 2 Tablespoons lemon juice
- 2 Tablespoons extra virgin olive oil
- 2 Cups arugula

Directions:

⇒ Combine the rice and chicken stock in a saucepan and cook until the liquid has been absorbed entirely.

⇒ Transfer the rice to a salad bowl.

⇒ Season the prawns with salt and pepper and drizzle them with lemon juice and oil.

⇒ Heat a grill pan over a medium flame.

⇒ Place the prawns on the hot pan and cook on each side for 2-3 minutes.

⇒ For the salad, combine the rice with arugula and prawns and mix well.

⇒ Serve the salad fresh.

Nutrition: Calories: 207 Fat: 4g Protein: 20.6g Carbohydrates: 17g

31) Beet Salad (from Israel)

Preparation Time: 5 Minutes   **Cooking Time: 0 Minutes**   **Servings:2**

Ingredients:

- 2–3 Fresh, raw beets grated or shredded in food processor
- 3 Tablespoons olive oil
- 2 Tablespoons balsamic vinegar
- ¼ Teaspoon salt
- 1/3 Teaspoon cumin
- Dash stevia powder or liquid
- Dash pepper

Directions:

⇒ Mix all ingredients together for the best raw beet salad.

Nutrition: Calories: 156 Protein: 8g Carbohydrate: 40g Fat: 5g

32) Greek Salad

Preparation Time: 15 Minutes   **Cooking Time: 15 Minutes**   **Servings:5**

Ingredients:

For the Dressing:
- ½ Teaspoon black pepper
- ¼ Teaspoon salt
- ½ Teaspoon oregano
- 1 Tablespoon garlic powder
- 2 Tablespoons Balsamic
- 1/3 Cup olive oil

For the Salad:
- ½ Cup sliced black olives

- ½ Cup chopped parsley, fresh
- 1 Small red onion, thin-sliced
- 1 Cup cherry tomatoes, sliced
- 1 Bell pepper, yellow, chunked
- 1 Cucumber, peeled, quartered, and sliced
- 4 Cups chopped romaine lettuce
- ½ Teaspoon salt
- 2 Tablespoons olive oil

Directions:

⇒ In a small bowl, blend all of the ingredients for the dressing and let this set in the refrigerator while you make the salad.

⇒ To assemble the salad, mix together all the ingredients in a large-sized bowl and toss the veggies gently but thoroughly to mix.

⇒ Serve the salad with the dressing in amounts as desired

Nutrition: Calories: 234 Fat: 16.1g Protein: 5g Carbs: 48g

33) Norwegian Niçoise Salad Smoked Salmon Cucumber Egg and Asparagus

Preparation Time: 20 Minutes   **Cooking Time: 5 Minutes**   Servings:4

Ingredients:

For the vinaigrette:

- 3 Tablespoons walnut oil
- 2 Tablespoons champagne vinegar
- 1 Tablespoon chopped fresh dill
- ½ Teaspoon kosher salt
- ¼ Teaspoon ground mustard
- Freshly ground black pepper

For the salad:

- Handful green beans, trimmed
- 1 (3- to 4-ounce) Package spring greens
- 12 Spears pickled asparagus
- 4 Large soft-boiled eggs, halved
- 8 Ounces smoked salmon, thinly sliced
- 1 Cucumber, thinly sliced
- 1 Lemon, quartered

Directions:

⇒ To make the dressing. In a small bowl, whisk the oil, vinegar, dill, salt, ground mustard, and a few grinds of pepper until emulsified. Set aside.

⇒ To make the salad. Start by blanching the green beans, bring a pot of salted water to a boil. Drop in the beans

⇒ Cook for 1 to 2 minutes until they turn bright green, then immediately drain and rinse under cold water. Set aside.

⇒ Divide the spring greens among four plates. Toss each serving with dressing to taste. Arrange three asparagus spears, one egg, 2 ounces of salmon, one-fourth of the cucumber slices, and a lemon wedge on each plate. Serve immediately.

Nutrition: Calories: 257 Total fat: 18g Total carbs: 6g Cholesterol: 199mg Fiber: 2g Protein: 19g Sodium: 603mg

34) Mediterranean Chickpea Salad

Preparation Time: 5 Minutes   **Cooking Time: 20 Minutes**   Servings:6

Ingredients:

- 1 Can chickpeas, drained
- 1 Fennel bulb, sliced
- 1 Red onion, sliced
- 1 Teaspoon dried basil
- 1 Teaspoon dried oregano

- 2 Tablespoons chopped parsley
- 4 Garlic cloves, minced
- 2 Tablespoons lemon juice
- 2 Tablespoons extra virgin olive oil
- Salt and pepper to taste

Directions:

⇒ Combine the chickpeas, fennel, red onion, herbs, garlic, lemon juice, and oil in a salad bowl.

⇒ Add salt and pepper and serve the salad fresh.

Nutrition: Calories: 200 Fat: 9g Protein: 4g Carbohydrates: 28g

35) Romaine Lettuce and Radicchios Mix

Preparation Time: 6 Minutes   **Cooking Time: 0 Minutes**   **Servings: 4**

Ingredients:

- 2 Tablespoons olive oil
- A pinch of salt and black pepper
- 2 Spring onions, chopped
- 3 Tablespoons Dijon mustard
- Juice of 1 lime
- ½ Cup basil, chopped
- 4 Cups romaine lettuce heads, chopped
- 3 Radicchios, sliced

Directions:

⇒ In a salad bowl, mix the lettuce with the spring onions and the other ingredients, toss and serve.

Nutrition: Calories: 87 Fats: 2g Fiber: 1g Carbs: 1g Protein: 2g

36) Chicken Broccoli Salad With Avocado Dressing

Preparation Time: 5 Minutes   **Cooking Time: 40 Minutes**   **Servings: 6**

Ingredients:

- 2 Chicken breasts
- 1 Pound broccoli, cut into florets
- 1 Avocado, peeled and pitted
- ½ Lemon, juiced
- 2 Garlic cloves
- ¼ Teaspoon chili powder
- ¼ Teaspoon cumin powder
- Salt and pepper to taste

Directions:

⇒ Cook the chicken in a large pot of salty water.

⇒ Drain and cut the chicken into small cubes—place in a salad bowl.

⇒ Add the broccoli and mix well.

⇒ Combine the avocado, lemon juice, garlic, chili powder, cumin powder, salt, and pepper in a blender. Pulse until smooth.

⇒ Spoon the dressing over the salad and mix well.

⇒ Serve the salad fresh.

Nutrition: Calories: 195 Fat: 11g Protein: 14g Carbohydrates: 3g

37) Zucchini Salmon Salad

Preparation Time: 5 Minutes   **Cooking Time: 10 Minutes**   **Servings: 3**

Ingredients:

- 2 Salmon fillets
- 2 Tablespoons soy sauce
- 2 Zucchinis, sliced
- Salt and pepper to taste
- 2 Tablespoons extra virgin olive oil
- 2 Tablespoons sesame seeds

Directions:

⇒ Drizzle the salmon with soy sauce.

⇒ Heat a grill pan over a medium flame. Cook salmon on the grill on each side for 2-3 minutes.

⇒ Season the zucchini with salt and pepper and place it on the grill as well.

⇒ Cook on each side until golden.

⇒ Place the zucchini, salmon, and the rest of the ingredients in a bowl.

⇒ Serve the salad fresh.

Nutrition: Calories: 224 Fat: 19g Protein: 18g Carbohydrates: 0g

38) Warm Chorizo Chickpea Salad

Preparation Time: 5 Minutes   **Cooking Time: 20 Minutes**   **Servings:6**

Ingredients:

- 1 Tablespoon extra-virgin olive oil
- 4 Chorizo links, sliced
- 1 Red onion, sliced
- 4 Roasted red bell peppers, chopped

- 1 Can chickpeas, drained
- 2 Cups cherry tomatoes
- 2 Tablespoons balsamic vinegar
- Salt and pepper to taste

Directions:

⇒ Heat the oil in a skillet and add the chorizo. Cook briefly just until fragrant, then add the onion, bell peppers, and chickpeas and cook for two additional minutes.

⇒ Transfer the mixture to a salad bowl, then add the tomatoes, vinegar, salt, and pepper.

⇒ Mix well and serve the salad right away.

Nutrition: Calories: 359 Fat: 18g Protein: 15g Carbohydrates: 21g

39) Broccoli Salad

Preparation Time: 5 Minutes   **Cooking Time: 0 Minutes**   **Servings:2**

Ingredients:

- 1 Head broccoli, chopped
- 2–3 Slices of fried bacon, crumbled
- 1 Diced green onion
- ½ Cup raisins or craisins
- ½–1 Cup of chopped pecans
- ¾ Cups sunflower seeds

- ½ Cup of pomegranate

Dressing:

- 1 Cup Organic Mayonnaise
- ¼ Cup Baking Stevia
- 2 Teaspoons White Vinegar

Directions:

⇒ Mix all ingredients together. Mix dressing and fold into the salad.

Nutrition: Calories: 239 Protein: 10g Carbohydrate: 33g Fat: 2g

40) Loaded Caesar Salad With Crunchy Chickpeas

Preparation Time: 5 Minutes **Cooking Time: 20 Minutes** **Servings: 6**

Ingredients:

For the chickpeas:

- 2 (15-ounce) cans chickpeas, drained and rinsed
- 2 Tablespoons extra-virgin olive oil
- 1 Teaspoon kosher salt
- 1 Teaspoon garlic powder
- 1 Teaspoon onion powder
- 1 Teaspoon dried oregano

For the dressing:

- ½ Cup Mayonnaise
- 2 Tablespoons Grated Parmesan Cheese

- 2 Tablespoons Freshly Squeezed Lemon Juice
- 1 Clove Garlic, Peeled and Smashed
- 1 Teaspoon Dijon Mustard
- ½ Tablespoon Worcestershire Sauce
- ½ Tablespoon Anchovy Paste

For the salad:

- 3 Heads romaine lettuce, cut into bite-size pieces

Directions:

⇒ To make the chickpeas:

⇒ Preheat the oven to 450°F. Line a baking sheet with parchment paper.

⇒ In a medium bowl, toss together the chickpeas, oil, salt, garlic powder, onion powder, and oregano. Scatter the coated chickpeas on the prepared baking sheet.

⇒ Roast for about 20 minutes, occasionally tossing until the chickpeas are golden and have a bit of crunch.

⇒ To make the dressing:

⇒ In a small bowl, whisk the mayonnaise, Parmesan, lemon juice, garlic, mustard, Worcestershire sauce, and anchovy paste until combined.

⇒ To make the salad:

⇒ In a large bowl, combine the lettuce and dressing. Toss to coat. Top with the roasted chickpeas and serve.

Nutrition: Calories: 367 Total fat: 22g Total carbs: 35g Cholesterol: 9mg Fiber: 13g Protein: 12g Sodium: 407mg

41) Taste of Normandy Salad

Preparation Time: 25 Minutes   **Cooking Time: 5 Minutes**   **Servings:4-6**

Ingredients:

For the walnuts:

- 2 Tablespoons butter
- ¼ Cup sugar or honey
- 1 Cup walnut pieces
- ½ Teaspoon kosher salt

For the dressing:

- 3 Tablespoons extra-virgin olive oil
- 1½ Tablespoons champagne vinegar
- 1½ Tablespoons Dijon mustard

- ¼ Teaspoon kosher salt

For the salad:

- 1 Head red leaf lettuce, torn into pieces
- 3 Heads endive, ends trimmed and leaves separated
- 2 Apples, cored and cut into thin wedges
- 1 (8-ounce) Camembert wheel, cut into thin wedges

Directions:

⇒ To make the walnuts:

⇒ In a skillet over medium-high heat, melt the butter. Stir in the sugar and cook until it dissolves. Add the walnuts and cook for about 5 minutes, stirring, until toasty—season with salt and transfer to a plate to cool.

⇒ To make the dressing:

⇒ In a large bowl, whisk the oil, vinegar, mustard, and salt until combined.

⇒ To make the salad:

⇒ Add the lettuce and endive to the bowl with the dressing and toss to coat. Transfer to a serving platter.

⇒ Decoratively arrange the apple and Camembert wedges over the lettuce and scatter the walnuts on top. Serve immediately.

Nutrition: Calories: 699 Total fat: 52g Total carbs: 44g Cholesterol: 60mg Fiber: 17g Protein: 23g Sodium: 1170mg

Chapter 5 -

42) Easy Cauliflower Soup

Preparation Time: 5 Minutes   **Cooking Time: 15 Minutes**   **Servings:4**

Ingredients:

- 2 Tbsp. olive oil (1/4 condiment)
- 1 Tsp. garlic, minced (1/4 condiment)
- 1-pound cauliflower, cut into florets (1green)
- 1 Cup kale, chopped (½ green)
- 4 Cups vegetable broth (1 condiment)

- ½ Cup almond milk (½ healthy fat)
- ½ Tsp. salt (1/8 condiment)
- ½ Tsp. red pepper flakes (1/8 condiment)
- 1 Tbsp. fresh chopped parsley (1/4green)

Directions:

⇒ Set a pot over medium heat and warm the oil.

⇒ Add garlic and onions and sauté until browned and softened.

⇒ Place in vegetable broth, kale, and cauliflower; cook for 10 minutes until the mixture boils.

⇒ Stir in the pepper flakes, salt, and almond milk; reduce the heat and simmer the soup for 5 minutes.

⇒ Transfer the soup to an immersion blender and blend to achieve the desired consistency; top with parsley and serve immediately.

Nutrition: Calories: 172 Fats: 10.3g Protein: 8.1g

43) Tofu Stir Fry With Asparagus Stew

Preparation Time: 15 Minutes   **Cooking Time: 30 Minutes**   **Servings:4**

Ingredients:

- 1-pound Asparagus, cut off stems (1green)
- 2 Tbsp. olive oil (1/8 condiment)
- 2 Blocks tofu, pressed and cubed (1 lean)
- 2 Garlic cloves, minced (1/8 condiment)
- 1 Tsp. Cajun spice mix (1/8 condiment)

- 1 Tsp. mustard (1/8 condiment)
- 1 Bell pepper, chopped (1/4green)
- 1/4 Cup vegetable broth (1green)
- Salt and black pepper, to taste (1/8 condiment)

Directions:

⇒ Using a huge saucepan with lightly salted water, place in asparagus and cook until tender for 10 minutes; drain.

⇒ Set a wok over high heat and warm olive oil; stir in tofu cubes and cook for 6 minutes.

⇒ Place in garlic and cook for 30 seconds until soft.

⇒ Stir in the remaining ingredients, including reserved asparagus, and cook for four more minutes.

⇒ Divide among plates and serve.

Nutrition: Calories: 138 Fat: 8.9g Protein: 6.4g

44) Cream of Thyme Tomato Soup

Preparation Time: 5 Minutes   **Cooking Time: 20 Minutes**   **Servings:6**

Ingredients:

- 2 Tbsp. ghee (½ healthy fat)
- ½ Cup raw cashew nuts, diced (½ healthy fat)
- 2 (28 oz.) Cans tomatoes (1green)
- 1 Tsp. fresh thyme leaves + extra to garnish (1/4green)
- 1 ½ Cups water (½ healthy fat)
- Salt and black pepper to taste (1/8 condiment)

Directions:

⇒ Cook ghee in a pot over medium heat and sauté the onions for 4 minutes until softened.

⇒ Stir in the tomatoes, thyme, water, cashews, and season with salt and black pepper.

⇒ Cover and bring to simmer for 10 minutes until thoroughly cooked.

⇒ Open, turn the heat off, and puree the ingredients with an immersion blender.

⇒ Adjust to taste and stir in the heavy cream.

⇒ Spoon into soup bowls and serve.

Nutrition: Calories: 310 Fats: 27g Protein: 11g

45) Lime-Mint Soup

Preparation Time: 5 Minutes   **Cooking Time: 20 Minutes**   **Servings:4**

Ingredients:

- 4 Cups vegetable broth (1 condiment)
- 1/4 Cup fresh mint leaves (1/8 condiment)
- 1/4 Cup scallions (1/4green)
- 3 Garlic cloves, minced (1/8 condiment)
- 3 Tablespoons freshly squeezed lime juice (1/4 condiment)

Directions:

⇒ In a large stockpot, combine the broth, mint, scallions, garlic, and lime juice.

⇒ Bring to a boil over medium-high heat.

⇒ Cover, set heat to low, simmer for 15 minutes, and serve.

Nutrition: Fat: 2g Protein: 5g Calories: 214

46) Cauliflower Soup

Preparation Time: 5 Minutes   **Cooking Time: 20 Minutes**   **Servings:4**

Ingredients:

- 2 Cups cauliflower florets, diced (1green)
- 1 Cup heavy cream (½ healthy fat)
- 2 Cups vegetable stock (1 condiment)
- 1 Tbsp. chives, minced (1/8 condiment)
- Salt and pepper to taste (1/8 condiment)
- 1 Garlic clove, minced (1/8 condiment)
- 1 Tbsp. almond butter (1/4 healthy fat)

Directions:

⇒ In a large saucepan, add the almond butter.

⇒ Toss the garlic until it turns golden.

⇒ Add the cauliflower and toss for 2 minutes.

⇒ Add the vegetable stock and cook on high heat for 10 minutes.

⇒ Add the heavy cream, chives, salt, pepper, and cook for 8 minutes.

⇒ Serve hot.

Nutrition: Fat: 5.5g Protein: 16g Calories: 291

47) Pork Cacciatore

Preparation Time: 10 Minutes   **Cooking Time: 6 Hours**   **Servings:6**

Ingredients:

- 1 ½ lbs. Pork chops (1 lean)
- 1 Teaspoon dried oregano (1/4green)
- 1 Cup beef broth (1 condiment)
- 3 Tablespoon tomato paste (1/4 condiment)
- 14 oz. Can tomato, diced (1/4 healthy fat)
- 2 Cups mushrooms, sliced (1/4 healthy fat)
- 1 Garlic clove, minced (1/8 condiment)
- 2 Tablespoon olive oil (1/8 condiment)
- ¼ Teaspoon pepper (1/8 condiment)
- ½ Teaspoon salt (1/8 condiment)

Directions:

⇒ Cook oil in a pan over medium heat.

⇒ Stir in pork chops in the pan and cook until brown on both sides.

⇒ Transfer pork chops into the crockpot.

⇒ Pour remaining ingredients over the pork chops.

⇒ Cover and cook on low heat for 6 hours.

⇒ Serve and enjoy.

Nutrition: Calories: 440 Fat: 33g Protein: 28g

48) Classic Beef Stroganoff

Preparation Time: 10 Minutes   **Cooking Time: 8 Hours**   **Servings:2**

Ingredients:

- ½ lb. Beef stew meat (1 lean)
- 10 oz. Mushroom soup, homemade (2 healthy fat)
- ½ Cup sour cream (½ condiment)
- 2.5 oz. Mushrooms, sliced (½ healthy fat)
- Pepper and salt (1/4 condiment)

Directions:

⇒ Add all ingredients except sour cream into the crockpot and mix well.

⇒ Cover and cook on low heat for 8 hours.

⇒ Add sour cream and stir well.

⇒ Serve and enjoy.

Nutrition: Calories: 470 Fat: 25g Protein: 49g

49) Savory Split Pea Soup

Preparation Time: 5 Minutes   **Cooking Time: 50 Minutes**   **Servings:6**

Ingredients:

- 1 (16-ounce) package dried green split peas, soaked overnight (1 healthy fat)
- 5 Cups vegetable broth or water (2 condiments)
- 2 Teaspoons garlic powder (1/8 condiment)
- 2 Teaspoons onion powder (1/8 condiment)
- 1 Teaspoon dried oregano (1/8green)
- 1 Teaspoon dried thyme (1/8green)
- 1/4 Teaspoon freshly ground black pepper (1/8 condiment)

Directions:

⇒ In a large stockpot, combine the split peas, broth, garlic powder, onion powder, oregano, thyme, and pepper.

⇒ Bring to a boil over medium-high heat.

⇒ Cover, set heat to medium-low, and simmer for 45 minutes, stirring every 5 to 10 minutes. Serve warm.

Nutrition: Fat: 2g Protein: 23g Calories: 301

50) Pork and Tomatillo Stew

Preparation Time: 10 Minutes   **Cooking Time: 20 Minutes**   **Servings:4**

Ingredients:

- 2 Scallions, chopped (½ green)
- 2 Cloves of garlic (1/8 condiment)
- 1 lb. Tomatillos, trimmed and chopped (1green)
- 8 Large romaine or green lettuce leaves, divided (2green)
- 2 Serrano chilies, seeds, and membranes (1 healthy fat)
- ½ Tsp. of dried Mexican oregano (½ green)
- 1 ½ lb. of boneless pork loin, to be cut into bite-sized cubes (1 lean)
- ¼ Cup of cilantro, chopped (1/8green)
- ¼ Tablespoon (each) salt and pepper (1/8 condiment)
- 1 Jalapeno, seeds and membranes to be removed and thinly sliced (1/8 healthy fat)
- 1 Cup of sliced radishes (1green)
- 4 Lime wedges (1/4 condiment)

Directions:

⇒ Combine scallions, garlic, tomatillos, four lettuce leaves, serrano chilies, and oregano in a blender. Then puree until smooth

⇒ Put pork and tomatillo mixture in a medium pot. 1-inch of puree should cover the pork; if not, add water until it covers it. Season with pepper, salt and cover it to simmer on heat for approximately 20 minutes.

⇒ Now, finely shred the remaining lettuce leaves.

⇒ When the stew is done cooking, garnish with cilantro, radishes, finely shredded lettuce, sliced jalapenos, and lime wedges.

Nutrition: Calories: 370 Protein: 36g Fat: 19g

51) Bok Choy With Tofu Stir Fry

Preparation Time: 15 Minutes   **Cooking Time: 15 Minutes**   **Servings:4**

Ingredients:

- 1 lb. Super-firm tofu (1 lean)
- One tablespoon coconut oil (1/4 condiment)
- 1Clove of garlic (1/4 condiment)
- 3 Heads Baby bok choy (1 healthy fat)
- Low-sodium vegetable broth (1 condiment)
- 2 Teaspoons maple syrup (1/4 condiment)
- Braggs liquid aminos (1/4 condiment)
- 1 to 2 Teaspoons Sambal oelek (1/8 condiment)
- 1 Scallion or green onion(1green)
- 1 Teaspoon Freshly grated ginger (1/4 condiment)
- Quinoa/rice, for serving (1 healthy fat)

Directions:

⇒ With paper towels, Pat pressed the tofu dry and cut it into tiny pieces of bite-size around ½ inch wide.

⇒ Heat coconut oil in a wide skillet in a warm.

⇒ Remove tofu and stir-fry until painted softly.

⇒ Stir-fry for 1-2 minutes before the bok choy starts to wilt.

⇒ When this occurs, you'll want to apply the vegetable broth and all the remaining ingredients to the skillet.

⇒ Hold the mixture stir-frying until all components are well coated and the bulk of the liquid evaporates, around 5-6 min.

⇒ Serve over brown rice or quinoa.

Nutrition: Calories: 263 Fat: 4.2g Protein: 3.57g

Chapter 6 -   Vegan Recipes

52) Cinnamon Butternut Squash Fries

Preparation Time: 10 Minutes   **Cooking Time: 10 Minutes**   **Servings:2**

Ingredients:

- 1 Pinch of salt
- 1 Tbsp. powdered unprocessed sugar
- ½ Tsp. nutmeg
- ½ Tsp. cinnamon
- 1 Tbsp. coconut oil
- 0.5 Ounces pre-cut butternut squash fries

Directions:

⇒ In a plastic bag, pour in all ingredients. Cover fries with other components till coated and sugar is dissolved.

⇒ Spread coated fries into a single layer in the air fryer, cook 10 minutes at 390 degrees until crispy.

Nutrition: Calories: 175 Fat: 8g Protein: 1g Sugar: 5g

53) Carrot & Zucchini Muffins

Preparation Time: 5 Minutes   **Cooking Time: 14 Minutes**   **Servings:4**

Ingredients:

- 2 Tablespoons butter, melted
- ¼ Cup carrots, shredded
- ½ Cup zucchini, shredded
- 1 ½ Cups almond flour
- 1 Tablespoon liquid Stevia
- ½ Teaspoons baking powder
- Pinch of salt
- 2 Eggs
- 1 Tablespoon yogurt
- 1 Cup milk

Directions:

⇒ Preheat your air fryer to 350 degrees Fahrenheit.

⇒ Beat the eggs, yogurt, milk, salt, pepper, baking soda, and Stevia.

⇒ Whisk in the flour gradually.

⇒ Add zucchini and carrots.

⇒ Grease muffin tins with butter and pour the muffin batter into tins. Cook for 14-minutes and serve.

Nutrition: Calories:224 Total Fats:12.3 Carbs: 11.2g Protein:14.2g

54) Curried Cauliflower Florets

Preparation Time: 5 Minutes   **Cooking Time: 10 Minutes**   **Servings:4**

Ingredients:

- 1/4 Cup sultanas or golden raisins
- ¼ Teaspoon salt
- 1 Tablespoon curry powder
- 1 Cauliflower head, broken into small florets
- ¼ Cup pine nuts
- ½ Cup olive oil

Directions:

⇒ In a cup of boiling water, soak your sultanas to plump. Preheat your air fryer to 350 degrees Fahrenheit.

⇒ Add oil and pine nuts to the air fryer and toast for a minute or so.

⇒ In a bowl, toss the cauliflower and curry powder as well as salt, then add the mix to the air fryer mixing well.

⇒ Cook for 10-minutes. Drain the sultanas, toss with cauliflower, and serve.

Nutrition: Calories: 275 Total Fat: 11.3g Carbs: 8.6g Protein: 9.5g

55) Feta & Mushroom Frittata

Preparation Time: 15 Minutes   **Cooking Time: 30 Minutes**   **Servings:4**

Ingredients:

- 1 Red onion, thinly sliced
- 2 Cups button mushrooms, thinly sliced
- Salt to taste
- 1 Tablespoons feta cheese, crumbled

- 3 Medium eggs
- Non-stick cooking spray
- 2 Tablespoons olive oil

Directions:

⇒ Saute the onion and mushrooms in olive oil over medium heat until the vegetables are tender.

⇒ Remove the vegetables from the pan and drain them on a paper towel-lined plate.

⇒ In a mixing bowl, whisk eggs and salt. Coat all sides of the baking dish with cooking spray.

⇒ Preheat your air fryer to 325 degrees Fahrenheit. Pour the beaten eggs into the prepared baking dish and scatter the sautéed vegetables and crumble feta on top—bake in the air fryer for 30-minutes. Allow to cool slightly and serve!

Nutrition: Calories: 226 Total Fat: 9.3g Carbs:8.7g Protein: 12.6g

56) Vegan Edamame Quinoa Collard Wraps

Preparation Time: 5 Minutes   **Cooking Time: 15 Minutes**   **Servings:4**

Ingredients:

For the wrap:
- 2 to 3 Collard leaves
- 1/4 Cup Grated carrot
- 1/4 Cup Sliced cucumber
- 1/4 Thin strips Red bell pepper
- 1/4 Thin strips Orange bell pepper
- 1/3 Cup Cooked Quinoa
- 1/3 Cup Shelled defrosted edamame

For the dressing:
- 3 Tablespoons Fresh ginger root, peeled and chopped

- 1 Cup Cooked chickpeas
- 1 Garlic clove
- 4 Tablespoons Rice vinegar
- 2 Tablespoons Low sodium tamari/coconut aminos
- 2 Tablespoons Lime juice
- 1/4 Cup Water
- Few pinches of chili flakes
- 1 Stevia pack

Directions:

⇒ For the dressing, combine all the ingredients and purée in a food processor until smooth.

⇒ Load into a little jar or tub, and set aside.

⇒ Place the collar leaves on a flat surface, covering one another to create a tighter tie.

⇒ Take one tablespoon of ginger dressing and blend it up with the prepared quinoa.

⇒ Spoon the prepared quinoa onto the leaves and shape a simple horizontal line at the closest end.

⇒ Supplement the edamame with all the veggie fillings left over.

⇒ Drizzle around one tablespoon of the ginger dressing on top, then fold the cover's sides inwards.

⇒ Pullover the fillings, the side of the cover closest to you, then turn the whole body away to seal it up.

Nutrition: Calories: 295 Sugar: 3g Sodium: 200mg Fat: 13g

57) Baked Cheesy Eggplant With Marinara

Preparation Time: 20 Minutes   **Cooking Time: 45 Minutes**   **Servings: 3**

Ingredients:

- 1 Clove garlic, sliced
- 1 Large eggplant
- 2 Tablespoons olive oil
- ½ Pinch salt, or as needed
- 1/4 Cup and 2 tablespoons dry bread crumbs
- 1/4 Cup and 2 tablespoons ricotta cheese
- 1/4 Cup grated Parmesan cheese

- 1/4 Cup water, plus more as needed
- 1/4 Teaspoon red pepper flakes
- 1-½ Cups prepared marinara sauce
- 1-½ Teaspoons olive oil
- 2 Tablespoons shredded pepper jack cheese
- Salt and freshly ground black pepper to taste

Directions:

⇒ Cut the eggplant crosswise into five pieces. Peel a pumpkin, grate it and cut it into two cubes.

⇒ Lightly turn skillet with one tablespoon olive oil. Heat the oil at 390°F for 5 minutes. Add half of the eggplants and cook for 2 minutes on each side. Transfer to a plate.

⇒ Add one tablespoon of olive oil and add garlic, cook for one minute. Add the chopped eggplants. Season with pepper flakes and salt. Cook for 4 minutes. Lower the heat to 330oF and continue cooking the eggplants until soft, about eight more minutes.

⇒ Stir in water and marinara sauce. Cook for 7 minutes until heated through. Stir every now and then. Transfer to a bowl.

⇒ In a bowl, whisk well pepper, salt, pepper jack cheese, Parmesan cheese, and ricotta. Evenly spread cheeses over eggplant strips and then fold in half.

⇒ Lay folded eggplant in baking pan. Pour the marinara sauce on top.

⇒ In a small bowl, whisk well olive oil and bread crumbs. Sprinkle all over the sauce.

⇒ Cook for 15 minutes at 390°F until tops are lightly browned.

⇒ Serve and enjoy.

Nutrition: Calories: 405 Carbs: 41.1g Protein: 12.7g Fat: 21.4g

58) Creamy Spinach and Mushroom Lasagna

Preparation Time: 60 Minutes   **Cooking Time: 20 Minutes**   **Servings:6**

Ingredients:

- 10 Lasagna noodles
- 1 Package whole milk ricotta
- 2 Packages of frozen chopped spinach.
- 4 Cups mozzarella cheese (divided and shredded)
- 3/4 Cups grated fresh Parmesan
- 3 Tablespoons chopped fresh parsley leaves (optional)

  For the Sauce:
- 1/4 Cup of butter (unsalted)

- 2 Garlic cloves
- 1 Pound of thinly sliced cremini mushroom
- 1 Diced onion
- 1/4 Cup flour
- 4 Cups milk, kept at room temperature
- 1 Teaspoon basil (dried)
- Pinch of nutmeg
- Salt and freshly ground black pepper, to taste

Directions:

⇒ Preheat oven to 352 degrees F.

⇒ To make the sauce, over medium heat, melt your butter. Add garlic, mushrooms, and onion. Cook and stir at intervals until it becomes tender at about 3-4 minutes.

⇒ Whisk in flour until lightly browned; it takes about 1 minute for it to become brown.

⇒ Next, whisk in the milk gradually, and cook, constantly whisking, about 2-3 minutes till it becomes thickened. Stir in basil, oregano, and nutmeg, season with salt and pepper for taste.

⇒ Then set aside.

⇒ In another pot of boiling salted water, cook lasagna noodles according to the package instructions.

⇒ Spread one cup mushroom sauce onto the bottom of a baking dish; top it with four lasagna noodles, ½ of the spinach, one cup mozzarella cheese, and 1/4 cup Parmesan.

⇒ Repeat this process with the remaining noodles, mushroom sauce, and cheeses.

⇒ Place into oven and bake for 35-45 minutes, or until it starts bubbling. Then boil for 2-3 minutes until it becomes brown and translucent.

⇒ Let cool for 15 minutes.

⇒ Serve it with garnished parsley (optional)

Nutrition: Calories: 488.3 Cal Fats: 19.3g Cholesterol: 88.4mg Sodium: 451.9mg Carbohydrates: 51.0g Dietary Fiber: 7.0g Protein: 25.0g

59) Zucchini Parmesan Chips

Preparation Time: 5 Minutes   **Cooking Time: 8 Minutes**   **Servings: 10**

Ingredients:

- ½ Tsp. Paprika
- ½ C. Grated parmesan cheese
- ½ C. Italian breadcrumbs
- 1 Lightly beaten egg
- Thinly sliced zucchinis

Directions:

⇒ Use a very sharp knife or mandolin slicer to slice zucchini as thinly as you can—pat off extra moisture.

⇒ Beat the egg with a pinch of pepper and salt and a bit of water.

⇒ Combine paprika, cheese, and breadcrumbs in a bowl.

⇒ Dip slices of zucchini into the egg mixture and then into the breadcrumb mixture. Press gently to coat.

⇒ With olive oil or cooking spray, mist-coated zucchini slices, then place them into your air fryer in a single layer.

⇒ Cook 8 minutes at 350 degrees.

⇒ Sprinkle with salt and serve with salsa.

Nutrition: Calories: 211 Fat: 16g Protein: 8g Sugar: 0g

60) Roasted Squash Puree

Preparation Time: 20 Minutes   **Cooking Time: 6 to 7 Hours**   **Servings: 8**

Ingredients:

- 1 (3-pound) Butternut squash, peeled, seeded, and cut into 1-inch pieces
- 3 (1-pound) Acorn squash, peeled, seeded, and cut into 1-inch pieces
- 2 Onions, chopped
- 3 Garlic cloves, minced
- 2 Tablespoons olive oil
- 1 Teaspoon dried marjoram leaves
- ½ Teaspoon salt
- 1/8 Teaspoon freshly ground black pepper

Directions:

⇒ In a 6-quart slow cooker, mix all of the ingredients.

⇒ Cover and cook on low for 6 to 7 hours or until the squash is tender when pierced with a fork.

⇒ Use a potato masher to mash the squash right in the slow cooker.

Nutrition: Calories: 175 Carbohydrates: 38g Sugar: 1g Fiber: 3g Fat: 4g Saturated Fat: 1g Protein: 3g Sodium: 149mg

61) Air Fryer Brussels Sprouts

Preparation Time: 5 Minutes   **Cooking Time: 10 Minutes**   **Servings: 5**

Ingredients:

- ¼ Tsp. salt
- 1 Tbsp. balsamic vinegar
- 1 Tbsp. olive oil
- C. Brussels sprouts

Directions:

⇒ Cut Brussels sprouts in half lengthwise. Toss with salt, vinegar, and olive oil till coated thoroughly.

⇒ Add coated sprouts to the air fryer, cooking 8-10 minutes at 400 degrees. Shake after 5 minutes of cooking.

⇒ Brussels sprouts are ready to devour when brown and crisp!

Nutrition: Calories: 118 Fat: 9g Protein: 11g Sugar: 1g

62) Thai Roasted Veggies

Preparation Time: 20 Minutes   **Cooking Time: 6 to 8 Hours**   **Servings:8**

Ingredients:

- 4 Large carrots, peeled and cut into chunks
- 2 Onions, peeled and sliced
- 6 Garlic cloves, peeled and sliced
- 2 Parsnips, peeled and sliced
- 2 Jalapeño peppers, minced

- ½ Cup Roasted Vegetable Broth
- 1/3 Cup canned coconut milk
- 3 Tablespoons lime juice
- 2 Tablespoons grated fresh ginger root
- 2 Teaspoons curry powder

Directions:

⇒ In a 6-quart slow cooker, mix the carrots, onions, garlic, parsnips, and jalapeño peppers.

⇒ In a small bowl, mix the vegetable broth, coconut milk, lime juice, ginger root, and curry powder until well blended. Pour this mixture into the slow cooker.

⇒ Cover and cook on low for 6 to 8 hours, do it until the vegetables are tender when pierced with a fork.

Nutrition: Calories: 69 Carbohydrates: 13g Sugar: 6g Fiber: 3g Fat: 3g Saturated Fat: 3g Protein: 1g Sodium: 95mg

63) Crispy Jalapeno Coins

Preparation Time: 10 Minutes   **Cooking Time: 10 Minutes**   **Servings:8-10**

Ingredients:

- 1 Egg
- 2-3 Tbsp. coconut flour
- 1 Sliced and seeded jalapeno
- Pinch of garlic powder

- Pinch of onion powder
- Pinch of Cajun seasoning (optional)
- Pinch of pepper and salt

Directions:

⇒ Ensure your air fryer is preheated to 400 degrees.

⇒ Mix together all dry ingredients.

⇒ Pat jalapeno slices dry. Dip coins into the egg wash and then into the dry mixture. Toss to thoroughly coat.

⇒ Add coated jalapeno slices to the air fryer in a singular layer. Spray with olive oil.

⇒ Cook just till crispy.

Nutrition: Calories: 128 Fat: 8g Protein: 7g Sugar: 0g

64) Crispy-Topped Baked Vegetables

Preparation Time: 10 Minutes   **Cooking Time: 40 Minutes**   **Servings: 4**

Ingredients:

- 2 Tbsp. Olive oil
- 1 Onion, chopped
- 1 Celery stalk, chopped
- 2 Carrots, grated
- ½-pound Turnips, sliced
- 1 Cup vegetable broth
- 1 Tsp. Turmeric
- Sea salt and black pepper, to taste
- ½ Tsp. Liquid smoke
- 1 Cup Parmesan cheese, shredded
- 2 Tbsp. Fresh chives, chopped

Directions:

⇒ Set oven to 360°F and grease a baking dish with olive oil.

⇒ Set a skillet over medium heat and warm olive oil.

⇒ Sweat the onion until soft, and place in the turnips, carrots, and celery; and cook for 4 minutes.

⇒ Remove the vegetable mixture from the baking dish.

⇒ Combine vegetable broth with turmeric, pepper, liquid smoke, and salt.

⇒ Spread this mixture over the vegetables.

⇒ Sprinkle with Parmesan cheese and bake for about 30 minutes.

⇒ Garnish with chives to serve.

Nutrition: Calories: 242 Cal Fats: 16.3g Carbohydrates: 8.6g Protein: 16.3g

65) Jicama Fries

Preparation Time: 10 Minutes   **Cooking Time: 20 Minutes**   **Servings: 8**

Ingredients:

- 1 Tbsp. Dried thyme
- ¾ C. Arrowroot flour
- ½ Large Jicama
- Eggs

Directions:

⇒ Sliced jicama into fries.

⇒ Whisk eggs together and pour over fries. Toss to coat.

⇒ Mix a pinch of salt, thyme, and arrowroot flour together. Toss egg-coated jicama into dry mixture, tossing to coat well.

⇒ Spray air fryer basket with olive oil and add fries—cook 20 minutes on the "CHIPS" setting. Toss halfway into the cooking process.

Nutrition: Calories: 211 Fat: 19g Protein: 9g Sugar: 1g

66) Spaghetti Squash Tots

Preparation Time: 5 Minutes   **Cooking Time: 15 Minutes**   **Servings: 8 to 10**

Ingredients:

- ¼ Tsp. pepper
- ½ Tsp. salt
- 1 Thinly sliced scallion
- 1 Spaghetti squash

Directions:

⇒ Wash and cut the squash in half lengthwise. Scrap out the seeds.

⇒ With a fork, remove spaghetti meat by strands and throw out skins.

⇒ In a clean towel, toss in squash and wring out as much moisture as possible. Place in a bowl and with a knife, slice through meat a few times to cut up smaller.

⇒ Add pepper, salt, and scallions to squash and mix well.

⇒ Create "tot" shapes with your hands and place them in the air fryer. Spray with olive oil.

⇒ Cook 15 minutes at 350 degrees until golden and crispy!

Nutrition: Calories: 231 Fat: 18g Protein: 5g Sugar: 0g

Chapter 7 -   Meat Recipes

67) Roasted Garlic Bacon and Potatoes

Preparation Time: 5 Minutes   **Cooking Time: 25 Minutes**   **Servings:4**

Ingredients:

- Medium-sized potatoes (1 healthy fat)
- 1 Strips of streaky bacon (1 lean)
- 2 tablespoon Sprigs of rosemary (1green)
- ½ Cloves of garlic unpeeled smashed, (½ condiment)
- 3 Tsp. of vegetable oil (½ condiment)

Directions:

⇒ Preheat Air fryer to 390°F.

⇒ Put the smashed garlic, bacon, potatoes, rosemary, and then the oil in a bowl. Stir thoroughly.

⇒ Place into air fryer basket and roast until golden for about 25 minutes.

Nutrition: Calories: 114 Fat: 8.1g Protein: 6.2g

68) Peppery Roasted Potatoes With Smoked Bacon

Preparation Time: 15 Minutes   **Cooking Time: 11 Minutes**   **Servings:2**

Ingredients:

- 38g Small rashers smoked bacon (1 lean)
- 1/3 Tsp. garlic powder (1/4 condiment)
- 1 Tsp. sea salt (1/4 condiment)
- 1 Tsp. Paprika (1/4 condiment)
- 1/3 Tsp. ground black pepper (1/4 condiment)
- 1 Bell pepper (½ green)
- 1 Tsp. mustard (1/4 condiment)
- 2 Habanero peppers, halved (½ green)

Directions:

⇒ Simply toss all the ingredients in a mixing dish, then transfer them to your air fryer's basket.

⇒ Air-fry at 375°F for 10 minutes, serve warm.

Nutrition: Calories: 122 Fat: 9g Protein: 10g

69) Pancetta Chops With Pineapple-Jalapeno Salsa

Preparation Time: 20 Minutes   **Cooking Time: 20 Minutes**   **Servings:3**

Ingredients:

- ½ pound Pieces of Pancetta Chops (roughly 10 ounces each) (1 lean)
- ½ Tablespoons parsley (½ green)
- 1 Tablespoon of ground Coriander (1/4 condiment)
- ¾ Cup of olive oil (1/4 condiment)
- 1 Tablespoon of finely chopped rosemary (1/4green)
- 1.5 Ounces of tomatoes, diced (1/4green)
- 2 Cloves of garlic, chopped (1/4 condiment)

- 8 Ounces of pineapple, diced (½ healthy fat)
- 1 Teaspoon of chopped Jalapenos (½ green)
- 2 Tsp. of Dijon Mustard (1/4 condiment)
- 1½ tsp. of sugar (1/8 condiment)
- 3.5 Ounces of lemon juice (1/8 condiment)
- ½ Tbsp. of finely chopped Cilantro (½ green)
- 2½ Tsp. of salt (1/8 condiment)

Directions:

⇒ Place the rosemary, sugar, mustard, ¼ cup of olive oil, one tablespoon of coriander, 1 ½ teaspoon of salt, cilantro, and one tablespoon of parsley in a mixing bowl and mix thoroughly. Add the pancetta chops and mix.

⇒ Fill a resealable plastic bag with the marinade and refrigerate for about 3 hours.

⇒ Heat your deep fryer to 390°F.

⇒ Place the jalapenos in a bowl and season with one teaspoon of oil to cover them evenly. Transfer the jalapenos to the air fryer and cook for about 7 minutes. Remove from the deep fryer and set aside to cool.

⇒ Once cooled, peel, remove the seeds and chop the jalapenos into small pieces and transfer them to a bowl. Add the pineapple, tomatoes, garlic, and lemon juice, the rest of the oil, parsley, coriander, and salt. Stir and set the sauce aside.

⇒ Remove the pancetta chops from the refrigerator and allow to rest for 30 minutes at room temperature before cooking.

⇒ Place the ribs in the air fryer and roast at 390°F for about 12 minutes. The pancetta chops are well cooked when the internal temperature is 140°F.

Nutrition: Calories: 104 Fat: 8.7g Protein: 6.7g

70) Cornbread With Pulled Pancetta

Preparation Time: 24 Minutes   **Cooking Time: 19 Minutes**   **Servings:2**

Ingredients:

- 2½ Cups pulled Pancetta (1 lean)
- 1 Tsp. dried rosemary (1/4green)
- ½ Tsp. chili powder (1/4 condiment)
- ½ Teaspoon Garlic cloves (1/4 condiment)

- ½ Recipe cornbread (1 healthy fat)
- ½ Tablespoon brown sugar (1/4 condiment)
- 1/3 Cup scallions, thinly sliced (½ green)
- 1 Tsp. sea salt (1/8 condiment)

Directions:

⇒ Preheat a large non-stick pan over medium heat; now, cook the scallions together with the garlic and the pulled pancetta.

⇒ Next, add the sugar, chili powder, rosemary, and salt. Cook, regularly stirring until thickened.

⇒ Preheat your air fryer to 3350°F. Now, coat two mini loaf pans with cooking spray. Add the pulled bacon mixture and spread over the bottom with a spatula.

⇒ Spread the previously prepared cornbread batter over the spicy pulled bacon mixture.

⇒ Bake this cornbread in a preheated air fryer until a centered tester is clean, or for 18 minutes.

Nutrition: Calories: 117 Fat: 9.4g Protein: 11g

71) Bacon and Garlic Pizzas

Preparation Time: 10 Minutes   **Cooking Time: 10 Minutes**   **Servings:4**

Ingredients:

- 32 oz. Dinner rolls, frozen
- ½ teaspoon Garlic cloves minced
- ½ Tsp. oregano dried
- ½ Tsp. garlic powder
- 1 Cup ketchup
- 2 Teaspoons Bacon slices, cooked and chopped
- 1 and ¼ Cups cheddar cheese, grated

Directions:

⇒ Place the rolls on a work surface and press them to obtain four ovals.

⇒ Spray each oval with cooking spray, transfer them to the air fryer and cook at 370°F for 2 minutes.

⇒ Spread the ketchup on each oval, divide the garlic, sprinkle with oregano and garlic powder, and garnish with bacon and cheese.

⇒ Return the pizzas to your hot air fryer and cook them at 370°F for another 8 minutes.

⇒ Serve hot for lunch.

Nutrition: Calories: 104 Fat: 9g Protein: 8.5g

72) Stuffed Meatballs

Preparation Time: 10 Minutes   **Cooking Time: 10 Minutes**   **Servings:4**

Ingredients:

- 1/3 Cup bread crumbs (1 healthy fat)
- 2 Tbsp. milk (½ condiment)
- 1 Tablespoon ketchup (1/4 condiment)
- 1 Egg (1 healthy fat)
- ½ Tsp. marjoram, dried (1/4 condiment)
- Salt and black pepper to the taste (1/8 condiment)
- 1-pound Lean beef, ground (1 lean)
- 20 Cheddar cheese cubes (½ healthy fat)
- 1 Tablespoon olive oil (1/8 condiment)

Directions:

⇒ In a bowl, mix the breadcrumbs with ketchup, milk, marjoram, salt, pepper, and egg and beat well.

⇒ Add the beef, mix and form 20 meatballs with this mixture.

⇒ Shape each meatball around a cube of cheese, sprinkle with oil and rub.

⇒ Place all the meatballs in your preheated air fryer and cook at 390°F for 10 minutes.

⇒ Serve them for lunch with a side of salad.

Nutrition: Calories: 112 Fat: 8.2g Protein: 7.7g

73) Low Carb Pork Dumplings With Dipping Sauce

Preparation Time: 30 Minutes   **Cooking Time: 20 Minutes**   **Servings:6**

Ingredients:

- 18 Dumpling wrappers (1 healthy fat)
- 1 Teaspoon olive oil (1/4 condiment)
- 4 Cups bok choy (chopped) (2 leans)
- 2 Tablespoons rice vinegar (½ condiment)
- 1 Tablespoon diced ginger (1/4 condiment)
- 1/4 Teaspoon crushed red pepper (½ green)

- 1 Tablespoon diced garlic (½ condiment)
- Lean ground pork ½ cup (2 leans)
- 2 Teaspoons Lite soy sauce (½ condiment)
- ½ Tsp. Honey (1/4 healthy fat)
- 1 Teaspoon Toasted sesame oil (1/4 condiment)
- Finely chopped scallions (1green)

Directions:

⇒ In a large skillet, heat the olive oil, add the bok choy, cook for 6 minutes and add the garlic, ginger and cook for one minute. Transfer this mixture to a paper towel and pat dry any excess oil

⇒ In a bowl, add the mixture of bok choy, red pepper, and lean ground pork and mix well.

⇒ Place dumplings wrap on a plate and add a spoon to fill half of the wrapper. With water, seal the edges and fold them.

⇒ Spray air fryer basket with oil, add dumplings into the air fryer basket and cook at 375°F for 12 minutes or until golden brown.

⇒ Meanwhile, to make the sauce, combine the sesame oil, rice vinegar, shallot, soy sauce, and honey in a mixing bowl.

⇒ Serve the dumplings with the sauce.

Nutrition: Calories: 140 Fat: 5g Protein: 12g

74) Gluten-Free Air Fryer Chicken Fried Brown Rice

Preparation Time: 10 Minutes   **Cooking Time: 20 Minutes**   **Servings:2**

Ingredients:

- 1 Cup Chicken Breast (1 lean)
- 1/4 Cup chopped White Onion (½ green)
- 1/4 Cup chopped Celery (½ green)

- 4 Cups Cooked brown rice (2 healthy fat)
- 1/4 Cup chopped Carrots (½ green)

Directions:

⇒ Place the foil on the air fryer basket, make sure to leave room for airflow, roll up on the sides

⇒ Spray the film with olive oil. Mix all the ingredients.

⇒ On top of the foil, add all the ingredients to the air fryer basket.

⇒ Give a splash of olive oil to the mixture.

⇒ Cook for five minutes at 390°F.

⇒ Open the air fryer and give the mixture a spin

⇒ Cook for another five minutes at 390°F.

⇒ Remove from the air fryer and serve hot.

Nutrition: Calories: 350 Fat: 6g Protein: 22g

75) Air Fryer Cheesy Pork Chops

Preparation Time: 5 Minutes   **Cooking Time: 8 Minutes**   **Servings:2**

Ingredients:

- 2 Lean pork chops
- Half teaspoon of Salt (1/4 condiment)
- ½ Tsp. Garlic powder (1/4 condiment)

- 4 Tbsp. Shredded cheese (1 healthy fat)
- Chopped cilantro (1green)

Directions:

⇒ Let the air fryer preheat to 350 degrees.

⇒ With garlic, coriander and salt, rub the pork chops. Put the air fryer on. Let it cook for four minutes. Turn them over and then cook for extra two minutes.

⇒ Drizzle the cheese on top and cook for another two minutes or until the cheese has melted.

⇒ Serve with salad.

Nutrition: Calories: 467 Protein: 61g Fat: 22g

Chapter 8 -   Snack Recipes

76) Glazed Bananas in Phyllo Nut Cups

Preparation Time: 30 Minutes   **Cooking Time: 45 Minutes**   **Servings: 6**

Ingredients:

- 3/4 Cups shelled pistachios
- ½ Cup sugar
- 1 Teaspoon. ground cinnamon
- 4 Sheets phyllo dough (14 inches x 9 inches)
- 1/4 Cup butter, melted

Sauce:
- 3/4 Cup butter, cubed
- 3/4 Cup packed brown sugar
- 3 Medium-firm bananas, sliced
- 1/4 Teaspoon. ground cinnamon
- 3 to 4 Cups vanilla ice cream

Directions:

⇒ Finely chop sugar and pistachios in a food processor; move to a bowl, then mix in cinnamon. Slice each phyllo sheet into six four-inch squares, get rid of the trimmings. Pile the squares, then use plastic wrap to cover.

⇒ Slather melted butter on each square one at a time, then scatter a heaping tablespoonful of pistachio mixture. Pile three squares, flip each at an angle to misalign the corners. Force each stack on the sides and bottom of an oiled eight ounces custard cup.

⇒ Bake for 15-20 minutes in a 350 degrees F oven until golden; cool for 5 minutes. Move to a wire rack to cool completely.

⇒ Melt and boil brown sugar and butter in a saucepan to make the sauce; lower heat. Mix in cinnamon and bananas gently; heat completely. Put ice cream in the phyllo cups until full, then put banana sauce on top. Serve right away.

Nutrition: Calories: 735 Total Carbohydrate: 82g Cholesterol: 111mg Total Fat: 45g Fiber: 3g Protein: 7g Sodium: 468mg

77) Salmon Cream Cheese and Onion on Bagel

Preparation Time: 15 Minutes   **Cooking Time: 10 Minutes**   **Servings: 4**

Ingredients:

- 8 Ounces (250g) smoked salmon fillet, thinly sliced
- ½ Cup (125g) cream cheese
- 1 Medium (110g) onion, thinly sliced
- 4 Bagels (about 80g each), split
- 2 Tablespoons (7g) fresh parsley, chopped
- Freshly ground black pepper, to taste

Directions:

⇒ Spread the cream cheese on each bottom's half of bagels. Top with salmon and onion, season with pepper, sprinkle with parsley and then cover with bagel tops.

⇒ Serve and enjoy.

Nutrition: Calories: 309 Fat: 14.1g Carbohydrates: 32.0g Protein: 14.7g Sodium: 571mg

78) Salmon Apple Salad Sandwich

Preparation Time: 15 Minutes   **Cooking Time: 10 Minutes**   **Servings:4**

Ingredients:

- 4 Ounces (125g) canned pink salmon, drained and flaked
- 1 Medium (180g) red apple, cored and diced
- 1 Celery stalk (about 60g), chopped
- 1 Shallot (about 40g), finely chopped
- 1/3 Cup (85g) light mayonnaise
- 8 Whole grain bread slices (about 30g each), toasted
- 8 (15g) Romaine lettuce leaves
- Salt and freshly ground black pepper

Directions:

⇒ Combine the salmon, apple, celery, shallot, and mayonnaise in a mixing bowl—season with salt and pepper.

⇒ Place one bread slice on a plate, top with lettuce and salmon salad, and then cover it with another slice of bread—repeat the procedure for the remaining ingredients.

⇒ Serve and enjoy.

Nutrition: Calories: 315 Fat: 11.3g Carbohydrates: 40.4g Protein: 15.1g Sodium: 469mg

79) Greek Baklava

Preparation Time: 20 Minutes   **Cooking Time: 20 Minutes**   **Servings:18**

Ingredients:

- 1 (16 oz.) Package phyllo dough
- 1 lb. Chopped nuts
- 1 Cup butter
- 1 Teaspoon ground cinnamon
- 1 Cup water
- 1 Cup white sugar
- 1 Teaspoon vanilla extract
- ½ Cup honey

Directions:

⇒ Preheat the oven to 175°C or 350°Fahrenheit. Spread butter on the sides and bottom of a 9- by 13-inch pan.

⇒ Chop the nuts, then mix with cinnamon; set it aside. Unfurl the phyllo dough, then halve the whole stack to fit the pan. Use a damp cloth to cover the phyllo to prevent drying as you proceed. Put two phyllo sheets in the pan, then butter well. Repeat to make eight layered phyllo sheets. Scatter 2-3 tablespoons of the nut mixture over the sheets, then place two more phyllo sheets on top, butter, sprinkle with nuts—layer as you go. The final layer should be six to eight phyllo sheets deep.

⇒ Make square or diamond shapes with a sharp knife up to the bottom of the pan. You can slice into four long rows for diagonal shapes. Bake until crisp and golden for 50 minutes.

⇒ Meanwhile, boil water and sugar until the sugar melts to make the sauce; mix in honey and vanilla. Let it simmer for 20 minutes.

⇒ Take the baklava out of the oven, then drizzle with sauce right away; cool. Serve the baklava in cupcake papers. You can also freeze them without cover. The baklava will turn soggy when wrapped.

Nutrition: Calories: 393 Total Carbohydrate: 37.5g Cholesterol: 27mg Total Fat: 25.9g Protein: 6.1g Sodium: 196mg

80) Easy Salmon Burger

Preparation Time: 15 minutes   **Cooking Time: 15 minutes**   **Servings:6**

Ingredients:

- 16 Ounces (450g) pink salmon, minced
- 1 Cup (250g) prepared mashed potatoes
- 1 Medium (110g) onion, chopped
- 1 Stalk celery (about 60g), finely chopped
- 1 Large egg (about 60g), lightly beaten

- 2 Tablespoons (7g) fresh cilantro, chopped
- 1 Cup (100g) breadcrumbs
- Vegetable oil, for deep frying
- Salt and freshly ground black pepper

Directions:

⇒ Combine the salmon, mashed potatoes, onion, celery, egg, and cilantro in a mixing bowl. Season to taste and mix thoroughly. Spoon about 2 Tablespoons of the mixture, roll in breadcrumbs, and then form into small patties.

⇒ Heat oil in a non-stick frying pan. Cook your salmon patties for 5 minutes on each side or until golden brown and crispy.

⇒ Serve in burger buns and with coleslaw on the side if desired.

⇒ Enjoy.

Nutrition: Calories: 230 Fat: 7.9g Carbs: 20.9g Protein: 18.9g Sodium: 298mg

81) White Bean Dip

Preparation Time: 10 Minutes   **Cooking Time: 0 Minutes**   **Servings:4**

Ingredients:

- 15 Ounces canned white beans, drained and rinsed
- 6 Ounces canned artichoke hearts, drained and quartered
- 4 Garlic cloves, minced
- 1 Tablespoon basil, chopped

- 2 Tablespoons olive oil
- Juice of ½ lemon
- Zest of ½ lemon, grated
- Salt and black pepper to the taste

Directions:

⇒ In your food processor, combine the beans with the artichokes and the rest of the ingredients except the oil and pulse well.

⇒ Add the oil gradually, pulse the mix again, divide into cups and serve as a party dip.

Nutrition: Calories: 274 Fat: 11.7g Fiber: 6.5g Carbs: 18.5g Protein: 16.5g

82) Grilled Salmon Burger

Preparation Time: 15 Minutes　　　**Cooking Time: 10 Minutes**　　　**Servings:4**

Ingredients:

- 16 Ounces (450g) pink salmon fillet, minced
- 1 Cup (250g) prepared mashed potatoes
- 1 Shallot (about 40g), chopped
- 1 Large egg (about 60g), lightly beaten
- 2 Tablespoons (7g) fresh coriander, chopped
- 4 Hamburger buns (about 60g each), split
- 1 Large tomato (about 150g), sliced
- 8 (15g) Romaine lettuce leaves
- 1/4 Cup (60g) mayonnaise
- Salt and freshly ground black pepper
- Cooking oil spray

Directions:

⇒ Combine the salmon, mashed potatoes, shallot, egg, and coriander in a mixing bowl—season with salt and pepper.

⇒ Spoon about two tablespoons of mixture and form into patties.

⇒ Preheat your grill or griddle on high—grease with cooking oil spray.

⇒ Grill the salmon patties for 4-5 minutes on each side or until cooked through. Transfer to a clean plate and cover to keep warm.

⇒ Spread some mayonnaise on the bottom half of the buns. Top with lettuce, salmon patty, and tomato. Cover with bun tops.

⇒ Serve and enjoy.

Nutrition:　　　Calories: 395 Fat: 18.0g Carbohydrates: 38.8g Protein: 21.8g Sodium: 383mg

83) Grilled Avocado Capers Crostini

Preparation Time: 10 Minutes　　　**Cooking Time: 20 Minutes**　　　**Servings:2**

Ingredients:

- 1 Avocado thinly sliced
- 9 Ounces ripened cherry tomatoes
- 1.50 Ounces fresh bocconcini in water
- 2 Tsp. Balsamic glaze
- 8 Pieces Italian baguette
- ½ Cup basil leaves

Directions:

⇒ Preheat your oven to 375 degrees Fahrenheit

⇒ Arrange your baking sheet properly before spraying them on top with olive oil.

⇒ Cut and bake your baguette until golden brown. Rub your crostini with the cut side of garlic while they are still warm, and you can season them with pepper and salt.

⇒ Divide the basil leaves on each piece of bread and top them up with tomato halves, avocado slices, and bocconcini. Season it with pepper and salt.

⇒ Broil it for 4 minutes, and when the cheese starts to melt through, remove and drizzle balsamic glaze before serving.

Nutrition:　　　Calories: 278 Fat: 10g Carbohydrates: 37g Proteins: 10g Sodium: 342mg Potassium: 277mg

84) Cheesy Garlic Sweet Potatoes

Preparation Time: 10 Minutes   **Cooking Time: 25 Minutes**   **Servings:4**

Ingredients:

- Sea salt
- ¼ Cup garlic butter melt
- ¾ Cup shredded mozzarella cheese
- ½ Cup of parmesan cheese freshly grated
- 4 Medium sized sweet potatoes
- 2 Tsp. freshly chopped parsley

Directions:

⇒ Heat the oven to 400 degrees Fahrenheit and brush the potatoes with garlic butter, and season each with pepper and salt. Arrange the cut side down on a greased baking sheet until the flesh is tender or they turn golden brown.

⇒ Remove them from the oven, flip the cut side up and top up with parsley and parmesan cheese.

⇒ Change the settings of your instant fryer oven to broil and on medium heat, add the cheese and melt it. Sprinkle salt and pepper to taste. Serve them warm.

Nutrition: Calories: 356 Fat: 9g Carbohydrates: 13g Proteins: 5g Potassium: 232mg Sodium: 252mg

85) Crispy Garlic Baked Potato Wedges

Preparation Time: 5 Minutes   **Cooking Time: 10 Minutes**   **Servings:3**

Ingredients:

- 3 Tsp. salt
- 1 Tsp. minced garlic
- 6 Large russet
- ¼ Cup olive oil
- 1 Tsp. Paprika
- 2/3 Finely grated parmesan cheese
- 2 Tsp. Freshly chopped parsley

Directions:

⇒ Preheat the oven to 350 degrees Fahrenheit and line the baking sheet with parchment paper.

⇒ Cut the potatoes into half-length and cut each half in half lengthways again. Make eight wedges.

⇒ In a small jug, combine garlic, oil, paprika, and salt and place your wedges in the baking sheets. Pour the oil mixture over the potatoes and toss them to ensure that they are evenly coated.

⇒ Arrange the potato wedges in a single layer on the baking tray and sprinkle salt and parmesan cheese if needed. Bake for 35 minutes and turn the wedges once half side is cooked.

⇒ Flip the other side until they are both golden brown.

⇒ Sprinkle parsley and the remaining parmesan before serving.

Nutrition: Calories: 324 Fat: 6g Carbs: 8g Proteins: 2g Sodium: 51mg Potassium: 120mg

86) Cheesy Mashed Sweet Potato Cakes

Preparation Time: 10 Minutes   **Cooking Time: 30 Minutes**   **Servings:4**

Ingredients:

- ¾ Cup bread crumbs
- 4 Cups mashed potatoes
- ½ Cup onions
- 2 Cup of grated mozzarella cheese
- ¼ Cup fresh grated parmesan cheese
- 2 Large garlic cloves finely chopped
- 1 Egg
- 2 Tsp. Finely chopped parsley
- Salt and pepper to taste

Directions:

⇒ Line your baking sheet with foil. Wash, peel and cut the sweet potatoes into six pieces. Arrange them inside the baking sheet and drizzle a small amount of oil on top before seasoning with salt and pepper.

⇒ Cover with a baking sheet and bake it for 45 minutes; once cooked, transfer them into a mixing bowl and mash them well with a potato masher.

⇒ Put the sweet potatoes in a bowl, add green onions, parmesan, mozzarella, garlic, egg, parsley, and bread crumbs. Mash and combine the mixture together using the masher.

⇒ Put the remaining ¼ cup of the breadcrumbs in place. Scoop a teaspoon of the mixture into your palm and form round patties around ½ an inch thick. Dredge your patties in the breadcrumbs to cover both sides and set them aside.

⇒ Heat a tablespoon of oil in a medium nonstick pan. When the oil is hot, begin to cook the patties in batches 4 or 5 per session and cook each side for 6 minutes until they turn golden brown. Use a spoon or spatula to flip them. Add oil to prevent burning.

Nutrition: Calories:126 Fat:6g Carbs: 15g Proteins 3g Sodium: 400mg

87) Sticky Chicken Thai Wings

Preparation Time: 10 Minutes   **Cooking Time: 30 Minutes**   **Servings:6**

Ingredients:

- 3 Pounds chicken wings removed
- 1 Tsp. sea salt to taste
- For the glaze:
- ¾ Cup Thai sweet chili sauce
- ¼ Cup soy sauce
- 4 Tsp. brown sugar
- 4 Tsp. rice wine vinegar
- 3 Tsp. fish sauce
- 2 Tsp. lime juice
- 1 Tsp. lemongrass minced
- 2 Tsp. sesame oil
- 1 Tsp. garlic minced

Directions:

⇒ Preheat the oven to 350 degrees Fahrenheit. Lightly spray your baking tray with the cooking spray and set it aside. To prepare the glaze, combine the ingredients in a small bowl and whisk them until they are well combined. Pour half of the mixture into a pan and reserve the rest.

⇒ Trim any excess skin off the wing edges and season it with pepper and salt. Add the wings to a baking tray and pour the sauce over the wings tossing them for the sauce to coat evenly. Arrange them in a single layer and bake them for 15 minutes.

⇒ While the wings are in the oven, bring your glaze to simmer in medium heat until there are visible bubbles.

⇒ Once the wings are cooked on one side, rotate each piece and bake for an extra 10 minutes. Baste them and return them into the oven to allow for more cooking until they are golden brown. Garnish with onion slices, cilantro, chili flakes, and sprinkle the remaining salt. Serve with some glaze as you desire.

Nutrition: Calories: 256 Fat: 16g Carbohydrates 19g Proteins: 20g Potassium: 213mg Sodium: 561mg

88) Caprese Stuffed Garlic Butter Portobellos

Preparation Time: 5 Minutes   **Cooking Time: 10 Minutes**   **Servings:6**

Ingredients:

For the garlic butter:

- 2 Tsp. of butter
- 2 Cloves garlic
- 1 Tsp. parsley finely chopped

For the mushrooms:

- 6 Large portobello mushrooms, washed and dried well with a paper towel
- 6 Mozzarella cheese balls thinly sliced

- 1 Cup grape tomatoes thinly sliced
- Fresh basil for garnishing

For the balsamic glaze:

- 2 Tsp. brown sugar
- ¼ Cup balsamic vinegar

Directions:

⇒ Preheat the oven to broil, setting on high heat. Arrange the oven shelf and place it in the right direction.

⇒ Combine the garlic butter ingredients in a small pan and melt until the garlic begins to be fragrant. Brush the bottoms of the mushroom and place them on the buttered section of the baking tray.

⇒ Flip and brush the remaining garlic over each cap. Fill each mushroom with tomatoes and mozzarella slices and grill until the cheese has melted. Drizzle the balsamic glaze and sprinkle some salt to taste.

⇒ If you are making the balsamic glaze from scratch, combine the sugar and vinegar in a small pan and reduce the heat to low. Allow it to simmer for 6 minutes or until the mixture has thickened well.

Nutrition: Calories: 101 Fat: 5g Carbohydrates: 12g Proteins: 2g Sodium: 58mg Potassium: 377mg

89) Veggie Fritters

Preparation Time: 10 Minutes   **Cooking Time: 10 Minutes**   **Servings:4**

Ingredients:

- 2 Garlic cloves, minced
- 2 Yellow onions, chopped
- 4 Scallions, chopped
- 2 Carrots, grated
- 2 Teaspoons cumin, ground
- ½ Teaspoon turmeric powder
- Salt and black pepper to the taste
- ¼ Teaspoon coriander, ground

- 2 Tablespoons parsley, chopped
- ¼ Teaspoon lemon juice
- ½ Cup almond flour
- 2 Beets, peeled and grated
- 2 Eggs, whisked
- ¼ Cup tapioca flour
- 3 Tablespoons olive oil

Directions:

⇒ In a bowl, combine the garlic with the onions, scallions, and the rest of the ingredients except the oil; stir well and shape medium fritters out of this mix.

⇒ Heat up a pan with the oil over medium-high heat, add the fritters, cook for 5 minutes on each side, arrange on a platter and serve.

Nutrition: Calories: 209 Fat: 11.2g Fiber: 3g Carbs: 4.4g Protein: 4.8g

90) Eggplant Dip

Preparation Time: 10 Minutes   **Cooking Time: 40 Minutes**   **Servings:4**

Ingredients:

- 1 Eggplant, poked with a fork
- 2 Tablespoons tahini paste
- 2 Tablespoons lemon juice
- 2 Garlic cloves, minced
- 1 Tablespoon olive oil
- Salt and black pepper to the taste
- 1 Tablespoon parsley, chopped

Directions:

⇒ Put the eggplant in a roasting pan, bake at 400°F for 40 minutes, cool down, peel, and transfer to your food processor.

⇒ Add the rest of the ingredients except the parsley, pulse well, divide into small bowls and serve as an appetizer with the parsley sprinkled on top.

Nutrition: Calories: 121 Fat: 4.3g Fiber: 1g Carbs: 1.4g Protein:4.3g

91) Coconut Shrimp

Preparation Time: 15 Minutes   **Cooking Time: 15 Minutes**   **Servings:6**

Ingredients:

- Salt and pepper
- 1-pound Jumbo shrimp peeled and deveined
- ½ Cup all-purpose flour

  For the batter:
- ½ Cup beer
- 1 Tsp. Baking powder
- ½ Cup all-purpose flour
- 1 Egg

  For the coating:
- 1 Cup panko bread crumbs
- 1 Cup shredded coconut

Directions:

⇒ Line the baking tray with parchment paper.

⇒ In a shallow bowl, add ½ cup flour for dredging, and in another bowl, whisk the batter ingredients. The batter should resemble a pancake consistency. If it is too thick, add a little mineral or beer whisking in between; in another bowl, mix together the shredded coconut and bread crumbs.

⇒ Dredge the shrimps in flour, shaking off any excess before dipping in the batter, and coat them with the bread crumb mixture. Lightly press the coconut into the shrimp.

⇒ Place them into the baking sheet and repeat the process until you have several.

⇒ In a Dutch oven skillet, heat vegetable oil until it is nice and hot, fry the frozen shrimp batches for 3 minutes per side. Drain them on a paper towel-lined plate.

⇒ Serve immediately with sweet chili sauce.

Nutrition: Calories: 409 Fat: 11g Carbohydrates: 46g Proteins: 30g Sodium: 767mg Potassium: 345mg

92) Salmon Sandwich With Avocado and Egg

Preparation Time: 15 Minutes   **Cooking Time: 10 Minutes**   **Servings:4**

Ingredients:

- 8 Ounces (250g) smoked salmon, thinly sliced

- 1 Medium (200g) ripe avocado, thinly sliced

- 4 Large poached eggs (about 60g each)

- 4 Slices whole wheat bread (about 30g each)

- 2 Cups (60g) arugula or baby rocket

- Salt and freshly ground black pepper

Directions:

⇒ Place one bread slice on a plate top with arugula, avocado, salmon, and poached egg—season with salt and pepper. Repeat the procedure for the remaining ingredients.

⇒ Serve and enjoy.

Nutrition: Calories: 310 Fat: 18.2g Carbohydrates: 16.4g Protein: 21.3g Sodium: 383mg

Chapter 9 - Dessert Recipes

93) Lemon Curd

Preparation Time: 10 Minutes   **Cooking Time: 10 Minutes**   **Servings: 2**

Ingredients:

- 4 Tbsp. Butter
- 1 Cup sugar
- 2/3 Cups lemon juice
- 3 Eggs
- 2 Tsp. Lemon zest
- 1 ½ Cups of water

Directions:

⇒ Whisk the butter and sugar thoroughly until smooth.

⇒ Add two whole eggs and incorporate just the yolk of the other egg.

⇒ Add the lemon juice.

⇒ Transfer the mixture into the two jars and tightly seal the tops

⇒ Pour 1 ½ cups of water into the bottom of the Instant Pot and place in a steaming rack. Put the jars on the rack and cook on HIGH PRESSURE for 10 minutes.

⇒ Natural-release the pressure for 10 minutes before quickly releasing the rest.

⇒ Stir in the zest and put the lids back on the jars.

Nutrition: Calories: 45 Fat: 1g Carbs: 8g Protein: 1g

94) Poached Pears

Preparation Time: 8 Minutes   **Cooking Time: 10 Minutes**   **Servings: 2**

Ingredients:

- 1 Tbsp. Lime juice
- 2 Tsp. Lime zest
- 1 Cinnamon stick
- 2 Whole pears, peeled
- 1 Cup of water
- Fresh mint leaves for garnish

Directions:

⇒ Add all ingredients except for the mint leaves to the Instant Pot.

⇒ Seal the Instant Pot and choose the MANUAL button.

⇒ Cook on HIGH for 10 minutes.

⇒ Perform a natural pressure release.

⇒ Remove the pears from the pot.

⇒ Serve in bowls and garnish with mint on top.

Nutrition: Calories: 59 Fat: 0.1g Carbs: 14g Protein: 0.3g

95) Delicious Brownie Bites

Preparation Time: 20 Minutes   **Cooking Time: 0 Minutes**   **Servings: 13**

Ingredients:

- 1/4 Cup unsweetened chocolate chips
- 1/4 Cup unsweetened cocoa powder
- 1 Cup pecans, chopped
- ½ Cup almond butter
- ½ Tsp. Vanilla
- 1/4 Cup monk fruit sweetener
- 1/8 Tsp. Pink salt

Directions:

⇒ Add pecans, sweetener, vanilla, almond butter, cocoa powder, and salt into the food processor and process until well combined.

⇒ Transfer the brownie mixture into a large bowl. Add chocolate chips and fold well.

⇒ Make small round shape balls from the brownie mixture and place them onto a baking tray.

⇒ Place in the freezer for 20 minutes.

⇒ Serve and enjoy.

Nutrition: Calories: 108 Fat: 9g Carbs: 4g Sugar: 1g Protein: 2g Cholesterol: 0mg

96) Pumpkin Balls

Preparation Time: 15 Minutes   **Cooking Time: 0 Minutes**   **Servings: 18**

Ingredients:

- 1 Cup almond butter
- 5 Drops liquid stevia
- 2 Tbsp. Coconut flour
- 2 Tbsp. Pumpkin puree
- 1 Tsp. Pumpkin pie spice

Directions:

⇒ Mix together pumpkin puree in a large bowl and almond butter until well combined.

⇒ Add liquid stevia, pumpkin pie spice, and coconut flour and mix well.

⇒ Make small balls from the mixture and place them onto a baking tray.

⇒ Place in the freezer for 1 hour.

⇒ Serve and enjoy.

Nutrition: Calories: 96 Fat: 8g Carbs: 4g Sugar: 1g Protein: 2g Cholesterol: 0mg

97) Smooth Peanut Butter Cream

Preparation Time: 10 Minutes   **Cooking Time: 0 Minutes**   **Servings: 8**

Ingredients:

- 1/4 Cup peanut butter
- 4 Overripe bananas, chopped
- 1/3 Cup cocoa powder
- 1/4 Tsp. vanilla extract
- 1/8 Tsp. salt

Directions:

⇒ In the blender, add all the listed ingredients and blend until smooth.

⇒ Serve immediately and enjoy.

Nutrition: Calories: 101 Fat: 5g Carbs: 14g Sugar: 7g Protein: 3g Cholesterol: 0mg

98) Vanilla Avocado Popsicles

Preparation Time: 20 Minutes   **Cooking Time: 0 Minutes**   **Servings: 6**

Ingredients:

- 2 Avocadoes
- 1 Tsp. Vanilla
- 1 Cup almond milk
- 1 Tsp. Liquid stevia
- ½ Cup unsweetened cocoa powder

Directions:

⇒ In the blender, add all the listed ingredients and blend smoothly.

⇒ Pour blended mixture into the Popsicle molds and place in the freezer until set.

⇒ Serve and enjoy.

Nutrition: Calories: 130 Fat: 12g Carbs: 7g Sugar: 1g Protein: 3g Cholesterol: 0mg

99) Chocolate Popsicle

Preparation Time: 20 Minutes   **Cooking Time: 10 Minutes**   **Servings:6**

Ingredients:

- 4 oz. Unsweetened chocolate, chopped
- 6 Drops liquid stevia
- 1 ½ Cups heavy cream

Directions:

⇒ Add heavy cream into the microwave-safe bowl and microwave until it just begins boiling.

⇒ Add chocolate into the heavy cream and set aside for 5 minutes.

⇒ Add liquid stevia into the heavy cream mixture and stir until chocolate is melted.

⇒ Pour the mixture into the Popsicle molds and place them in the freezer for 4 hours or until set.

⇒ Serve and enjoy.

Nutrition: Calories: 198 Fat: 21g Carbs: 6g Sugar: 0.2g Protein: 3g Cholesterol: 41mg

100) Raspberry Ice Cream

Preparation Time: 10 Minutes   **Cooking Time: 0 Minutes**   **Servings:2**

Ingredients:

- 1 Cup frozen raspberries
- ½ Cup heavy cream
- 1/8 Tsp. Stevia powder

Directions:

⇒ Blend all the listed ingredients in a blender until smooth.

⇒ Serve immediately and enjoy.

Nutrition: Calories: 144 Fat: 11g Carbs: 10g Sugar: 4g Protein: 2g Cholesterol: 41mg

101) Chocolate Frosty

Preparation Time: 20 Minutes   **Cooking Time: 0 Minutes**   **Servings:4**

Ingredients:

- 2 Tbsp. unsweetened cocoa powder
- 1 Cup heavy whipping cream
- 1 Tbsp. almond butter
- 5 Drops liquid stevia
- 1 Tsp. vanilla

Directions:

⇒ Add cream into the medium bowl and beat using the hand mixer for 5 minutes.

⇒ Add the remaining ingredients and blend until you get a thick cream form.

⇒ Pour in serving bowls and place them in the freezer for 30 minutes.

⇒ Serve and enjoy.

Nutrition: Calories: 137 Fat: 13g Carbs: 3g Sugar: 0.5g Protein: 2g Cholesterol: 41mg

102)   Bread Dough and Amaretto Dessert

Preparation Time: 15 Minutes   **Cooking Time: 8 Minutes**   **Servings:12**

Ingredients:

- 1 lb. Bread dough
- 1 Cup sugar
- ½ Cup butter

- 1 Cup heavy cream
- 12 oz. Chocolate chips
- 2 Tbsp. amaretto liqueur

Directions:

⇒ Turn dough, cut into 20 slices and cut each piece in halves.

⇒ Put the dough pieces with spray sugar and butter, put this into the air fryer's basket, and cook them at 350°F for 5 minutes. Turn them, cook for 3 minutes still. Move to a platter.

⇒ Melt the heavy cream in a pan over medium heat, put chocolate chips and turn until they melt.

⇒ Put in liqueur, turn and move to a bowl.

⇒ Serve bread dippers with the sauce.

Nutrition: Calories: 179 Total Fat: 18g Total carbs: 17g

103)   Bread Pudding

Preparation Time: 10 Minutes   **Cooking Time: 10 Minutes**   **Servings:4**

Ingredients:

- 6 Glazed doughnuts
- 1 Cup cherries
- 4 Egg yolks
- 1 and ½ Cups whipping cream

- ½ Cup raisins
- ¼ Cup sugar
- ½ Cup chocolate chips

Directions:

⇒ Mix in cherries with whipping cream and egg in a bowl, then turn properly.

⇒ Mix in raisins with chocolate chips, sugar, and doughnuts in a bowl, then stir.

⇒ Combine the two mixtures, pour into an oiled pan, then into the air fryer, and cook at 310°F for 1 hour.

⇒ Cool pudding before cutting.

⇒ Serve.

Nutrition: Calories: 456 Total Fat: 11g Total carbs: 6g

Chapter 10 - L & G McAdams Meal Plan – for Men

Day 1

11) Barley Breakfast Bowl With Lemon Yogurt Sauce | Calories 432

23) Greek Style Mini Burger Pies | Calories 270

30) Wild Rice Prawn Salad | Calories 207

43) Tofu Stir Fry With Asparagus Stew | Calories 138

69) Pancetta Chops With Pineapple-Jalapeno Salsa | Calories 104

92) Salmon Sandwich With Avocado and Egg | Calories 310

Total Calories 1461

Day 3

8) Apple Oatmeal | Calories 277

28) Barley and Lentil Salad | Calories 213

29) Blueberry Cantaloupe Avocado Salad | Calories 406

52) Cinnamon Butternut Squash Fries | Calories 175

68) Peppery Roasted Potatoes With Smoked Bacon | Calories 122

93) Lemon Curd | Calories 45

Total Calories 1238

Day 5

14) Omelette à la Margherita | Calories 402

20) Chicken Omelet | Calories 400

39) Broccoli Salad | Calories 239

55) Feta & Mushroom Frittata | Calories 226

70) Cornbread With Pulled Pancetta | Calories 117

81) White Bean Dip | Calories 274

Total Calories 1658

Day 7

10) Oatmeal-Applesauce Muffins | Calories 115

19) Lemony Parmesan Salmon | Calories 290

35) Romaine Lettuce and Radicchios Mix | Calories 87

62) Thai Roasted Veggies | Calories 69

71) Bacon and Garlic Pizzas | Calories 104

90) Eggplant Dip | Calories 121

Total Calories 786

Day 2

16) Tuna Spinach Casserole | Calories 400

25) Mouth-watering Pie | Calories 198

33) Norwegian Niçoise Salad Smoked Salmon Cucumber Egg and Asparagus | Calories 257

65) Jicama Fries | Calories 211

75) Air Fryer Cheesy Pork Chops | Calories 467

89) Veggie Fritters | Calories 209

Total Calories 1742

Day 4

5) Flaxseed Porridge With Cinnamon | Calories 171

17) Lean and Green Chicken Pesto Pasta | Calories 244

41) Taste of Normandy Salad | Calories 699

61) Air Fryer Brussels Sprouts | Calories 118

72) Stuffed Meatballs | Calories 112

78) Salmon Apple Salad Sandwich | Calories 315

Total Calories 1659

Day 6

7) Banana Cashew Toast | Calories 634

22) Tasty WW Pancakes | Calories 344

40) Loaded Caesar Salad With Crunchy Chickpeas | Calories 367

57) Feta & Mushroom Frittata | Calories 405

74) Gluten-Free Air Fryer Chicken Fried Brown Rice | Calories 350

85) Crispy Garlic Baked Potato Wedges | Calories 324

Total Calories 2424

Chapter 11 -   Conclusion

Warning, remember to consult with your medical professional before starting this diet, he/she knows what is best for you and what special requirements you may have.

I hope this cookbook has been useful and that you enjoy it as much as I did when I was writing it and testing it on myself.

In order to get the best results, I recommend you to accompany the diet with an exercise routine and trust in the process, I am sure you will see the results you expect by following these recipes.

I also recommend you to adopt this diet as part of your lifestyle, since it is a diet both in the beginning and in the maintenance of the results. That's right, you will be able to lose weight and stay in shape.

Adopting a healthy lifestyle increases your life expectancy, your quality of life and prevents diseases.

Best wishes,

Lorely McAdams

Lean and Green Diet Cookbook for Athletes

Dr. McAdams Sport Diet Plan | 100+ Amazing Recipes and Fueling Hacks Meal to Boost Your Metabolism and Lose Weight with No-Stress

By Lorely McAdams

Chapter 1 - Introduction

If you have an athletic lifestyle you are probably always looking for new and better diets that will give you energy and allow you to stay healthy and fit. I understand you because I've been through the same thing, and after trying several diets suitable for an athletic lifestyle I came across the lean and green diet.

In the following pages you will learn what this diet consists of and what are its main benefits for athletes.

The lean and green diet basically consists of increasing your protein intake and reducing the consumption of carbohydrates, trans fats and sugars. As you probably know trans fats and sugars, far from providing energy to the body make you get tired faster and inactivate your appetite.

Trainers know perfectly well that protein is important for muscle development and repair of body tissues. It can also be used by the body for energy, but you have to have a balance with carbohydrate intake, so the lean and green diet gives you a healthy balance between carbohydrates and protein, because protein intake without carbohydrates can seriously affect your health, especially if you have an athletic life where it is normal to burn carbohydrates.

Keep in mind that athletes, even bodybuilders, need just a little extra protein to support muscle development. As for the consumption of carbohydrates, it is better to consume the so-called good carbohydrates, which can often be found in vegetables.

However, feel stress-free because in this cookbook you will find a meal plan with the exact portions of protein and carbohydrates for each recipe, so you can focus only on your workouts.

In summary, the main benefits, of the lean and green diet, for athletes are:
- *Helping muscle development*
- *Helps you repair body tissues*
- *It allows you to stay in shape in a healthy way*
- *It gives you the energy you need for your workout.*

So, what are you waiting for! Never give up, go ahead, achieve your goals and maintain a healthy nutrition with the lean and green diet.

Chapter 2 -   Breakfast Recipes

1) Cinnamon-Apple Granola With Greek Yogurt

Preparation Time: 5 Minutes　　　**Cooking Time: 10 Minutes**　　　**Servings:2**

Ingredients:

- ½ C. Raw almonds, chopped (or raw nuts of choice)
- ½ C. Raw walnuts, chopped (or raw nuts of choice)
- ½ Apple, peeled and diced
- 1 Tbsp. Almond flour
- 2 Tbsp. Vanilla protein powder
- 1 Tsp. Ground cinnamon
- 1/8 C. Applesauce, unsweetened preferred
- 2 Tsp. Honey
- 2 Tsp. Almond butter
- 1/16 Tsp. Vanilla extract
- Dash of sea salt
- 1 Cup Greek plain or vanilla yogurt (or flavor of choice)

Directions:

⇒ In a mixing bowl, combine the chopped almonds, chopped walnuts (or preferred raw nuts), diced apple, vanilla protein powder, almond flour, lucuma (opt), and cinnamon and salt in a bowl. Mix well.

⇒ In a second bowl, combine the apple sauce, almond butter, honey, and vanilla extract. Mix well. Pour the bowl with the nuts into the bowl with the wet ingredients and blend together thoroughly. Make sure all dry ingredients get coated.

⇒ Place the granola mixture onto a parchment paper-lined baking sheet and bake until the desired crunch is obtained for approximately 8 to 10 minutes. Take off from the oven and let cool or eat hot. Place ½ cup of Greek yogurt into two bowls. Divide the granola and sprinkle over the yogurt in each bowl. Serve immediately.

Nutrition:　　　Calories: 312 kcal Protein: 11.72g Fat: 22.37g Carbohydrates: 19.92g

2) Greek Yogurt With Cherry-Almond Syrup Parfait

Preparation Time: 25 Minutes　　　**Cooking Time: 5 Minutes**　　　**Servings:2**

Ingredients:

- 1 C. Fresh black or red cherries, pitted
- 2 Tbsp. Almond syrup
- 2 Tbsp. Coconut palm sugar
- 1 Tsp. Fresh-squeezed lemon juice
- 2 C. Greek plain yogurt, stir to loosen
- 2 Tbsp. Sliced almonds to garnish
- 4 Tbsp. Granola of choice, to garnish (opt.)

Directions:

⇒ Place a saucepan over medium-high heat and combine cherries, almond syrup, sugar, lemon juice, and one tablespoon of water. Stir to combine, then place it to simmer, constantly stirring until sugar is dissolved. Continue to simmer for further 5 minutes until liquid starts to turn into a syrupy mixture, but the cherries are still holding firm.

⇒ Place the mixture in a bowl and let cool for 5 minutes at room temperature, then bring it in the refrigerator to chill until it is completely cold.

⇒ Place one cup of Greek yogurt into two serving bowls and spoon ½ of the cherries and their syrupy juices over the yogurt. Garnish with sliced almonds or granola, if desired. Serve immediately.

Nutrition:　　　Calories: 185 kcal Protein: 4.75g Fat: 4.88g Carbohydrates: 33.07g

3) Omelette With Tomatoes and Spring Onions

Preparation Time: 5 Minutes   **Cooking Time: 20 Minutes**   **Servings:**

Ingredients:

- 6 Eggs
- 2 Tomatoes
- 2 Spring onions
- 1 Shallot
- 2 Tbsp. Butter

- 1 Tbsp. Olive oil
- 1 Pinch of nutmeg
- Salt
- Pepper

Directions:

⇒ Whisk the eggs in a bowl.

⇒ Mix them together and season them with salt and pepper.

⇒ Peel the shallot and chop it up.

⇒ Clean the onions and cut them into rings.

⇒ Wash the tomatoes and cut them into pieces.

⇒ Heat butter and oil in a pan.

⇒ Braise half of the shallots in it.

⇒ Add half of the egg mixture.

⇒ Let everything set over medium heat.

⇒ Scatter a few tomatoes and onion rings on top.

⇒ Repeat with the second half of the egg mixture.

⇒ In the end, spread the grated nutmeg over the whole thing.

Nutrition: Kcal: 263 Carbohydrates: 8g Protein: 20.3g Fat: 24g

4) Swiss Chard and Spinach With Egg

Preparation Time: 5 Minutes   **Cooking Time: 10 Minutes**   **Servings:4**

Ingredients:

- 4 Egg whites
- 4 Pieces of rice bread
- 20 Pieces spinach leaves
- 20 Pieces Swiss chard leaves

- 4 Tbsp. Parsley (fresh)
- 1 Tsp. Olive oil
- Sea salt, ground pepper, and dried mint

Directions:

⇒ Bring to a boil 2 cups of water in a pan just below the boiling point. Open an egg, separate the whites from the yolks. Put the whites in a small bowl. Lower the bowl towards the heated water, and gently pour the egg into the pan. Do the same with the other eggs. Poach the eggs for 4 minutes. After that, gently take the eggs, one at a time, and transfer them to a plate. Do the same with the remaining two eggs.

⇒ Chop the parsley and sauté the leaves in a pan for 6 minutes. Toast the bread while doing this. When done, make a layer of the sautéed greens and the chopped parsley on top of the toasted rice bread. Put the poached eggs above the bed of greens. Sprinkle each serving with ground pepper, sea salt, and dried mint.

Nutrition: Calories: 49 kcal Protein: 5.31g Fat: 2.73g Carbohydrates: 0.48g

5) Omega-3-rich Cold Banana Breakfast

Preparation Time: 10 Minutes   **Cooking Time: 0 Minutes**   **Servings:2**

Ingredients:

- ½ Cup cold milk
- 4 Tbsp. Sesame seeds
- 2 Tbsp. Flaxseeds

- 4 Tbsp. Sunflower seeds
- 2 Tbsp. Ground coconut
- 1 Large Sliced Banana

Directions:

⇒ Mix the milk and honey in your breakfast bowl. Use your coffee grinder to grind all the seeds. Add the ground seeds to the honey and milk mixture.

⇒ Place the sliced bananas neatly on top. Sprinkle the ground coconuts for added flavor.

Nutrition: Calories: 393 kcal Protein: 14.85g Fat: 27.63g Carbohydrates: 27.37g

6) Breakfast Pitas

Preparation Time: 4 Minutes   **Cooking Time: 6 Minutes**   **Servings:4**

Ingredients:

- 8 Egg whites
- 2 C. Bell peppers, chopped (any color)
- 1 Tsp. Garlic powder
- 1 Tsp. Onion powder

- 1 C. Raw spinach (cook if you prefer)
- 2 Tsp. Extra virgin olive oil
- 4 Whole-wheat pita pockets

Directions:

⇒ Put the olive oil into a large sauté pan and place it over medium heat. When the oil is hot in glistening, toss in the bell pepper and sauté for about 3 minutes or until tender. Add in the spinach now (if you want it cooked) and sauté for about 1 to 3 minutes or just up to the sides starts to wilt.

⇒ Place the egg whites into a small bowl, whisk well. Add in spices; whisk well. Pour the egg mixture into the sauté pan and scramble everything together.

⇒ Remove from heat and stuff ½ to one cup of mixture into a pita pocket and serve.

Nutrition: Calories: 153 kcal Protein: 12.4g Fat: 3.41g Carbohydrates: 19.32g

7) Strawberry Yogurt Treat

Preparation Time: 10 Minutes   **Cooking Time: 0 Minutes**   **Servings:2**

Ingredients:

- 4 Cups 0% fat plain yogurt
- 1 Cup sliced strawberries
- 8 Tbsp. of Flax meal

- 4 Tbsp. Honey
- 8 Tbsp. Walnuts (chopped)

Directions:

⇒ Distribute 2 cups of the yogurt into your serving bowls. Neatly layer the flax meal and the walnut in the middle. Add a drizzle of half of the honey before covering with the last layer of yogurt.

⇒ Add the honey and strawberries on top of the yogurt to add color when you serve.

Nutrition: Calories: 733 kcal Protein: 38.42g Fat: 30.57g Carbohydrates: 83.44g

8) Chia Seed Gel With Pomegranate and Nuts

Preparation Time: 5 minutes   **Cooking Time: 10 minutes**   **Servings:3**

Ingredients:

- 20g Hazelnuts
- 20g Walnuts
- 120ml Almond milk
- 4 Tbsp. Chia seeds
- 4 Tbsp. Pomegranate seeds
- 1 Teaspoon agave syrup
- Some lime juice

Directions:

⇒ Finely chop the nuts.

⇒ Mix the almond milk with the chia seeds.

⇒ Let everything soak for 10 to 20 minutes.

⇒ Occasionally stir the mixture with the chia seeds.

⇒ Stir in the agave syrup and a little lime juice.

⇒ Pour two tablespoons of each mixture into a dessert glass.

⇒ Layer the chopped nuts on top.

⇒ Cover the nuts with one tablespoon each of the chia mass.

⇒ Sprinkle the pomegranate seeds on top and serve everything.

Nutrition: Kcal: 248 Carbohydrates: 7g Protein: 1g Fat: 19g

9) Lavender Blueberry Chia Seed Pudding

Preparation Time: 1 Hour 10 Minutes   **Cooking Time: 0 Minutes**   **Servings:4**

Ingredients:

- 100g Blueberries
- 70g Organic quark
- 50g Soy yogurt
- 30g Hazelnuts
- 200ml Almond milk
- 2 Tbsp. chia seeds
- 2 Teaspoons agave syrup
- 2 Teaspoons of lavender

Directions:

⇒ Bring the almond milk to a boil along with the lavender.

⇒ Let the mixture simmer for 10 minutes at a reduced temperature.

⇒ Let them cool down afterward.

⇒ If the milk is cold, add the blueberries and puree everything.

⇒ Mix the whole thing with the chia seeds and agave syrup.

⇒ Let everything soak in the refrigerator for an hour.

⇒ Mix the yogurt and organic quark together.

⇒ Add both to the mixture.

⇒ Divide the pudding into glasses.

⇒ Finely chop the hazelnuts and sprinkle them on top.

Nutrition: Kcal: 252 Carbohydrates: 12g Protein: 1g Fat: 11g

10) Quinoa Porridge

Preparation Time: 5 Minutes   **Cooking Time: 25 Minutes**   **Servings: 2**

Ingredients:

- 2 Cups coconut milk
- 1 Cup rinsed quinoa
- 1/8 Tsp. Ground cinnamon
- 1 Cup fresh blueberries

Directions:

⇒ In a saucepan, boil the coconut milk over high heat.

⇒ Add the quinoa to the milk, then bring the mixture to a boil.

⇒ Let it simmer for 15 minutes on medium heat until the milk is reduced.

⇒ Add the cinnamon, then mix it properly in the saucepan.

⇒ Cover the saucepan and cook for at least 8 minutes until the milk is completely absorbed.

⇒ Add in the blueberries, then cook for 30 more seconds.

⇒ Serve.

Nutrition: Calories: 271 kcal Fat: 3.7g Carbs: 54g Protein: 6.5g

11) Eel on Scrambled Eggs and Bread

Preparation Time: 5 Minutes   **Cooking Time: 10 Minutes**   **Servings: 2**

Ingredients:

- 4 Eggs
- 1 Shallot
- 4 Slices of low carb bread
- 2 Sticks of dill
- 200g Smoked eel
- 1 Tbsp. oil
- Salt
- White pepper

Directions:

⇒ Mix the eggs in a bowl and season with salt and pepper.

⇒ Peel the shallot and cut it into fine cubes.

⇒ Chop the dill.

⇒ Remove the skin from the eel and cut it into pieces.

⇒ Heat the oil in a pan and steam the shallot in it.

⇒ Add the eggs and let them set.

⇒ Use the spatula to turn the eggs several times.

⇒ Reduce the heat and add the dill.

⇒ Stir everything.

⇒ Spread the scrambled eggs over four slices of bread.

⇒ Put the eel pieces on top.

⇒ Add some fresh dill and serve everything.

Nutrition: Kcal: 830 Carbohydrates: 8g Protein: 45g Fat: 64g

12) Coconut Pancakes

Preparation Time: 5 Minutes   **Cooking Time: 15 Minutes**   **Servings:4**

Ingredients:

- 1 Cup coconut flour
- 2 Tbsp. Arrowroot powder
- 1 Tsp. Baking powder
- 1 Cup coconut milk
- 3 Tbsp. Coconut oil

Directions:

⇒ In a medium container, mix in all the dry ingredients.

⇒ Add the coconut milk and two tablespoons of coconut oil, then mix properly.

⇒ In a skillet, melt one tablespoon of coconut oil.

⇒ Pour a ladle of the batter into the skillet, then swirl the pan to spread the batter evenly into a smooth pancake.

⇒ Cook it for like 3 minutes on medium heat until it becomes firm.

⇒ Turn the pancake to the other side, then cook it for another 2 minutes until it turns golden brown.

⇒ Cook the remaining pancakes in the same process.

Nutrition: Calories: 377 kcal Fat: 14.9g Carbs: 60.7g Protein: 6.4g

13) Coconut Chia Pudding With Berries

Preparation Time: 20 Minutes   **Cooking Time: 45 Minutes**   **Servings:2**

Ingredients:

- 150g Raspberries and blueberries
- 60g Chia seeds
- 500ml Coconut milk
- 1 Teaspoon agave syrup
- ½ Teaspoon ground bourbon vanilla

Directions:

⇒ Put the chia seeds, agave syrup, and vanilla in a bowl.

⇒ Pour in the coconut milk.

⇒ Mix thoroughly and let it soak for 30 minutes.

⇒ Meanwhile, wash the berries and let them drain well.

⇒ Divide the coconut chia pudding between two glasses.

⇒ Put the berries on top.

Nutrition: Kcal: 662 Carbohydrates: 18g Protein: 8g Fat: 55g

14) Alkaline Blueberry Spelt Pancakes

Preparation Time: 6 Minutes   **Cooking Time: 20 Minutes**   **Servings: 3**

Ingredients:

- 2 Cups Spelt Flour
- 1 Cup Coconut Milk
- ½ Cup Alkaline Water
- 2 Tbsp. Grapeseed Oil
- ½ Cup Agave
- ½ Cup Blueberries
- 1/4 Tsp. Sea Moss

Directions:

⇒ Mix the spelt flour, agave, grape seed oil, hemp seeds, and the sea moss together in a bowl.

⇒ Add in 1 cup of hemp milk and alkaline water to the mixture until you get the consistent mixture you like.

⇒ Crimp the blueberries into the batter.

⇒ Heat the skillet to moderate heat, then lightly coat it with the grapeseed oil.

⇒ Pour the batter into the skillet, then let them cook for approximately 5 minutes on every side.

⇒ Serve and Enjoy.

Nutrition: Calories: 203 kcal Fat: 1.4g Carbs: 41.6g Proteins: 4.8g

15) Yogurt With Granola and Persimmon

Preparation Time: 5 Minutes   **Cooking Time: 5 Minutes**   **Servings: 1**

Ingredients:

- 150g Greek-style yogurt
- 20g Oatmeal
- 60g Fresh persimmons
- 30ml of tap water

Directions:

⇒ Put the oatmeal in the pan without any fat.

⇒ Toast them, constantly stirring, until golden brown.

⇒ Then put them on a plate and let them cool down briefly.

⇒ Peel the persimmon and put it in a bowl with the water. Mix the whole thing into a fine puree.

⇒ Put the yogurt, the toasted oatmeal, and then puree in layers in a glass and serve.

Nutrition: Kcal: 286 Carbohydrates: 29g Protein: 1g Fat: 11g

16) Pancakes With Berries

Preparation Time: 5 Minutes   **Cooking Time: 20 Minutes**   **Servings:2**

Ingredients:

For the Pancake:

- 1 Egg
- 50g Spelled flour
- 50g Almond flour
- 15g Coconut flour
- 150ml of water
- Salt

For Filling:

- 40g Mixed berries
- 10g Chocolate
- 5g Powdered sugar
- 4 Tbsp. yogurt

Directions:

⇒ Put the flour, egg, and some salt in a blender jar.

⇒ Add 150ml of water.

⇒ Mix everything with a whisk.

⇒ Mix everything into a batter.

⇒ Heat a coated pan.

⇒ Put in half of the batter.

⇒ Once the pancake is firm, turn it over.

⇒ Take out the pancake, add the second half of the batter to the pan, and repeat.

⇒ Melt chocolate over a water bath.

⇒ Let the pancakes cool.

⇒ Brush the pancakes with the yogurt.

⇒ Wash the berry and let it drain.

⇒ Put berries on the yogurt.

⇒ Roll up the pancakes.

⇒ Sprinkle them with powdered sugar.

⇒ Decorate the whole thing with the melted chocolate.

Nutrition: Kcal: 298 Carbohydrates: 26g Protein: 21g Fat: 9g

17) Millet Porridge

Preparation Time: 10 Minutes   **Cooking Time: 20 Minutes**   **Servings:2**

Ingredients:

- Sea salt
- 1 Tbsp. finely chopped coconuts
- ½ Cup unsweetened coconut milk

- ½ Cup rinsed and drained millet
- 1-½ Cups alkaline water
- 3 Drops liquid stevia

Directions:

⇒ Sauté the millet in a non-stick skillet for about 3 minutes.

⇒ Add salt and water, then stir.

⇒ Let the meal boil, then reduce the amount of heat.

⇒ Cook for 15 minutes, then add the remaining ingredients. Stir.

⇒ Cook the meal for four extra minutes.

⇒ Serve the meal with toping of the chopped nuts.

Nutrition: Calories: 219 kcal Fat: 4.5g Carbs: 38.2g Protein: 6.4g

Chapter 3 -   Side Recipes

18) Awesome Avocado Muffins

Preparation Time: 10 Minutes   **Cooking Time: 20 Minutes**   **Servings: 12**

Ingredients:

- 6 Bacon slices; chopped.
- 1 Yellow onion; chopped.
- ½ Teaspoon baking soda
- ½ Cup coconut flour
- 1 Cup coconut milk
- 2 Cups avocado; pitted, peeled, and chopped.
- 4 Eggs
- Salt and black pepper, to the taste

Directions:

⇒ Heat up a pan, add onion and bacon, stir and brown for a few minutes.

⇒ In a bowl, mash avocado pieces with a fork and whisk well with the eggs.

⇒ Add milk, salt, pepper, baking soda, and coconut flour and stir everything.

⇒ Add the bacon mixture and stir again.

⇒ Add coconut oil to muffin tray, divide eggs and avocado mix into the tray, heat oven at 350 degrees F and bake for 20 minutes.

⇒ Divide muffins between plates and serve them for breakfast.

Nutrition: Calories: 200 Fat: 7 Fiber: 4 Carbs: 7 Protein: 5

19) Bacon and Brussels Sprout Breakfast

Preparation Time: 10 Minutes   **Cooking Time: 15 Minutes**   **Servings: 3**

Ingredients:

- 1½ Tbsp. Apple cider vinegar
- Salt
- 2 Minced shallots
- 2 Minced garlic cloves
- 3 Medium eggs
- 12 oz. Sliced Brussels sprouts
- Black pepper
- 2 oz. Chopped bacon
- 1 Tbsp. Melted butter

Directions:

⇒ Over medium heat, quickly fry the bacon until crispy, then reserve on a plate.

⇒ Put the pan on the heat again to fry garlic and shallots for 30 seconds.

⇒ Stir in apple cider vinegar, Brussels sprouts, and seasoning to cook for five minutes.

⇒ Add the bacon to cook for five minutes, then stir in the butter and set a hole at the center.

⇒ Crack the eggs into the pan and let cook fully.

⇒ Enjoy.

Nutrition: Calories: 275 Fat: 16.5 Fiber: 4.3 Carbs: 17.2 Protein: 17.4

20) Bacon and Lemon spiced Muffins

Preparation Time: 10 Minutes   **Cooking Time: 20 Minutes**   **Servings: 12**

Ingredients:

- 2 Tsp. Lemon thyme
- Salt
- 3 Cups Almond flour
- ½ Cup Melted butter

- 1 Tsp. Baking soda
- Black pepper
- 4 Medium eggs
- 1 Cup diced bacon

Directions:

⇒ Set a mixing bowl in place and stir in the eggs and baking soda to incorporate well.

⇒ Whisk in the seasonings, butter, bacon, and lemon thyme.

⇒ Set the mixture in a well-lined muffin pan.

⇒ Set the oven for 20 minutes at 350°F, allow to bake.

⇒ Allow the muffins to cool before serving.

Nutrition: Calories: 186 Fat: 17.1 Fiber: 0.8 Carbs: 1.8 Protein: 7.4

21) Special Almond Cereal

Preparation Time: 5 Minutes   **Cooking Time: 5 Minutes**   **Servings: 1**

Ingredients:

- 2 Tablespoons almonds; chopped.
- 1/3 Cup coconut milk
- 1 Tablespoon chia seeds
- 2 Tablespoons pepitas; roasted

- A handful blueberries
- 1 Small banana; chopped.
- 1/3 Cup water

Directions:

⇒ In a bowl, mix chia seeds with coconut milk and leave aside for 5 minutes

⇒ In your food processor, mix half of the pepitas with almonds and pulse them well.

⇒ Add this to the chia seeds mix.

⇒ Also, add the water and stir.

⇒ Top with the rest of the pepitas, banana pieces, and blueberries to serve

Nutrition: Calories: 200 Fat: 3 Fiber: 2 Carbs: 5 Protein: 4

22) WW Salad in a Jar

Preparation Time: 10 Minutes   **Cooking Time: 5 Minutes**   **Servings: 1**

Ingredients:

- 1 Ounce favorite greens
- 1 Ounce red bell pepper; chopped
- 4 Ounces rotisserie chicken; roughly chopped
- 4 Tablespoons extra virgin olive oil

- ½ Scallion; chopped
- 1-Ounce cucumber; chopped
- 1-Ounce cherry tomatoes; halved
- Salt and black pepper to the taste

Directions:

⇒ In a bowl, mix greens with bell pepper, tomatoes, scallion, cucumber, salt, pepper, and olive oil and toss to coat well.

⇒ Transfer this to a jar, top with chicken pieces, and serve for breakfast.

Nutrition: Calories: 180 Fat: 12 Fiber: 4 Carbs: 5 Protein: 17

23) WW Breakfast Cereal

Preparation Time: 10 Minutes   **Cooking Time: 3 Minutes**   **Servings: 2**

Ingredients:

- ½ Cup coconut; shredded
- 1/3 cup macadamia nuts; chopped
- 4 Teaspoons ghee
- 2 Cups almond milk
- 1 Tablespoon stevia
- 1/3 Cup walnuts; chopped
- 1/3 Cup flax seed
- A pinch of salt

Directions:

⇒ Heat a pot over medium heat. Add the milk, coconut, salt, macadamia nuts, walnuts, flax seeds, and stevia, and mix well.

⇒ Cook for 3 minutes. Stir again, remove from heat for 10 minutes.

⇒ Divide into two bowls and serve

Nutrition: Calories: 140 Fat: 3 Fiber: 2 Carbs: 1.5 Protein: 7

24) Yummy Smoked Salmon

Preparation Time: 10 Minutes   **Cooking Time: 10 Minutes**   **Servings: 3**

Ingredients:

- 4 Eggs; whisked
- ½ Teaspoon avocado oil
- 4 Ounces smoked salmon; chopped.

  For the sauce:
- ½ Cup cashews; soaked; drained
- 1/4 Cup green onions; chopped
- 1 Teaspoon garlic powder
- 1 Cup coconut milk
- 1 Tablespoon lemon juice
- Salt and black pepper to the taste

Directions:

⇒ In your blender, mix cashews with coconut milk, garlic powder, and lemon juice and blend well.

⇒ Add salt, pepper, and green onions, blend again well, transfer to a bowl and keep in the fridge for now.

⇒ Heat up a pan with the oil over medium-low heat; add eggs, whisk a bit and cook until they are almost done

⇒ Introduce in your preheated broiler and cook until the eggs are done.

⇒ Divide eggs on plates, top with smoked salmon, and serve with the green onion sauce on top.

Nutrition: Calories: 200 Fat: 10 Fiber: 2 Carbs: 11 Protein: 15

25) Almond Coconut Cereal

Preparation Time: 5 Minutes   **Cooking Time: 5 Minutes**   **Servings: 2**

Ingredients:

- 1/3 Cup Water
- 1/3 Cup Coconut milk
- 2 Tbsp. Roasted sunflower seeds
- 1 Tbsp. Chia seeds
- ½ Cup Blueberries
- 2 Tbsp. Chopped almonds

Directions:

⇒ Set a medium bowl in position to add coconut milk and chia seeds, then reserve for five minutes

⇒ Set the blender in position to blend almond with sunflower seeds

⇒ Stir the combination to chia seeds mixture, then add water to mix evenly.

⇒ Serve topped with the remaining sunflower seeds and blueberries

Nutrition: Calories: 181 Fat: 15.2 Fiber: 4 Carbs: 10.8 Protein: 3.7

26) Almond Porridge

Preparation Time: 10 Minutes   **Cooking Time: 5 Minutes**   **Servings: 1**

Ingredients:

- ¼ Tsp. Ground cloves
- ¼ Tsp. Nutmeg
- 1 Tsp. Stevia
- ¾ Cups coconut cream
- ½ Cup ground almonds
- ¼ Tsp. Ground cardamom
- 1 Tsp. Ground cinnamon

Directions:

⇒ Set your pan over medium heat to cook the coconut cream for a few minutes

⇒ Stir in almonds and stevia to cook for 5 minutes

⇒ Mix in nutmeg, cardamom, and cinnamon

⇒ Enjoy while still hot

Nutrition: Calories: 695 Fat: 66.7 Fiber: 11.1 Carbs: 22 Protein: 14.3

27) Asparagus Frittata Recipe

Preparation Time: 20 Minutes   **Cooking Time: 20 Minutes**   **Servings: 4**

Ingredients:

- 4 Bacon slices, chopped
- Salt and black pepper
- 8 Whisked eggs
- 1 Asparagus bunch, trimmed and chopped

Directions:

⇒ Heat a pan, add bacon, stir and cook for 5 minutes.

⇒ Add asparagus, salt, and pepper, stir and cook for another 5 minutes.

⇒ Add the whisked eggs, spread them in the pan, let them stand in the oven, and bake for 20 minutes at 350°F.

⇒ Share and divide between plates and serve for breakfast.

Nutrition: Calories: 251 Carbs: 16 Fat: 6 Fiber: 8 Protein: 7

28) Avocados Stuffed With Salmon

Preparation Time: 5 Minutes   **Cooking Time: 5 Minutes**   **Servings: 2**

Ingredients:

- 1 Avocado pitted and halved
- 2 Tablespoons Olive oil
- The juice of one lemon
- 2 Ounces Smoked salmon flaked
- 1 Ounce crumbled goat cheese
- Salt and black pepper

Directions:

⇒ Combine the salmon with lemon juice, oil, cheese, salt, and pepper in your food processor and pulsate well.

⇒ Divide this mixture into avocado halves and serve.

⇒ Dish and Enjoy!

Nutrition: Calories: 300 Fat: 15 Fiber: 5 Carbs: 8 Protein: 16

29)Buffalo Chicken Sliders

Preparation Time: 10 Minutes   **Cooking Time: 15 Minutes**   **Servings:12**

Ingredients:

- 2 lb. Cooked, shredded chicken breasts
- 1 Cup Wing sauce
- 1 Pack Ranch dressing mix
- 1/4 Cup low-fat Blue cheese dressing
- Lettuce for topping
- 12 Slider Buns

Directions:

⇒ Add the chicken breasts (shredded, cooked) in a large bowl along with the ranch dressing and wing sauce.

⇒ Stir well to incorporate, then place a piece of lettuce onto each slider roll.

⇒ Top off using the chicken mixture.

⇒ Drizzle blue cheese dressing over chicken, then top off using top buns of slider rolls

⇒ Serve.

Nutrition: Calories: 300 Fat: 14g Cholesterol: 25mg

30)Three-Bean Medley

Preparation Time: 15 Minutes   **Cooking Time: 6 to 8 Hours**   **Servings:8**

Ingredients:

- 11/4 Cups dried kidney beans, rinsed and drained
- 11/4 Cups dried black beans, rinsed and drained
- 11/4 Cups dried black-eyed peas, rinsed and drained
- 1 Onion, chopped
- 1 Leek, chopped
- 2 Garlic cloves, minced
- 2 Carrots, peeled and chopped
- 6 Cups low-sodium vegetable broth
- 1½ cups water
- ½ Teaspoon dried thyme leaves

Directions:

⇒ In a 6-quart slow cooker, mix all of the ingredients.

⇒ Cover and cook on low for 6 to 8 hours, or until the beans are tender and the liquid is absorbed.

Nutrition: Calories: 284 Carbohydrates: 56g Sugar: 6g Fiber: 19g Fat: 0g Saturated Fat: 0g Protein: 19g Sodium: 131mg

Chapter 4 -   Salads Recipes

31) Coleslaw Worth a Second Helping

Preparation Time: 20 Minutes   **Cooking Time: 10 Minutes**   **Servings:6**

Ingredients:

- 5 Cups shredded cabbage
- 2 Carrots, shredded
- 1/3 Cup chopped fresh flat-leaf parsley
- ½ Cup mayonnaise
- ½ Cup sour cream
- 3 Tablespoons apple cider vinegar
- 1 Teaspoon kosher salt
- ½ Teaspoon celery seed

Directions:

⇒ In a large bowl, combine the cabbage, carrots, and parsley.

⇒ In a small bowl, whisk the mayonnaise, sour cream, vinegar, salt, and celery seed until smooth.

⇒ Pour the dressing over the vegetables and toss until coated. Transfer to a serving bowl and chill until ready to serve.

Nutrition: Calories: 192 Total fat: 18g Total carbs: 7g Cholesterol: 18mg Fiber: 3g Protein: 2g Sodium: 543mg

32) Barley and Lentil Salad

Preparation Time: 5 Minutes   **Cooking Time: 0 Minutes**   **Servings:2**

Ingredients:

- 1 Head romaine lettuce
- ¾ Cup cooked barley
- 2 Cups cooked lentils
- 1 Diced carrot
- ¼ Chopped red onion
- ¼ Cup olives
- ½ Chopped cucumber
- 3 Tablespoons olive oil
- 2 Tablespoons fresh lemon juice

Directions:

⇒ Mix all ingredients together. Add kosher salt and black pepper to taste.

Nutrition: Calories: 213 Protein: 21g Carbohydrate: 6g Fat: 9g

33) Blueberry Cantaloupe Avocado Salad

Preparation Time: 5 Minutes   **Cooking Time: 0 Minutes**   **Servings:2**

Ingredients:

- 1 Diced cantaloupe
- 2–3 Chopped avocados
- 1 Package of blueberries
- ¼ Cup olive oil
- 1/8 Cup balsamic vinegar

Directions:

⇒ Mix all ingredients.

Nutrition: Calories: 406 Protein: 9g Carbohydrate: 32g Fat: 5g

34) Wild Rice Prawn Salad

Preparation Time: 5 Minutes   **Cooking Time: 35 Minutes**   **Servings: 6**

Ingredients:

- ¾ Cup wild rice
- 1¾ Cups chicken stock
- 1 Pound prawns
- Salt and pepper to taste

- 2 Tablespoons lemon juice
- 2 Tablespoons extra virgin olive oil
- 2 Cups arugula

Directions:

⇒ Combine the rice and chicken stock in a saucepan and cook until the liquid has been absorbed entirely.

⇒ Transfer the rice to a salad bowl.

⇒ Season the prawns with salt and pepper and drizzle them with lemon juice and oil.

⇒ Heat a grill pan over a medium flame.

⇒ Place the prawns on the hot pan and cook on each side for 2-3 minutes.

⇒ For the salad, combine the rice with arugula and prawns and mix well.

⇒ Serve the salad fresh.

Nutrition: Calories: 207 Fat: 4g Protein: 20.6g Carbohydrates: 17g

35) Beet Salad (from Israel)

Preparation Time: 5 Minutes   **Cooking Time: 0 Minutes**   **Servings: 2**

Ingredients:

- 2–3 Fresh, raw beets grated or shredded in food processor
- 3 Tablespoons olive oil
- 2 Tablespoons balsamic vinegar
- ¼ Teaspoon salt

- 1/3 Teaspoon cumin
- Dash stevia powder or liquid
- Dash pepper

Directions:

⇒ Mix all ingredients together for the best raw beet salad.

Nutrition: Calories: 156 Protein: 8g Carbohydrate: 40g Fat: 5g

36) Greek Salad

Preparation Time: 15 Minutes   **Cooking Time: 15 Minutes**   **Servings:5**

Ingredients:

For the Dressing:

- ½ Teaspoon black pepper
- ¼ Teaspoon salt
- ½ Teaspoon oregano
- 1 Tablespoon garlic powder
- 2 Tablespoons Balsamic
- 1/3 Cup olive oil

For the Salad:

- ½ Cup sliced black olives
- ½ Cup chopped parsley, fresh

- 1 Small red onion, thin-sliced
- 1 Cup cherry tomatoes, sliced
- 1 Bell pepper, yellow, chunked
- 1 Cucumber, peeled, quartered, and sliced
- 4 Cups chopped romaine lettuce
- ½ Teaspoon salt
- 2 Tablespoons olive oil

Directions:

⇒ In a small bowl, blend all of the ingredients for the dressing and let this set in the refrigerator while you make the salad.

⇒ To assemble the salad, mix together all the ingredients in a large-sized bowl and toss the veggies gently but thoroughly to mix.

⇒ Serve the salad with the dressing in amounts as desired

Nutrition: Calories: 234 Fat: 16.1g Protein: 5g Carbs: 48g

37) Norwegian Niçoise Salad Smoked Salmon Cucumber Egg and Asparagus

Preparation Time: 20 Minutes   **Cooking Time: 5 Minutes**   **Servings:4**

Ingredients:

For the vinaigrette:

- 3 Tablespoons walnut oil
- 2 Tablespoons champagne vinegar
- 1 Tablespoon chopped fresh dill
- ½ Teaspoon kosher salt
- ¼ Teaspoon ground mustard
- Freshly ground black pepper

For the salad:

- Handful green beans, trimmed

- 1 (3- to 4-ounce) Package spring greens
- 12 Spears pickled asparagus
- 4 Large soft-boiled eggs, halved
- 8 Ounces smoked salmon, thinly sliced
- 1 Cucumber, thinly sliced
- 1 Lemon, quartered

Directions:

⇒ To make the dressing. In a small bowl, whisk the oil, vinegar, dill, salt, ground mustard, and a few grinds of pepper until emulsified. Set aside.

⇒ To make the salad. Start by blanching the green beans, bring a pot of salted water to a boil. Drop in the beans. Cook for 1 to 2 minutes until they turn bright green, then immediately drain and rinse under cold water. Set aside.

⇒ Divide the spring greens among four plates. Toss each serving with dressing to taste. Arrange three asparagus spears, one egg, 2 ounces of salmon, one-fourth of the cucumber slices, and a lemon wedge on each plate. Serve immediately.

Nutrition: Calories: 257 Total fat: 18g Total carbs: 6g Cholesterol: 199mg Fiber: 2g Protein: 19g Sodium: 603mg

38) Mediterranean Chickpea Salad

Preparation Time: 5 Minutes　　　**Cooking Time: 20 Minutes**　　　**Servings: 6**

Ingredients:

- 1 Can chickpeas, drained
- 1 Fennel bulb, sliced
- 1 Red onion, sliced
- 1 Teaspoon dried basil
- 1 Teaspoon dried oregano

- 2 Tablespoons chopped parsley
- 4 Garlic cloves, minced
- 2 Tablespoons lemon juice
- 2 Tablespoons extra virgin olive oil
- Salt and pepper to taste

Directions:

⇒ Combine the chickpeas, fennel, red onion, herbs, garlic, lemon juice, and oil in a salad bowl.

⇒ Add salt and pepper and serve the salad fresh.

Nutrition:　　　Calories: 200 Fat: 9g Protein: 4g Carbohydrates: 28g

39) Romaine Lettuce and Radicchios Mix

Preparation Time: 6 Minutes　　　**Cooking Time: 0 Minutes**　　　**Servings: 4**

Ingredients:

- 2 Tablespoons olive oil
- A pinch of salt and black pepper
- 2 Spring onions, chopped
- 3 Tablespoons Dijon mustard

- Juice of 1 lime
- ½ Cup basil, chopped
- 4 Cups romaine lettuce heads, chopped
- 3 Radicchios, sliced

Directions:

⇒ In a salad bowl, mix the lettuce with the spring onions and the other ingredients, toss and serve.

⇒

Nutrition:　　　Calories: 87 Fats: 2g Fiber: 1g Carbs: 1g Protein: 2g

40) Chicken Broccoli Salad With Avocado Dressing

Preparation Time: 5 Minutes　　　**Cooking Time: 40 Minutes**　　　**Servings: 6**

Ingredients:

- 2 Chicken breasts
- 1 Pound broccoli, cut into florets
- 1 Avocado, peeled and pitted
- ½ Lemon, juiced

- 2 Garlic cloves
- ¼ Teaspoon chili powder
- ¼ Teaspoon cumin powder
- Salt and pepper to taste

Directions:

⇒ Cook the chicken in a large pot of salty water.

⇒ Drain and cut the chicken into small cubes—place in a salad bowl.

⇒ Add the broccoli and mix well.

⇒ Combine the avocado, lemon juice, garlic, chili powder, cumin powder, salt, and pepper in a blender. Pulse until smooth.

⇒ Spoon the dressing over the salad and mix well.

⇒ Serve the salad fresh.

Nutrition:　　　Calories: 195 Fat: 11g Protein: 14g Carbohydrates: 3g

41)Zucchini Salmon Salad

Preparation Time: 5 Minutes   **Cooking Time: 10 Minutes**   **Servings:3**

Ingredients:

- 2 Salmon fillets
- 2 Tablespoons soy sauce
- 2 Zucchinis, sliced

- Salt and pepper to taste
- 2 Tablespoons extra virgin olive oil
- 2 Tablespoons sesame seeds

Directions:

⇒ Drizzle the salmon with soy sauce.

⇒ Heat a grill pan over a medium flame. Cook salmon on the grill on each side for 2-3 minutes.

⇒ Season the zucchini with salt and pepper and place it on the grill as well. Cook on each side until golden.

⇒ Place the zucchini, salmon, and the rest of the ingredients in a bowl.

⇒ Serve the salad fresh.

Nutrition: Calories: 224 Fat: 19g Protein: 18g Carbohydrates: 0g

Chapter 5 - Soup and Stew Recipes

42) Stewed Herbed Fruit

Preparation Time: 15 Minutes   **Cooking Time: 6 to 8 Hours**   **Servings: 12**

Ingredients:

- 2 Cups dried apricots (1 healthy fat)
- 2 Cups prunes (1 healthy fat)
- 2 Cups dried unsulfured pears (½ healthy fat)
- 2 Cups dried apples (½ healthy fat)
- 1 Cup dried cranberries (½ healthy fat)
- 1/4 Cup honey (1/4 condiment)
- 6 Cups water (1 condiment)
- 1 Teaspoon dried thyme leaves (1/4 green)
- 1 Teaspoon dried basil leaves (1/4 green)

Directions:

⇒ In a 6-quart slow cooker, mix all of the ingredients.

⇒ Cover and cook over low heat for 7 hours

⇒ Store in the refrigerator for up to 1 week.

⇒ You can freeze the fruit in 1-cup portions for more extended storage.

Nutrition: Calories: 242 Fat: 0.1g Protein: 2g

43) Roasted Tomato Soup

Preparation Time: 20 Minutes   **Cooking Time: 50 Minutes**   **Servings: 6**

Ingredients:

- 3 Pounds of tomatoes, halved (1 green)
- 6 Garlic(smashed) (½ condiment)
- 4 Teaspoons of cooking oil or virgin oil (1/8 condiment)
- Salt to taste (1/8 condiment)
- 1/4 Cup of heavy cream (optional) (½ healthy fat)
- Sliced fresh basil leaves for garnish (1/8 green)

Directions:

⇒ Set the oven at medium heat of about 427°F and let it preheat

⇒ In your mixing bowl, mix the halved tomatoes, garlic, olive oil, salt, and pepper

⇒ Spread the tomato mixture on the already prepared baking sheet

⇒ For a process of 20- 28 minutes, roast and stir

⇒ Then remove it from the oven, and the roasted vegetables should now be transferred to a soup pot

⇒ Stir in the basil leaves

⇒ Blend in small portions in a blender

⇒ Serve immediately

Nutrition: Fat: 5.9g Protein: 2.3g Calories: 126

44) Lemon-Garlic Chicken

Preparation Time: 5 Minutes   **Cooking Time: 45 Minutes**   **Servings:4**

Ingredients:

- 1 Small lemon, juiced (1/8 condiment)
- 1 3/4 lb. of bone-in, skinless chicken thighs (1 lean)
- 2 Tablespoons of fresh oregano, minced (1/8green)

- 2 Cloves of garlic, minced (1/8 condiment)
- 2 lbs. of asparagus, trimmed (1/8green)
- 1/4 Teaspoon each or less for black pepper and salt (1/8 condiment)

Directions:

⇒ Preheat the oven to about 350°F. Put the chicken in a medium-sized bowl.

⇒ Now, add the garlic, oregano, lemon juice, pepper, and salt and toss together to combine.

⇒ Roast for 40 minutes.

⇒ Once the chicken thighs have been cooked, remove and keep them aside to rest.

⇒ Now, steam the asparagus on a stovetop or in a microwave to the desired doneness.

⇒ Serve asparagus with roasted chicken thighs.

Nutrition: Calories: 350 Fat: 10g Protein: 32g

45) Quick Lentil Chili

Preparation Time: 15 Minutes   **Cooking Time: 1 Hour and 20 Minutes**   **Servings:10**

Ingredients:

- 1½ Cups of seeded or diced pepper (1green)
- 5 Cups of vegetable broth (it should have a low sodium content) (1 condiment)
- 1 Tablespoon of garlic (1/8 condiment)
- 1/4 Teaspoon of freshly ground pepper (1/8 condiment)

- 1 Cup of red lentils (1/4green)
- 3 Filled teaspoons of chili powder (1/8 condiment)
- 1 Tablespoon of grounded cumin (1/8 condiment)

Directions:

⇒ Place your pot over medium heat

⇒ Combine your onions, red peppers, low sodium vegetable broth, garlic, salt, and pepper

⇒ Cook and always stir until the onions are more translucent and all the liquid evaporated. This will take about 10mins.

⇒ Add the remaining broth, lime juice, chili powder, lentils, cumin, and boil.

⇒ Reduce heat at this point, cover it for about 15 minutes to simmer until the lentils are appropriately cooked

⇒ Drizzle a little water if the mixture seems to be thick.

⇒ The chili will be appropriately done when most of the water is absorbed.

⇒ Serve and enjoy.

Nutrition: Protein: 2.3g Calories: 121 Fat: 2.9g

46) Creamy Cauliflower Soup

Preparation Time: 15 Minutes   **Cooking Time: 30 Minutes**   **Servings: 6**

Ingredients:

- 5 Cups cauliflower rice (1green)
- 8 oz. Cheddar cheese, grated (1 healthy fat)
- 2 Cups unsweetened almond milk (½ healthy fat)
- 2 Cups vegetable stock (1 condiment)

- 2 Tbsp. water (½ condiment)
- 2 Garlic cloves, minced (1/4 condiment)
- 1 Tbsp. olive oil (1/8 condiment)

Directions:

⇒ Cook olive oil in a large stockpot over medium heat.

⇒ Add garlic and cook for 1-2 minutes. Add cauliflower rice and water.

⇒ Cover and cook for 5-7 minutes.

⇒ Now add vegetable stock and almond milk and stir well.

⇒ Bring to a boil.

⇒ Turn heat to low and simmer for 5 minutes.

⇒ Turn off the heat.

⇒ Slowly add cheddar cheese and stir until smooth.

⇒ Season soup with pepper and salt.

⇒ Stir well and serve hot.

Nutrition: Calories: 214 Fat: 16.5g Protein: 11.6g

47) Crackpot Chicken Taco Soup

Preparation Time: 15 Minutes   **Cooking Time: 6 Hours**   **Servings: 6**

Ingredients:

- 2 Frozen boneless chicken breasts (1 lean)
- 2 Cans of white beans or black beans (1 healthy fat)
- 1 Can of diced tomatoes (1 healthy fat)
- ½ Packet of taco seasoning (1/8 condiment)

- ½ Teaspoon of Garlic salt (1/8 condiment)
- 1 Cup of chicken broth (1 condiment)
- Salt and pepper to taste (1/8 condiment)
- Tortilla chips, sour cream cheese, and cilantro as toppings (1 healthy fat)

Directions:

⇒ Put your frozen chicken into the crockpot and place the other ingredients into the pool too.

⇒ Leave to cook for about 6-8 hours.

⇒ After cooking, take out the chicken and shred it to the size you want.

⇒ Finally, place the shredded chicken into the crockpot and put it on a slow cooker. Stir and allow to cook.

⇒ You can add more beans and tomatoes also to help stretch the meat and make it tastier.

Nutrition: Protein: 29g Fat: 4g Calories: 171

48) Cheeseburger Soup

Preparation Time: 15 Minutes   **Cooking Time: 45 Minutes**   **Servings:4**

Ingredients:

- 1 14.5 oz. can diced tomato (1green)
- 1 lb. of 90% lean ground beef (1 lean)
- 3/4 Cup of chopped celery (½ green)
- 2 Teaspoons of Worcestershire sauce (1/8 condiment)
- 3 Cups of low sodium chicken broth (1 condiment)
- 1/4 Teaspoon of salt (1/8 condiment)
- 1 Teaspoon of dried parsley (1/8green)
- 7 Cups of baby spinach (1green)
- 1/4 Teaspoon of ground pepper (1/8 condiment)
- 4 oz. of reduced-fat shredded cheddar cheese (½ healthy fat)

Directions:

⇒ Get a large soup pot and cook the beef until it becomes brown.

⇒ Add the celery and sauté until it becomes tender.

⇒ Remove from the heat and drain excess liquid. Stir in the broth, tomatoes, parsley, Worcestershire sauce, pepper, and salt.

⇒ Cover with the lid and allow it to simmer on low heat for about 20 minutes.

⇒ Add spinach and leave it to cook until it becomes wilted in about 1-3 minutes.

⇒ Top each of your servings with 1 ounce of cheese.

Nutrition: Calories: 400 Protein: 44g Fat: 20g

Chapter 6 -   Vegan Recipes

49) Cheesy Cauliflower Fritters

Preparation Time: 5 Minutes   **Cooking Time: 14 Minutes**   **Servings:8**

Ingredients:

- ½ C. Chopped parsley
- 1 C. Italian breadcrumbs
- 1/3 C. Shredded mozzarella cheese
- 1/3 C. Shredded sharp cheddar cheese
- 1 Egg
- Minced garlic cloves
- Chopped scallions
- 1 Head of cauliflower

Directions:

⇒ Cut the cauliflower up into florets. Wash well and pat dry. Place into a food processor and pulse 20-30 seconds till it looks like rice.

⇒ Place the cauliflower rice in a bowl and mix with pepper, salt, egg, cheeses, breadcrumbs, garlic, and scallions.

⇒ With your hands, form 15 patties of the mixture, add more breadcrumbs if needed.

⇒ With olive oil, spritz patties, and place into your air fryer in a single layer.

⇒ Cook 14 minutes at 390 degrees, flip after 7 minutes.

Nutrition: Calories: 209 Fat: 17g Protein: 6g Sugar: 0.5g

50) Oat and Chia Porridge

Preparation Time: 5 Minutes   **Cooking Time: 5 Minutes**   **Servings:4**

Ingredients:

- 2 Tablespoons peanut butter
- ½ Teaspoons liquid Stevia
- 1 Tablespoon butter, melted
- 2 Cups milk
- ½ Cups oats
- 1 Cup chia seeds

Directions:

⇒ Preheat your air fryer to 390 degrees Fahrenheit.

⇒ Whisk the peanut butter, butter, milk, and Stevia in a bowl.

⇒ Stir in the oats and chia seeds.

⇒ Pour the mixture into an oven-proof bowl and place in the air fryer, and cook for 5-minutes.

Nutrition: Calories: 228 Total Fats: 11.4g Carbs: 10.2g Protein: 14.5g

51) Roasted Root Vegetables

Preparation Time: 20 Minutes   **Cooking Time: 6 to 8 Hours**   **Servings:8**

Ingredients:

- 6 Carrots, cut into 1-inch chunks
- 2 Yellow onions, each cut into 8 wedges
- 2 Sweet potatoes, peeled and cut into chunks
- 6 Yukon Gold potatoes, cut into chunks
- 8 Whole garlic cloves, peeled
- 4 Parsnips, peeled and cut into chunks
- 3 Tablespoons olive oil
- 1 Teaspoon dried thyme leaves
- ½ Teaspoon salt
- 1/8 Teaspoon freshly ground black pepper

Directions:

⇒ In a 6-quart slow cooker, mix all of the ingredients.

⇒ Cover and cook on low for 6 to 8 hours or until the vegetables are tender.

⇒ Serve and enjoy!

Nutrition: Calories: 214 Carbohydrates: 40g Sugar: 7g Fiber: 6g Fat: 5g Saturated Fat: 1g Protein: 4g Sodium: 201mg

52) Hummus

Preparation Time: 10 Minutes   **Cooking Time: 10 Minutes**   **Servings: 32**

Ingredients:

- 4 Cups of cooked garbanzo beans
- 1 Cup of water
- 1½ Tablespoons of lemon juice
- 2 Teaspoons of ground cumin
- 1 ½ Teaspoon of ground coriander
- 1 Teaspoon of finely chopped garlic
- ½ Teaspoon of salt
- 1/4 Teaspoon of fresh ground pepper
- Paprika for garnish

Directions:

⇒ On a food processor, place the garbanzo beans together with lemon juice, water, cumin, coriander, garlic, salt, and pepper and process it until it becomes smooth and creamy.

⇒ To achieve the desired consistency, add more water.

⇒ Then spoon out the hummus in a serving bowl.

⇒ Sprinkle your paprika and serve.

Nutrition: Protein: 0.7g Carbohydrates: 2.5g Dietary Fiber: 0.6g Sugars: 0g Fat: 1.7g

53) Butter Glazed Carrots

Preparation Time: 20 Minutes   **Cooking Time: 15 Minutes**   **Servings: 4**

Ingredients:

- 2 Cups Baby carrots
- 1 Tbsp. Brown sugar
- ½ Tbsp. Butter; melted
- A pinch of salt and black pepper

Directions:

⇒ Take a baking dish suitable to fit in your air fryer.

⇒ Toss carrots with sugar, butter, salt, and black pepper in that baking dish.

⇒ Place this dish in the air fryer basket and seal the fryer.

⇒ Cook the carrots for 10 minutes at 350°F on Air fryer mode.

⇒ Enjoy.

Nutrition: Calories:151 Fat:2 Fiber: 4 Carbs: 14 Protein:4

54) Cinnamon Butternut Squash Fries

Preparation Time: 10 Minutes   **Cooking Time: 10 Minutes**   **Servings: 2**

Ingredients:

- 1 Pinch of salt
- 1 Tbsp. powdered unprocessed sugar
- ½ Tsp. nutmeg
- ½ Tsp. cinnamon
- 1 Tbsp. coconut oil
- 0.5 Ounces pre-cut butternut squash fries

Directions:

⇒ In a plastic bag, pour in all ingredients. Cover fries with other components till coated and sugar is dissolved.

⇒ Spread coated fries into a single layer in the air fryer, cook 10 minutes at 390 degrees until crispy.

Nutrition: Calories: 175 Fat: 8g Protein: 1g Sugar: 5g

55) Carrot & Zucchini Muffins

Preparation Time: 5 Minutes   **Cooking Time: 14 Minutes**   **Servings: 4**

Ingredients:

- 2 Tablespoons butter, melted
- ¼ Cup carrots, shredded
- ½ Cup zucchini, shredded
- 1 ½ Cups almond flour
- 1 Tablespoon liquid Stevia

- ½ Teaspoons baking powder
- Pinch of salt
- 2 Eggs
- 1 Tablespoon yogurt
- 1 Cup milk

Directions:

⇒ Preheat your air fryer to 350 degrees Fahrenheit.

⇒ Beat the eggs, yogurt, milk, salt, pepper, baking soda, and Stevia.

⇒ Whisk in the flour gradually.

⇒ Add zucchini and carrots.

⇒ Grease muffin tins with butter and pour the muffin batter into tins. Cook for 14-minutes and serve.

Nutrition: Calories:224 Total Fats:12.3 Carbs: 11.2g Protein:14.2g

56) Curried Cauliflower Florets

Preparation Time: 5 Minutes   **Cooking Time: 10 Minutes**   **Servings: 4**

Ingredients:

- 1/4 Cup sultanas or golden raisins
- ¼ Teaspoon salt
- 1 Tablespoon curry powder

- 1 Cauliflower head, broken into small florets
- ¼ Cup pine nuts
- ½ Cup olive oil

Directions:

⇒ In a cup of boiling water, soak your sultanas to plump. Preheat your air fryer to 350 degrees Fahrenheit.

⇒ Add oil and pine nuts to the air fryer and toast for a minute or so.

⇒ In a bowl, toss the cauliflower and curry powder as well as salt, then add the mix to the air fryer mixing well.

⇒ Cook for 10-minutes. Drain the sultanas, toss with cauliflower, and serve.

Nutrition: Calories: 275 Total Fat: 11.3g Carbs: 8.6g Protein: 9.5g

57) Feta & Mushroom Frittata

Preparation Time: 15 Minutes   **Cooking Time: 30 Minutes**   **Servings: 4**

Ingredients:

- 1 Red onion, thinly sliced
- 2 Cups button mushrooms, thinly sliced
- Salt to taste
- 1 Tablespoons feta cheese, crumbled

- 3 Medium eggs
- Non-stick cooking spray
- 2 Tablespoons olive oil

Directions:

⇒ Saute the onion and mushrooms in olive oil over medium heat until the vegetables are tender.

⇒ Remove the vegetables from the pan and drain them on a paper towel-lined plate.

⇒ In a mixing bowl, whisk eggs and salt. Coat all sides of the baking dish with cooking spray.

⇒ Preheat your air fryer to 325 degrees Fahrenheit. Pour the beaten eggs into the prepared baking dish and scatter the sautéed vegetables and crumble feta on top—bake in the air fryer for 30-minutes. Allow to cool slightly and serve!

Nutrition: Calories: 226 Total Fat: 9.3g Carbs:8.7g Protein: 12.6g

58) Vegan Edamame Quinoa Collard Wraps

Preparation Time: 5 Minutes   **Cooking Time: 15 Minutes**   **Servings:4**

Ingredients:

For the wrap:

- 2 to 3 Collard leaves
- 1/4 Cup Grated carrot
- 1/4 Cup Sliced cucumber
- 1/4 Thin strips Red bell pepper
- 1/4 Thin strips Orange bell pepper
- 1/3 Cup Cooked Quinoa
- 1/3 Cup Shelled defrosted edamame

For the dressing:

- 3 Tablespoons Fresh ginger root, peeled and chopped
- 1 Cup Cooked chickpeas
- 1 Garlic clove
- 4 Tablespoons Rice vinegar
- 2 Tablespoons Low sodium tamari/coconut aminos
- 2 Tablespoons Lime juice
- 1/4 Cup Water
- Few pinches of chili flakes
- 1 Stevia pack

Directions:

⇒ For the dressing, combine all the ingredients and purée in a food processor until smooth.

⇒ Load into a little jar or tub, and set aside.

⇒ Place the collar leaves on a flat surface, covering one another to create a tighter tie.

⇒ Take one tablespoon of ginger dressing and blend it up with the prepared quinoa.

⇒ Spoon the prepared quinoa onto the leaves and shape a simple horizontal line at the closest end.

⇒ Supplement the edamame with all the veggie fillings left over.

⇒ Drizzle around one tablespoon of the ginger dressing on top, then fold the cover's sides inwards.

⇒ Pullover the fillings, the side of the cover closest to you, then turn the whole body away to seal it up.

Nutrition: Calories: 295 Sugar: 3g Sodium: 200mg Fat: 13g

59) Baked Cheesy Eggplant With Marinara

Preparation Time: 20 Minutes   **Cooking Time: 45 Minutes**   **Servings: 3**

Ingredients:

- 1 Clove garlic, sliced
- 1 Large eggplant
- 2 Tablespoons olive oil
- ½ Pinch salt, or as needed
- 1/4 Cup and 2 tablespoons dry bread crumbs
- 1/4 Cup and 2 tablespoons ricotta cheese
- 1/4 Cup grated Parmesan cheese
- 1/4 Cup water, plus more as needed
- 1/4 Teaspoon red pepper flakes
- 1-½ Cups prepared marinara sauce
- 1-½ Teaspoons olive oil
- 2 Tablespoons shredded pepper jack cheese
- Salt and freshly ground black pepper to taste

Directions:

⇒ Cut the eggplant crosswise into five pieces. Peel a pumpkin, grate it and cut it into two cubes.

⇒ Lightly turn skillet with one tablespoon olive oil. Heat the oil at 390°F for 5 minutes. Add half of the eggplants and cook for 2 minutes on each side. Transfer to a plate.

⇒ Add one tablespoon of olive oil and add garlic, cook for one minute. Add the chopped eggplants. Season with pepper flakes and salt. Cook for 4 minutes. Lower the heat to 330oF and continue cooking the eggplants until soft, about eight more minutes.

⇒ Stir in water and marinara sauce. Cook for 7 minutes until heated through. Stir every now and then. Transfer to a bowl.

⇒ In a bowl, whisk well pepper, salt, pepper jack cheese, Parmesan cheese, and ricotta. Evenly spread cheeses over eggplant strips and then fold in half.

⇒ Lay folded eggplant in baking pan. Pour the marinara sauce on top.

⇒ In a small bowl, whisk well olive oil and bread crumbs. Sprinkle all over the sauce.

⇒ Cook for 15 minutes at 390°F until tops are lightly browned.

⇒ Serve and enjoy.

Nutrition: Calories: 405 Carbs: 41.1g Protein: 12.7g Fat: 21.4g

60) Creamy Spinach and Mushroom Lasagna

Preparation Time: 60 Minutes　　　**Cooking Time: 20 Minutes**　　　**Servings:6**

Ingredients:

- 10 Lasagna noodles
- 1 Package whole milk ricotta
- 2 Packages of frozen chopped spinach.
- 4 Cups mozzarella cheese (divided and shredded)
- 3/4 Cups grated fresh Parmesan
- 3 Tablespoons chopped fresh parsley leaves (optional)

  For the Sauce:
- 1/4 Cup of butter (unsalted)

- 2 Garlic cloves
- 1 Pound of thinly sliced cremini mushroom
- 1 Diced onion
- 1/4 Cup flour
- 4 Cups milk, kept at room temperature
- 1 Teaspoon basil (dried)
- Pinch of nutmeg
- Salt and freshly ground black pepper, to taste

Directions:

⇒ Preheat oven to 352 degrees F.

⇒ To make the sauce, over medium heat, melt your butter. Add garlic, mushrooms, and onion. Cook and stir at intervals until it becomes tender at about 3-4 minutes.

⇒ Whisk in flour until lightly browned; it takes about 1 minute for it to become brown.

⇒ Next, whisk in the milk gradually, and cook, constantly whisking, about 2-3 minutes till it becomes thickened. Stir in basil, oregano, and nutmeg, season with salt and pepper for taste.

⇒ Then set aside.

⇒ In another pot of boiling salted water, cook lasagna noodles according to the package instructions.

⇒ Spread one cup mushroom sauce onto the bottom of a baking dish; top it with four lasagna noodles, ½ of the spinach, one cup mozzarella cheese, and 1/4 cup Parmesan.

⇒ Repeat this process with the remaining noodles, mushroom sauce, and cheeses.

⇒ Place into oven and bake for 35-45 minutes, or until it starts bubbling. Then boil for 2-3 minutes until it becomes brown and translucent.

⇒ Let cool for 15 minutes.

⇒ Serve it with garnished parsley (optional)

Nutrition:　　Calories: 488.3 Cal Fats: 19.3g Cholesterol: 88.4mg Sodium: 451.9mg Carbohydrates: 51.0g Dietary Fiber: 7.0g

Protein: 25.0g

61)Zucchini Parmesan Chips

Preparation Time: 5 Minutes   **Cooking Time: 8 Minutes**   **Servings:10**

Ingredients:

- ½ Tsp. Paprika
- ½ C. Grated parmesan cheese
- ½ C. Italian breadcrumbs

- 1 Lightly beaten egg
- Thinly sliced zucchinis

Directions:

⇒ Use a very sharp knife or mandolin slicer to slice zucchini as thinly as you can—pat off extra moisture.

⇒ Beat the egg with a pinch of pepper and salt and a bit of water.

⇒ Combine paprika, cheese, and breadcrumbs in a bowl.

⇒ Dip slices of zucchini into the egg mixture and then into the breadcrumb mixture. Press gently to coat.

⇒ With olive oil or cooking spray, mist-coated zucchini slices, then place them into your air fryer in a single layer.

⇒ Cook 8 minutes at 350 degrees.

⇒ Sprinkle with salt and serve with salsa.

Nutrition: Calories: 211 Fat: 16g Protein: 8g Sugar: 0g

Chapter 7 - Meat Recipes

62) Air Fryer Pork Chop & Broccoli

Preparation Time: 20 Minutes   **Cooking Time: 20 Minutes**   **Servings: 2**

Ingredients:

- 2 Cups Broccoli florets (1green)
- 2 Pieces Bone-in pork chop (1 lean)
- ½ Tsp. Paprika (1/4 condiment)
- 2 Tbsp. Avocado oil (1 healthy fat)
- ½ Tsp. Garlic powder (1/4 condiment)
- ½ Tsp. Onion powder (1/4 condiment)
- Two cloves of crushed garlic (1/4 condiment)
- 1 Teaspoon of Salt divided (1/4 condiment)

Directions:

⇒ Let the air fryer preheat to 350 degrees. Spray the basket with cooking oil

⇒ Add an oil spoon, onion powder, half a teaspoon. of salt, garlic powder, and paprika in a bowl mix well, rub this spice mixture on the sides of the pork chop

⇒ Add the pork chops to the fryer basket and cook for five minutes

⇒ Meanwhile, add an oil teaspoon, garlic, a half teaspoon of salt, and broccoli in a bowl and coat them well

⇒ Turn the pork chop and add the broccoli, let it cook for another five minutes.

⇒ Remove from the air fryer and serve.

Nutrition: Calories: 483 Fat: 20g Protein: 23g

63) Mustard Glazed Air Fryer Pork Tenderloin

Preparation Time: 10 Minutes   **Cooking Time: 18 Minutes**   **Servings: 4**

Ingredients:

- ¼ Cup Yellow mustard (½ green)
- One pork tenderloin (1 lean)
- ¼ Tsp. Salt (1/4 condiment)
- 3 Tbsp. Honey (½ healthy fat)
- 1/8 Tsp. Black pepper (1/4 condiment)
- 1 Tbsp. Minced garlic (1/4 condiment)
- 1 Tsp. Dried rosemary (1/4green)
- 1 Tsp. Italian seasoning (1/8 condiment)

Directions:

⇒ Using a knife, cut the top of the pork tenderloin. Add the garlic (minced) into the cuts. Then sprinkle with kosher salt and pepper.

⇒ In a bowl, add the honey, mustard, rosemary, and Italian seasoning mixture until well blended. Rub this mustard mix all over the pork.

⇒ Leave to marinate in the refrigerator for at least two hours.

⇒ Place the pork tenderloin in the basket of the air fryer. Cook for 18-20 minutes at 400°F. With an instant-read thermometer, verify that the internal temperature of the pig should be 145°F.

⇒ Remove from the air fryer and serve with a side of salad.

Nutrition: Calories: 390 Protein: 59g Fat: 11g

64) Air Fryer Pork Taquitos

Preparation Time: 10 Minutes   **Cooking Time: 20 Minutes**   **Servings: 10**

Ingredients:

- 3 Cups of Pork tenderloin, cooked & shredded (2 leans)
- 2 and ½ cups, fat-free Shredded mozzarella (1 healthy fat)
- 10 Small tortillas (1 healthy fat)

- Salsa for dipping (1 condiment)
- Juice of a lime (1/4 condiment)

Directions:

⇒ Allow the air fryer to preheat to 380°F.

⇒ Add the lime juice to the pork and mix well

⇒ With a damp towel over the tortilla, microwave for ten seconds to soften it

⇒ Add the pork filling and cheese on top in a tortilla, roll the tortilla tightly.

⇒ Situate the tortillas on a greased baking sheet

⇒ Sprinkle oil on the tortillas. Bake for 7-10 minutes or until the tortillas are golden; turn them halfway.

⇒ Serve with salad.

Nutrition: Calories: 253 Fat: 18g Protein: 20g

65) Pork Rind Nachos

Preparation Time: 5 Minutes   **Cooking Time: 5 Minutes**   **Servings: 2**

Ingredients:

- Tbsp. Of pork rinds (1 lean)
- 1/4 Cup shredded cooked chicken (½ lean)
- ½ Cup shredded Monterey jack cheese (1/4 healthy fat)

- 1/4 Cup sliced pickled jalapeños (1/4 green)
- 1/4 Cup guacamole (1/4 healthy fat)
- 1/4 Cup full-fat sour cream (1/4 healthy fat)

Directions:

⇒ Place the pork rinds in a 6-inch round pan. Fill with grilled chicken and Monterey jack cheese. Place the pan in the basket with the air fryer.

⇒ Set the temperature to 370°F and set the timer for 5 minutes or until the cheese has melted.

⇒ Eat immediately with jalapeños, guacamole, and sour cream.

Nutrition: Calories: 295 Protein: 30g Fat: 27g

66) Air Fried Jamaican Jerk Pork

Preparation Time: 10 Minutes   **Cooking Time: 20 Minutes**   **Servings: 4**

Ingredients:

- Pork, cut into three-inch pieces (1 lean)

- ¼ Cup Jerk paste (1/4 condiment)

Directions:

⇒ Rub the jerk dough on all the pork pieces.

⇒ Chill to marinate for 4 hours in the refrigerator.

⇒ Allow the air fryer to preheat to 390°F. Spray with olive oil

⇒ Before placing it in the air fryer, allow the meat to rest for 20 minutes at room temperature.

⇒ Cook for 20 minutes at 390°F in the air fryer, turn halfway.

⇒ Remove from the air fryer and let sit for ten minutes before slicing.

⇒ Serve with microgreens.

Nutrition: Calories: 234 Protein: 31g Fat: 9g

67) Beef Lunch Meatballs

Preparation Time: 10 Minutes   **Cooking Time: 15 Minutes**   **Servings:4**

Ingredients:

- ½ Pound beef, ground (½ lean)
- ½ Pound Italian sausage, chopped (½ lean)
- ½ Tsp. Garlic powder (1/4 condiment)
- ½ Tsp. Onion powder (1/4 condiment)
- Salt and black pepper to the taste (1/4 condiment)
- ½ Cup cheddar cheese, grated (½ healthy fat)
- Mashed potatoes for serving (½ healthy fat)

Directions:

⇒ In a bowl, mix the beef with the sausage, garlic powder, onion powder, salt, pepper, and cheese, mix well and form 16 meatballs with this mixture.

⇒ Place the meatballs in your air fryer and cook them at 370°F for 15 minutes.

⇒ Serve the meatballs with some mashed potatoes on the side.

Nutrition: Calories: 132 Fat: 6.7g Protein: 5.5g

68) Air Fryer Whole Wheat Crusted Pork Chops

Preparation Time: 10 Minutes   **Cooking Time: 12 Minutes**   **Servings:4**

Ingredients:

- 1 Cup whole-wheat breadcrumbs (½ healthy fat)
- ¼ Teaspoon salt (1/4 condiment)
- 2-4 Pieces pork chops (center cut and boneless) (2 leans)
- ½ Teaspoon Chili powder (1/4 condiment)
- 1 Tablespoon parmesan cheese (1/4 healthy fat)
- 1 ½ Teaspoons paprika (½ condiment)
- 1 Egg beaten (1 healthy fat)
- ½ Teaspoon Onion powder (1/4 condiment)
- ½ Teaspoon Granulated garlic (1/4 condiment)

Directions:

⇒ Allow the air fryer to preheat to 400°F.

⇒ Rub kosher salt on each side of the pork chops, let them rest

⇒ Add the beaten egg to a large bowl

⇒ Add the parmesan, breadcrumbs, garlic, pepper, paprika, chili powder, and onion powder to a bowl and mix well

⇒ Dip the pork chop in the egg and then in the breadcrumbs

⇒ Put it in the air fryer and spray it with oil.

⇒ Leave them to cook for 12 minutes at 400°F. Turn them upside down halfway through cooking. Cook for another six minutes.

⇒ Serve with salad.

Nutrition: Calories: 425 Fat: 20g Protein: 31g

69) Air Fried Philly Cheesesteak Taquitos

Preparation Time: 20 Minutes   **Cooking Time: 6-8 Hours**   **Servings: 6**

Ingredients:

- 1 Package Dry Italian dressing mix (1 condiment)
- 1 Pack Super Soft Corn Tortillas (1 healthy fat)
- 2 Pieces green peppers chopped (½ green)
- 12 Cups lean beef steak strips (3 leans)
- 2 Cups Beef stock (1 condiment)
- 1 Cup Lettuce shredded (½ green)
- 10 Slices provolone cheese (1 healthy fat)
- 1 Onion, chopped

Directions:

⇒ In a slow cooker, add onion, beef, stock, pepper, and seasonings.

⇒ Cover, then cook at low heat for 6 or 8 hours.

⇒ Heat the tortillas for two minutes in the microwave.

⇒ Allow the air fryer to preheat to 350°F.

⇒ Remove the cheesesteak from the slow cooker, add 2-3 tablespoons of steak to the tortilla.

⇒ Add some cheese, roll the tortilla well, and place in a deep fryer basket.

⇒ Make all the tortillas you want.

⇒ Lightly brush with olive oil

⇒ Cook for 6-8 minutes.

⇒ Flip the tortillas over and brush more oil as needed.

⇒ Serve with chopped lettuce and enjoy.

Nutrition: Calories: 220 Protein: 21g Fat: 16g

70) Roasted Garlic Bacon and Potatoes

Preparation Time: 5 Minutes   **Cooking Time: 25 Minutes**   **Servings: 4**

Ingredients:

- Medium-sized potatoes (1 healthy fat)
- 1 Strips of streaky bacon (1 lean)
- 2 tablespoon Sprigs of rosemary (1green)
- ½ Cloves of garlic unpeeled smashed, (½ condiment)
- 3 Tsp. of vegetable oil (½ condiment)

Directions:

⇒ Preheat Air fryer to 390°F.

⇒ Put the smashed garlic, bacon, potatoes, rosemary, and then the oil in a bowl. Stir thoroughly.

⇒ Place into air fryer basket and roast until golden for about 25 minutes.

Nutrition: Calories: 114 Fat: 8.1g Protein: 6.2g

71) Peppery Roasted Potatoes With Smoked Bacon

Preparation Time: 15 Minutes   **Cooking Time: 11 Minutes**   **Servings: 2**

Ingredients:

- 38g Small rashers smoked bacon (1 lean)
- 1/3 Tsp. garlic powder (1/4 condiment)
- 1 Tsp. sea salt (1/4 condiment)
- 1 Tsp. Paprika (1/4 condiment)
- 1/3 Tsp. ground black pepper (1/4 condiment)
- 1 Bell pepper (½ green)
- 1 Tsp. mustard (1/4 condiment)
- 2 Habanero peppers, halved (½ green)

Directions:

⇒ Simply toss all the ingredients in a mixing dish, then transfer them to your air fryer's basket.

⇒ Air-fry at 375°F for 10 minutes, serve warm.

Nutrition: Calories: 122 Fat: 9g Protein: 10g

72) Pancetta Chops With Pineapple-Jalapeno Salsa

Preparation Time: 20 Minutes   **Cooking Time: 20 Minutes**   **Servings:3**

Ingredients:

- ½ pound Pieces of Pancetta Chops (roughly 10 ounces each) (1 lean)
- ½ Tablespoons parsley (½ green)
- 1 Tablespoon of ground Coriander (1/4 condiment)
- ¾ Cup of olive oil (1/4 condiment)
- 1 Tablespoon of finely chopped rosemary (1/4green)
- 1.5 Ounces of tomatoes, diced (1/4green)
- 2 Cloves of garlic, chopped (1/4 condiment)

- 8 Ounces of pineapple, diced (½ healthy fat)
- 1 Teaspoon of chopped Jalapenos (½ green)
- 2 Tsp. of Dijon Mustard (1/4 condiment)
- 1½ tsp. of sugar (1/8 condiment)
- 3.5 Ounces of lemon juice (1/8 condiment)
- ½ Tbsp. of finely chopped Cilantro (½ green)
- 2½ Tsp. of salt (1/8 condiment)

Directions:

⇒ Place the rosemary, sugar, mustard, ¼ cup of olive oil, one tablespoon of coriander, 1 ½ teaspoon of salt, cilantro, and one tablespoon of parsley in a mixing bowl and mix thoroughly. Add the pancetta chops and mix.

⇒ Fill a resealable plastic bag with the marinade and refrigerate for about 3 hours.

⇒ Heat your deep fryer to 390°F.

⇒ Place the jalapenos in a bowl and season with one teaspoon of oil to cover them evenly. Transfer the jalapenos to the air fryer and cook for about 7 minutes. Remove from the deep fryer and set aside to cool.

⇒ Once cooled, peel, remove the seeds and chop the jalapenos into small pieces and transfer them to a bowl. Add the pineapple, tomatoes, garlic, and lemon juice, the rest of the oil, parsley, coriander, and salt. Stir and set the sauce aside.

⇒ Remove the pancetta chops from the refrigerator and allow to rest for 30 minutes at room temperature before cooking.

⇒ Place the ribs in the air fryer and roast at 390°F for about 12 minutes. The pancetta chops are well cooked when the internal temperature is 140°F.

Nutrition: Calories: 104 Fat: 8.7g Protein: 6.7g

73) Cornbread With Pulled Pancetta

Preparation Time: 24 Minutes   **Cooking Time: 19 Minutes**   **Servings:2**

Ingredients:

- 2½ Cups pulled Pancetta (1 lean)
- 1 Tsp. dried rosemary (1/4green)
- ½ Tsp. chili powder (1/4 condiment)
- ½ Teaspoon Garlic cloves (1/4 condiment)

- ½ Recipe cornbread (1 healthy fat)
- ½ Tablespoon brown sugar (1/4 condiment)
- 1/3 Cup scallions, thinly sliced (½ green)
- 1 Tsp. sea salt (1/8 condiment)

Directions:

⇒ Preheat a large non-stick pan over medium heat; now, cook the scallions together with the garlic and the pulled pancetta.

⇒ Next, add the sugar, chili powder, rosemary, and salt. Cook, regularly stirring until thickened.

⇒ Preheat your air fryer to 3350°F. Now, coat two mini loaf pans with cooking spray. Add the pulled bacon mixture and spread over the bottom with a spatula.

⇒ Spread the previously prepared cornbread batter over the spicy pulled bacon mixture.

⇒ Bake this cornbread in a preheated air fryer until a centered tester is clean, or for 18 minutes.

Nutrition: Calories: 117 Fat: 9.4g Protein: 11g

Chapter 8 - Snack Recipes

74) Marinated Eggs

Preparation Time: 2 Hours and 10 Minutes

Cooking Time: 7 Minutes

Servings: 4

Ingredients:

- 6 Eggs
- 1 and ¼ Cups of water
- ¼ Cup unsweetened rice vinegar
- 2 Tablespoons coconut aminos
- Salt and black pepper to the taste
- 2 Garlic cloves, minced
- 1 Teaspoon stevia
- 4 Ounces cream cheese
- 1 Tablespoon chives, chopped

Directions:

⇒ Put the eggs in a pot, add water to cover, bring to a boil over medium heat, cover and cook for 7 minutes.

⇒ Rinse eggs with cold water and leave them aside to cool down.

⇒ In a bowl, mix one cup of water with coconut aminos, vinegar, stevia, and garlic and whisk well.

⇒ Put the eggs in this mix, cover with a kitchen towel, and leave them aside for 2 hours, rotating from time to time.

⇒ Peel eggs, cut in halves, and put egg yolks in a bowl.

⇒ Add ¼ cup water, cream cheese, salt, pepper, and chives, and stir well.

⇒ Stuff egg whites with this mix and serve them.

⇒ Enjoy!

Nutrition: Calories: 289 kcal Protein: 15.86g Fat: 22.62g Carbohydrates: 4.52g Sodium: 288mg

75) Pumpkin Muffins

Preparation Time: 10 Minutes

Cooking Time: 15 Minutes

Servings: 18

Ingredients:

- ¼ Cup sunflower seed butter
- ¾ Cup pumpkin puree
- 2 Tablespoons flaxseed meal
- ¼ Cup coconut flour
- ½ Cup erythritol
- ½ Teaspoon nutmeg, ground
- 1 Teaspoon cinnamon, ground
- ½ Teaspoon baking soda
- 1 Egg
- ½ Teaspoon baking powder
- A pinch of salt

Directions:

⇒ In a bowl, mix butter with pumpkin puree and egg and blend well.

⇒ Add flaxseed meal, coconut flour, erythritol, baking soda, baking powder, nutmeg, cinnamon, and a pinch of salt and stir well.

⇒ Spoon this into a greased muffin pan, introduce in the oven at 350 degrees Fahrenheit and bake for 15 minutes.

⇒ Leave muffins to cool down and serve them as a snack.

⇒ Enjoy!

Nutrition: Calories: 65 kcal Protein: 2.82g Fat: 5.42g Carbohydrates: 2.27g Sodium: 57mg

76) Salmon Spinach and Cottage Cheese Sandwich

Preparation Time: 15 Minutes   **Cooking Time: 10 Minutes**   **Servings:4**

Ingredients:

- 4 Ounces (125g) cottage cheese
- 1/4 Cup (15g) chives, chopped
- 1 Teaspoon (5g) capers
- ½ Teaspoon (2.5g) grated lemon rind
- 4 (2 oz. or 60g) Smoked salmon

- 2 Cups (60g) loose baby spinach
- 1 Medium (110g) red onion, sliced thinly
- 8 Slices rye bread (about 30g each)
- Kosher salt and freshly ground black pepper

Directions:

⇒ Preheat your griddle or Panini press.

⇒ Mix together cottage cheese, chives, capers, and lemon rind in a small bowl.

⇒ Spread and divide the cheese mixture on four bread slices. Top with spinach, onion slices, and smoked salmon.

⇒ Cover with remaining bread slices.

⇒ Grill the sandwiches until golden and grill marks form on both sides.

⇒ Transfer to a serving dish.

⇒ Serve and enjoy.

Nutrition: Calories: 261 Fat: 9.9g Carbohydrates: 22.9g Protein: 19.9g Sodium: 1226mg

77) Sausage and Cheese Dip

Preparation Time: 10 Minutes   **Cooking Time: 130 Minutes**   **Servings:28**

Ingredients:

- 8 Ounces cream cheese
- A pinch of salt and black pepper
- 16 Ounces sour cream
- 8 Ounces pepper jack cheese, chopped

- 15 Ounces canned tomatoes mixed with habaneros
- 1-pound Italian sausage, ground
- ¼ Cup green onions, chopped

Directions:

⇒ Heat up a pan over medium heat, add sausage, stir and cook until it browns.

⇒ Add tomatoes, mix, stir and cook for 4 minutes more.

⇒ Add a pinch of salt, pepper, and green onions, stir and cook for 4 minutes.

⇒ Spread the pepper jack cheese on the bottom of your slow cooker.

⇒ Add cream cheese, sausage mix, and sour cream, cover, and cook on High for 2 hours.

⇒ Uncover your slow cooker, stir dip, transfer to a bowl, and serve.

⇒ Enjoy!

Nutrition: Calories: 132 kcal Protein: 6.79g Fat: 9.58g Carbohydrates: 6.22g Sodium: 362mg

78) Pesto Crackers

Preparation Time: 10 Minutes   **Cooking Time: 17 Minutes**   **Servings: 6**

Ingredients:

- ½ Teaspoon baking powder
- Salt and black pepper to the taste
- 1 and ¼ Cups almond flour
- ¼ Teaspoon basil dried one garlic clove, minced
- 2 Tablespoons basil pesto
- A pinch of cayenne pepper
- 3 Tablespoons ghee

Directions:

⇒ In a bowl, mix salt, pepper, baking powder, and almond flour.

⇒ Add garlic, cayenne, and basil and stir.

⇒ Add pesto and whisk.

⇒ Also, add ghee and mix your dough with your finger.

⇒ Spread this dough on a lined baking sheet, introduce in the oven at 325 degrees F and bake for 17 minutes.

⇒ Leave aside to cool down, cut your crackers, and serve them as a snack.

⇒ Enjoy!

Nutrition: Calories: 9 kcal Protein: 0.41g Fat: 0.14g Carbohydrates: 1.86g Sodium: 2mg

79) Bacon Cheeseburger

Preparation Time: 10 Minutes   **Cooking Time: 30 Minutes**   **Servings: 4**

Ingredients:

- 1 lb. Lean ground beef
- 1/4 Cup chopped yellow onion
- 1 Clove garlic, minced
- 1 Tbsp. yellow mustard
- 1 Tbsp. Worcestershire sauce
- ½ Tsp. salt
- Cooking spray
- 4 Ultra-thin slices of cheddar cheese, cut into six equal-sized rectangular pieces
- 3 Pieces of turkey bacon, each cut into eight evenly-sized rectangular pieces
- 24 Dill pickle chips
- 4-6 Green leaf
- Lettuce leaves, torn into 24 small square-shaped pieces
- 12 Cherry tomatoes, sliced in half

Directions:

⇒ Pre-heat oven to 400°F.

⇒ Combine the garlic, salt, onion, Worcestershire sauce, and beef in a medium-sized bowl, and mix well.

⇒ Form the mixture into 24 small meatballs.

⇒ Put meatballs onto a foil-lined baking sheet and cook for 12-15 minutes.

⇒ Leave the oven on.

⇒ Top every meatball with a piece of cheese, then go back to the oven until cheese melts for about 2 to 3 minutes.

⇒ Let the meatballs cool.

⇒ To assemble bites, on a toothpick, put a cheese-covered meatball, a piece of bacon, a piece of lettuce, pickle chip, and a tomato half.

Nutrition: Fat: 14g Cholesterol: 41mg Carbohydrates: 30g Protein: 15g

80) Cheeseburger Pie

Preparation Time: 20 Minutes   **Cooking Time: 90 Minutes**   **Servings:4**

Ingredients:

- 1 Large spaghetti squash
- 1 lb. Lean ground beef
- 1/4 Cup diced onion
- 2 Eggs
- 1/3 Cup low-fat, plain Greek yogurt

- 2 Tablespoons tomato sauce
- ½ Tsp. Worcestershire sauce
- 2/3 Cups reduced-fat, shredded cheddar cheese
- 2 oz. Dill pickle slices
- Cooking spray

Directions:

⇒ Preheat oven to 400°F. Slice spaghetti squash in half lengthwise; dismiss pulp and seeds.

⇒ Spray insides with cooking spray.

⇒ Place squash halves cut-side-down onto a foil-lined baking sheet, and bake for 30 minutes.

⇒ Once cooked, let it cool before scraping squash flesh with a fork to remove spaghetti-like strands; set aside.

⇒ Push squash strands in the bottom and up sides of the greased pie pan, creating an even layer.

⇒ Meanwhile, set up pie filling.

⇒ In a lightly greased, medium-sized skillet, cook beef and onion over medium heat for 8 to 10 minutes, sometimes stirring, until meat is brown.

⇒ Drain and remove from heat.

⇒ In a medium-sized bowl, whisk together eggs, tomato sauce, Greek yogurt, and Worcestershire sauce. Stir in ground beef mixture.

⇒ Pour pie filling over the squash crust.

⇒ Sprinkle meat filling with cheese, and then top with dill pickle slices.

⇒ Bake for 40 minutes.

Nutrition: Calories: 409 Cal Fat: 24.49g Carbohydrates: 15.06g Protein: 30.69g

81) Smoked Salmon and Cheese on Rye Bread

Preparation Time: 15 Minutes   **Cooking Time: 10 Minutes**   **Servings:4**

Ingredients:

- 8 Ounces (250g) smoked salmon, thinly sliced
- 1/3 Cup (85g) mayonnaise
- 2 Tablespoons (30ml) lemon juice
- 1 Tablespoon (15g) Dijon mustard
- 1 Teaspoon (3g) garlic, minced

- 4 Slices cheddar cheese (about 2 oz. or 30g each)
- 8 Slices rye bread (about 2 oz. or 30g each)
- 8 (15g) Romaine lettuce leaves
- Salt and freshly ground black pepper

Directions:

⇒ Mix together the mayonnaise, lemon juice, mustard, and garlic in a small bowl. Flavor with salt and pepper and set aside.

⇒ Spread dressing on four bread slices. Top with lettuce, salmon, and cheese. Cover with remaining rye bread slices.

⇒ Serve and enjoy.

Nutrition: Calories: 365 Fat: 16.6g Carbohydrates: 31.6g Protein: 18.8g Sodium: 951mg

82) Chicken and Mushrooms

Preparation Time: 10 Minutes   **Cooking Time: 15 Minutes**   **Servings:6**

Ingredients:

- 2 Chicken breasts
- 1 Cup of sliced white champignons
- 1 Cup of sliced green chilies
- ½ Cup scallions hacked
- 1 Teaspoon of chopped garlic

- 1 Cup of low-fat cheddar shredded cheese (1-1,5 lb. grams fat / ounce)
- 1 Tablespoon of olive oil
- 1 Tablespoon of butter

Directions:

⇒ Fry the chicken breasts with olive oil.

⇒ When needed, add salt and pepper.

⇒ Grill the chicken breasts on a plate with a grill.

⇒ For every serving, weigh 4 ounces of chicken. (Make two servings, save leftovers for another meal).

⇒ In a buttered pan, stir in mushrooms, green peppers, scallions, and garlic until smooth and a little dark.

⇒ Place the chicken on a baking platter.

⇒ Cover with the mushroom combination.

⇒ Top on ham.

⇒ Place the cheese in a 350 oven until it melts.

Nutrition: Carbohydrates: 2g Protein: 23g Fat: 11g Cholesterol: 112mg Sodium: 198mg Potassium: 261mg

83) Chicken Enchilada Bake

Preparation Time: 20 Minutes   **Cooking Time: 50 Minutes**   **Servings:5**

Ingredients:

- 5 oz. Shredded chicken breast (boil and shred ahead) or 99 percent fat-free white chicken can be used in a pan.
- 1 Can tomato paste
- 1 Low sodium chicken broth can be fat-free
- 1/4 Cup cheese with low-fat mozzarella

- 1 Tablespoon oil
- 1 Tbsp. of salt
- Ground cumin, chili powder, garlic powder, oregano, and onion powder (all to taste)
- 1 to 2 Zucchinis sliced longways (similar to lasagna noodles) into thin lines
- Sliced (optional) olives

Directions:

⇒ Add olive oil in a saucepan over medium/high heat, stir in tomato paste and seasonings, and heat in chicken broth for 2-3 min.

⇒ Stirring regularly to boil, turn heat to low for 15 min.

⇒ Set aside and cool to ambient temperature.

⇒ Dredge a zucchini strip through enchilada sauce and lay flat on the pan's bottom in a small baking pan.

⇒ Next, add the chicken a little less than 1/4 cup of enchilada sauce and mix it.

⇒ Attach the chicken to cover and end the baking tray.

⇒ Sprinkle some bacon over the chicken.

⇒ Add another layer of the soaked enchilada sauce zucchini (similar to lasagna making).

⇒ When needed, cover with the remaining cheese and olives on top—bake for 35 to 40 minutes.

⇒ Keep an eye on them.

⇒ When the cheese starts getting golden, cover with foil.

⇒ Serve and enjoy!

Nutrition: Calories: 312 Cal Carbohydrates: 21.3g Protein: 27g Fat: 10.2g

84) Salmon Feta and Pesto Wrap

Preparation Time: 15 Minutes   **Cooking Time: 10 Minutes**   **Servings:4**

Ingredients:

- 8 Ounces (250g) smoked salmon fillet, thinly sliced
- 1 Cup (150g) feta cheese
- 8 (15g) Romaine lettuce leaves
- 4 (6-inch) Pita bread
- 1/4 Cup (60g) basil pesto sauce

Directions:

⇒ Place one pita bread on a plate. Top with lettuce, salmon, feta cheese, and pesto sauce. Fold or roll to enclose filling. Repeat the procedure for the remaining ingredients.

⇒ Serve and enjoy.

Nutrition: Calories: 379 Fat: 17.7g Carbohydrates: 36.6g Protein: 18.4g Sodium: 554mg

85) Pan-Fried Trout

Preparation Time: 15 Minutes   **Cooking Time: 10 Minutes**   **Servings:4**

Ingredients:

- 1 ¼ Pounds trout fillets
- 1/3 Cup white, or yellow, cornmeal
- ¼ Teaspoon anise seeds
- ¼ Teaspoon black pepper
- ½ Cup minced cilantro, or parsley
- Vegetable cooking spray
- Lemon wedges

Directions:

⇒ Coat the fish with combined cornmeal, spices, and cilantro, pressing them gently into the fish. Spray a large skillet with cooking spray; heat over medium heat until hot.

⇒ Add fish and cook until it is tender and flakes with a fork, about 5 minutes on each side. Serve with lemon wedges.

Nutrition: Calories: 207 Total Carbohydrates: 19g Cholesterol: 27mg Total Fat: 16g Fiber: 4g Protein: 18g

86) Glazed Bananas in Phyllo Nut Cups

Preparation Time: 30 Minutes   **Cooking Time: 45 Minutes**   **Servings:6**

Ingredients:

- 3/4 Cups shelled pistachios
- ½ Cup sugar
- 1 Teaspoon. ground cinnamon
- 4 Sheets phyllo dough (14 inches x 9 inches)
- 1/4 Cup butter, melted

Sauce:

- 3/4 Cup butter, cubed
- 3/4 Cup packed brown sugar
- 3 Medium-firm bananas, sliced
- 1/4 Teaspoon. ground cinnamon
- 3 to 4 Cups vanilla ice cream

Directions:

⇒ Finely chop sugar and pistachios in a food processor; move to a bowl, then mix in cinnamon. Slice each phyllo sheet into six four-inch squares, get rid of the trimmings. Pile the squares, then use plastic wrap to cover.

⇒ Slather melted butter on each square one at a time, then scatter a heaping tablespoonful of pistachio mixture. Pile three squares, flip each at an angle to misalign the corners. Force each stack on the sides and bottom of an oiled eight ounces custard cup. Bake for 15-20 minutes in a 350 degrees F oven until golden; cool for 5 minutes. Move to a wire rack to cool completely.

⇒ Melt and boil brown sugar and butter in a saucepan to make the sauce; lower heat. Mix in cinnamon and bananas gently; heat completely. Put ice cream in the phyllo cups until full, then put banana sauce on top. Serve right away.

Nutrition: Calories: 735 Total Carbohydrate: 82g Cholesterol: 111mg Total Fat: 45g Fiber: 3g Protein: 7g Sodium: 468mg

87) Salmon Cream Cheese and Onion on Bagel

Preparation Time: 15 Minutes   **Cooking Time: 10 Minutes**   **Servings:4**

Ingredients:

- 8 Ounces (250g) smoked salmon fillet, thinly sliced
- ½ Cup (125g) cream cheese
- 1 Medium (110g) onion, thinly sliced
- 4 Bagels (about 80g each), split
- 2 Tablespoons (7g) fresh parsley, chopped
- Freshly ground black pepper, to taste

Directions:

⇒ Spread the cream cheese on each bottom's half of bagels. Top with salmon and onion, season with pepper, sprinkle with parsley and then cover with bagel tops.

⇒ Serve and enjoy.

Nutrition: Calories: 309 Fat: 14.1g Carbohydrates: 32.0g Protein: 14.7g Sodium: 571mg

88) Salmon Apple Salad Sandwich

Preparation Time: 15 Minutes   **Cooking Time: 10 Minutes**   **Servings: 4**

Ingredients:

- 4 Ounces (125g) canned pink salmon, drained and flaked
- 1 Medium (180g) red apple, cored and diced
- 1 Celery stalk (about 60g), chopped
- 1 Shallot (about 40g), finely chopped
- 1/3 Cup (85g) light mayonnaise
- 8 Whole grain bread slices (about 30g each), toasted
- 8 (15g) Romaine lettuce leaves
- Salt and freshly ground black pepper

Directions:

⇒ Combine the salmon, apple, celery, shallot, and mayonnaise in a mixing bowl—season with salt and pepper.

⇒ Place one bread slice on a plate, top with lettuce and salmon salad, and then cover it with another slice of bread—repeat the procedure for the remaining ingredients.

⇒ Serve and enjoy.

Nutrition: Calories: 315 Fat: 11.3g Carbohydrates: 40.4g Protein: 15.1g Sodium: 469mg

89) Greek Baklava

Preparation Time: 20 Minutes   **Cooking Time: 20 Minutes**   **Servings: 18**

Ingredients:

- 1 (16 oz.) Package phyllo dough
- 1 lb. Chopped nuts
- 1 Cup butter
- 1 Teaspoon ground cinnamon
- 1 Cup water
- 1 Cup white sugar
- 1 Teaspoon vanilla extract
- ½ Cup honey

Directions:

⇒ Preheat the oven to 175°C or 350°Fahrenheit. Spread butter on the sides and bottom of a 9- by 13-inch pan.

⇒ Chop the nuts, then mix with cinnamon; set it aside. Unfurl the phyllo dough, then halve the whole stack to fit the pan. Use a damp cloth to cover the phyllo to prevent drying as you proceed. Put two phyllo sheets in the pan, then butter well. Repeat to make eight layered phyllo sheets. Scatter 2-3 tablespoons of the nut mixture over the sheets, then place two more phyllo sheets on top, butter, sprinkle with nuts—layer as you go. The final layer should be six to eight phyllo sheets deep.

⇒ Make square or diamond shapes with a sharp knife up to the bottom of the pan. You can slice into four long rows for diagonal shapes. Bake until crisp and golden for 50 minutes.

⇒ Meanwhile, boil water and sugar until the sugar melts to make the sauce; mix in honey and vanilla. Let it simmer for 20 minutes.

⇒ Take the baklava out of the oven, then drizzle with sauce right away; cool. Serve the baklava in cupcake papers. You can also freeze them without cover. The baklava will turn soggy when wrapped.

Nutrition: Calories: 393 Total Carbohydrate: 37.5g Cholesterol: 27mg Total Fat: 25.9g Protein: 6.1g Sodium: 196mg

90) Easy Salmon Burger

Preparation Time: 15 minutes   **Cooking Time: 15 minutes**   **Servings:6**

Ingredients:

- 16 Ounces (450g) pink salmon, minced
- 1 Cup (250g) prepared mashed potatoes
- 1 Medium (110g) onion, chopped
- 1 Stalk celery (about 60g), finely chopped
- 1 Large egg (about 60g), lightly beaten

- 2 Tablespoons (7g) fresh cilantro, chopped
- 1 Cup (100g) breadcrumbs
- Vegetable oil, for deep frying
- Salt and freshly ground black pepper

Directions:

⇒ Combine the salmon, mashed potatoes, onion, celery, egg, and cilantro in a mixing bowl. Season to taste and mix thoroughly. Spoon about 2 Tablespoons of the mixture, roll in breadcrumbs, and then form into small patties.

⇒ Heat oil in a non-stick frying pan. Cook your salmon patties for 5 minutes on each side or until golden brown and crispy.

⇒ Serve in burger buns and with coleslaw on the side if desired.

⇒ Enjoy.

Nutrition: Calories: 230 Fat: 7.9g Carbs: 20.9g Protein: 18.9g Sodium: 298mg

91) White Bean Dip

Preparation Time: 10 Minutes   **Cooking Time: 0 Minutes**   **Servings:4**

Ingredients:

- 15 Ounces canned white beans, drained and rinsed
- 6 Ounces canned artichoke hearts, drained and quartered
- 4 Garlic cloves, minced
- 1 Tablespoon basil, chopped

- 2 Tablespoons olive oil
- Juice of ½ lemon
- Zest of ½ lemon, grated
- Salt and black pepper to the taste

Directions:

⇒ In your food processor, combine the beans with the artichokes and the rest of the ingredients except the oil and pulse well.

⇒ Add the oil gradually, pulse the mix again, divide into cups and serve as a party dip.

Nutrition: Calories: 274 Fat: 11.7g Fiber: 6.5g Carbs: 18.5g Protein: 16.5g

92) Grilled Salmon Burger

Preparation Time: 15 Minutes   **Cooking Time: 10 Minutes**   **Servings:4**

Ingredients:

- 16 Ounces (450g) pink salmon fillet, minced
- 1 Cup (250g) prepared mashed potatoes
- 1 Shallot (about 40g), chopped
- 1 Large egg (about 60g), lightly beaten
- 2 Tablespoons (7g) fresh coriander, chopped
- 4 Hamburger buns (about 60g each), split

- 1 Large tomato (about 150g), sliced
- 8 (15g) Romaine lettuce leaves
- 1/4 Cup (60g) mayonnaise
- Salt and freshly ground black pepper
- Cooking oil spray

Directions:

⇒ Combine the salmon, mashed potatoes, shallot, egg, and coriander in a mixing bowl—season with salt and pepper.

⇒ Spoon about two tablespoons of mixture and form into patties.

⇒ Preheat your grill or griddle on high—grease with cooking oil spray.

⇒ Grill the salmon patties for 4-5 minutes on each side or until cooked through. Transfer to a clean plate and cover to keep warm.

⇒ Spread some mayonnaise on the bottom half of the buns. Top with lettuce, salmon patty, and tomato. Cover with bun tops.

⇒ Serve and enjoy.

Nutrition: Calories: 395 Fat: 18.0g Carbohydrates: 38.8g Protein: 21.8g Sodium: 383mg

Chapter 9 -   Dessert Recipes

93) Wrapped Pears

Preparation Time: 10 Minutes   **Cooking Time: 10 Minutes**   **Servings:4**

Ingredients:

- 4 Puff pastry sheets
- 14 oz. Vanilla custard
- 2 Pears

- 1 Egg
- ½ Tbsp. cinnamon powder
- 2 Tbsp. sugar

Directions:

⇒ Put wisp pastry slices on a flat surface, add a spoonful of vanilla custard at the center of each, add pear halves and wrap.

⇒ Combine pears with egg, cinnamon, and spray sugar, put into the air fryer's basket, then cook at 320°F for 15 minutes.

⇒ Split portions on plates.

⇒ Serve.

Nutrition: Calories: 285 Total Fat: 14g Total carbs: 30g

94) Air Fried Bananas

Preparation Time: 5 Minutes   **Cooking Time: 10 Minutes**   **Servings:4**

Ingredients:

- 3 Tbsp. butter
- 2 Eggs
- 8 Bananas

- ½ Cup corn flour
- 3 Tbsp. cinnamon sugar
- 1 Cup panko

Directions:

⇒ Heat a pan with the butter over medium heat, put panko, turn and cook for 4 minutes, then move to a bowl.

⇒ Dredge each in flour, panko, and egg mixture, place in the basket of the air fryer, gratinate with cinnamon sugar, and cook at 280°F for 10 minutes.

⇒ Serve immediately.

Nutrition: Calories: 337 Total fat: 3g Total carbs: 23g

95) Tasty Banana Cake

Preparation Time: 10 Minutes   **Cooking Time: 30 Minutes**   **Servings:4**

Ingredients:

- 1 Tbsp. butter, soft
- 1 Egg
- 1/3 Cup brown sugar
- 2 Tbsp. honey
- 1 Banana

- 1 Cup white flour
- 1 Tbsp. baking powder
- ½ Tbsp. cinnamon powder
- Cooking spray

Directions:

⇒ Grease the cake pan with cooking spray.

⇒ Mix in butter with honey, sugar, banana, cinnamon, egg, flour, and baking powder in a bowl, then beat.

⇒ Put the mix in a cake pan with cooking spray, put into the air fryer, and cook at 350°F for 30 minutes.

⇒ Allow to cool, then slice it.

⇒ Serve.

Nutrition: Calories: 435 Total Fat: 7g Total carbs: 15g

96) Peanut Butter Fudge

Preparation Time: 10 Minutes **Cooking Time: 10 Minutes** **Servings:20**

Ingredients:

- 1/4 Cup almonds, toasted and chopped
- 12 oz. Smooth peanut butter
- 15 Drops liquid stevia
- 3 Tbsp. coconut oil
- 4 Tbsp. coconut cream
- Pinch of salt

Directions:

⇒ Line a baking tray with parchment paper.

⇒ Melt coconut oil in a pan over low heat. Add peanut butter, coconut cream, stevia, and salt to a saucepan. Stir well.

⇒ Pour fudge mixture into the prepared baking tray and sprinkle chopped almonds on top.

⇒ Place the tray in the refrigerator for 1 hour or until set.

⇒ Slice and serve.

Nutrition: Calories: 131 Fat: 12g Carbs: 4g Sugar: 2g Protein: 5g Cholesterol: 0mg

97) Cocoa Cake

Preparation Time: 5 Minutes **Cooking Time: 17 Minutes** **Servings:6**

Ingredients:

- 4 oz. Butter
- 3 Eggs
- 3 oz. Sugar
- 1 Tbsp. cocoa powder
- 3 oz. Flour
- ½ Tbsp. lemon juice

Directions:

⇒ Mix in 1 tablespoon butter with cocoa powder in a bowl and beat.

⇒ Mix in the rest of the butter with eggs, flour, sugar, and lemon juice in another bowl, blend properly and move the half into a cake pan

⇒ Put half of the cocoa blend, spread, add the rest of the butter layer, and crest with remaining cocoa.

⇒ Put into the air fryer and cook at 360° F for 17 minutes.

⇒ Allow it to cool before slicing.

⇒ Serve.

Nutrition: Calories: 221 Total Fat: 5g Total carbs: 12g

98) Avocado Pudding

Preparation Time: 20 Minutes **Cooking Time: 0 Minutes** **Servings:8**

Ingredients:

- 2 Ripe avocados, pitted and cut into pieces
- 1 Tbsp. fresh lime juice
- 14 oz. Can coconut milk
- 2 Tsp. liquid stevia
- 2 Tsp. vanilla

Directions:

⇒ Inside the blender, add all ingredients and blend until smooth.

⇒ Serve immediately and enjoy.

Nutrition: Calories: 317 Fat: 30g Carbs: 9g Sugar: 0.5g Protein: 3g Cholesterol: 0mg

99) Bounty Bars

Preparation Time: 20 Minutes   **Cooking Time: 0 Minutes**   **Servings: 12**

Ingredients:

- 1 Cup coconut cream
- 3 Cups shredded unsweetened coconut
- 1/4 Cup extra virgin coconut oil
- ½ Teaspoon vanilla powder

- 1/4 Cup powdered erythritol
- 1 ½ oz. Cocoa butter
- 5 oz. Dark chocolate

Directions:

⇒ Heat the oven at 350°F and toast the coconut in it for 5-6 minutes. Remove from the oven once toasted and set aside to cool.

⇒ Take a bowl of medium size and add coconut oil, coconut cream, vanilla, erythritol, and shredded coconut. Mix the ingredients well to prepare a smooth mixture.

⇒ Make 12 bars of equal size with the help of your hands from the prepared mixture and adjust in the tray lined with parchment paper.

⇒ Place the tray in the fridge for around one hour and, in the meantime, put the cocoa butter and dark chocolate in a glass bowl.

⇒ Heat a cup of water in a saucepan over medium heat and place the bowl over it to melt the cocoa butter and the dark chocolate.

⇒ Remove from the heat once melted properly, mix well until blended, and set it aside to cool.

⇒ Take the coconut bars and coat them with dark chocolate mixture one by one using a wooden stick. Adjust on the tray lined with parchment paper and drizzle the remaining mixture over them.

⇒ Refrigerate for around one hour before you serve the delicious bounty bars.

Nutrition: Calories: 230 Fat: 25g Carbohydrates: 5g Protein: 32g

100)   Simple Cheesecake

Preparation Time: 10 Minutes   **Cooking Time: 15 Minutes**   **Servings: 15**

Ingredients:

- 1 lb. Cream cheese
- ½ Tbsp. vanilla extract
- 2 Eggs

- 4 Tbsp. sugar
- 1 Cup graham crackers
- 2 Tbsp. butter

Directions:

⇒ Mix in butter with crackers in a bowl.

⇒ Compress crackers blend to the bottom of a cake pan, put into the air fryer, and cook at 350°F for 4 minutes.

⇒ Mix cream cheese with sugar, vanilla, egg in a bowl and beat properly.

⇒ Sprinkle filling on crackers crust and cook the cheesecake in the air fryer at 310°F for 15 minutes.

⇒ Keep the cake in the fridge for 3 hours, slice.

⇒ Serve.

Nutrition: Calories: 257 Total Fat: 18g Total carbs: 22g

101) Chocolate Almond Butter Brownie

Preparation Time: 10 Minutes   **Cooking Time: 16 Minutes**   **Servings:4**

Ingredients:

- 1 Cup bananas, overripe
- ½ Cup almond butter, melted
- 1 Scoop protein powder
- 2 Tbsp. unsweetened cocoa powder

Directions:

⇒ Preheat the air fryer to 325°F. Grease the air fryer baking pan and set it aside.

⇒ Blend all ingredients in a blender until smooth.

⇒ Pour the batter into the prepared pan and place it in the air fryer basket to cook for 16 minutes.

⇒ Serve and enjoy.

Nutrition: Calories: 82 Fat: 2g Carbs: 11g Sugar: 5g Protein: 7g Cholesterol: 16mg

102) Almond Butter Fudge

Preparation Time: 10 Minutes   **Cooking Time: 10 Minutes**   **Servings:18**

Ingredients:

- 3/4 Cup creamy almond butter
- 1 ½ Cups unsweetened chocolate chips

Directions:

⇒ Line 8x4-inch pan with parchment paper and set aside.

⇒ Add chocolate chips and almond butter into the double boiler and cook over medium heat until the chocolate-butter mixture is melted. Stir well.

⇒ Place the mixture into the prepared pan and place in the freezer until set.

⇒ Slice and serve.

Nutrition: Calories: 197 Fat: 16g Carbs: 7g Sugar: 1g Protein: 4g Cholesterol: 0mg

103) Apple Bread

Preparation Time: 5 Minutes   **Cooking Time: 40 Minutes**   **Servings:6**

Ingredients:

- 3 Cups apples
- 1 Cup sugar
- 1 Tbsp. vanilla
- 2 Eggs
- 1 Tbsp. apple pie spice
- 2 Cups white flour
- 1 Tbsp. baking powder
- 1 Butter stick
- 1 Cup water

Directions:

⇒ Mix the eggs with one butter stick, sugar, vanilla, and apple pie spice, then turn using a mixer.

⇒ Put apples and turn properly.

⇒ Mix baking powder with flour in another bowl and turn.

⇒ Blend the two mixtures, turn and move it to a springform pan.

⇒ Put the pan into the air fryer and cook at 320°F for 40 minutes

⇒ Slice.

⇒ Serve.

Nutrition: Calories: 401 Total Fat: 9g Total carbs: 29g

104) Banana Bread

Preparation Time: 5 Minutes   **Cooking Time: 40 Minutes**   **Servings: 6**

Ingredients:

- ¾ Cup sugar
- 1/3 Cup butter
- 1 Tbsp. vanilla extract
- 1 Egg
- 2 Bananas
- 1 Tbsp. baking powder

- 1 and ½ Cups flour
- ½ Tbsp. baking soda
- 1/3 Cup milk
- 1 and ½ Tbsp. cream of tartar
- Cooking spray

Directions:

⇒ Mix the milk with cream of tartar, vanilla, egg, sugar, bananas, and butter in a bowl, then mix all.

⇒ Mix in flour with baking soda and baking powder.

⇒ Blend the two mixtures, turn properly, move into an oiled pan with cooking spray, put into the air fryer, and cook at 320°F for 40 minutes.

⇒ Remove the bread, allow to cool, slice.

⇒ Serve.

Nutrition: Calories: 540 Total Fat: 16g Total carbs: 28g

Chapter 10 - L & G McAdams Meal Plan – for Athletes

Day 1

3) Omelette With Tomatoes and Spring Onions | Calories 263

30) Three-Bean Medley | Calories 284

33) Blueberry Cantaloupe Avocado Salad | Calories 406

44) Lemon-Garlic Chicken | Calories 350

64) Air Fryer Pork Taquitos | Calories 253

90) Easy Salmon Burger | Calories 230

Total Calories 1786

Day 3

1) Cinnamon-Apple Granola With Greek Yogurt | Calories 312

27) Asparagus Frittata Recipe | Calories 251

41) Zucchini Salmon Salad | Calories 224

53) Butter Glazed Carrots | Calories 151

63) Mustard Glazed Air Fryer Pork Tenderloin | Calories 390

76) Salmon Spinach and Cottage Cheese Sandwich | Calories 261

Total Calories 1589

Day 5

18) Awesome Avocado Muffins | Calories 200

25) Almond Coconut Cereal | Calories 181

36) Greek Salad | Calories 234

60) Creamy Spinach and Mushroom Lasagna | Calories 488

68) Air Fryer Whole Wheat Crusted Pork Chops | Calories 425

88) Salmon Apple Salad Sandwich | Calories 315

Total Calories 1843

Day 7

7) Strawberry Yogurt Treat | Calories 733

29) Buffalo Chicken Sliders | Calories 300

35) Beet Salad (from Israel) | Calories 156

54) Cinnamon Butternut Squash Fries | Calories 175

69) Air Fried Philly Cheesesteak Taquitos | Calories 220

86) Glazed Bananas in Phyllo Nut Cups | Calories 735

Total Calories 2319

Day 2

17) Millet Porridge | Calories 219

20) Bacon and Lemon spiced Muffins | Calories 186

40) Chicken Broccoli Salad With Avocado Dressing | Calories 195

49) Cheesy Cauliflower Fritters | Calories 209

73) Cornbread With Pulled Pancetta | Calories 117

93) Wrapped Pears | Calories 285

Total Calories 1211

Day 4

15) Yogurt With Granola and Persimmon | Calories 286

19) Bacon and Brussels Sprout Breakfast | Calories 275

32) Barley and Lentil Salad | Calories 406

62) Air Fryer Pork Chop & Broccoli | Calories 483

74) Marinated Eggs | Calories 289

82) Chicken and Mushrooms | Calories

Total Calories 1739

Day 6

2) Greek Yogurt With Cherry-Almond Syrup Parfait | Calories 185

22) WW Salad in a Jar | Calories 180

38) Mediterranean Chickpea Salad | Calories 200

57) Feta & Mushroom Frittata | Calories 226

65) Pork Rind Nachos | Calories 295

75) Pumpkin Muffins | Calories 65

Total Calories 1151

Chapter 11 -   Conclusion

Warning, remember to consult with your medical professional before starting this diet, he/she knows what is best for you and what special requirements you may have.

I hope this cookbook has been useful and that you enjoy it as much as I did when I was writing it and testing it on myself.

In order to get the best results, I recommend you to accompany the diet with an exercise routine and trust in the process, I am sure you will see the results you expect by following these recipes.

I also recommend you to adopt this diet as part of your lifestyle, since it is a diet both in the beginning and in the maintenance of the results. That's right, you will be able to lose weight and stay in shape.

Adopting a healthy lifestyle increases your life expectancy, your quality of life and prevents diseases.

Best wishes,

Lorely McAdams

Lean and Green Diet Cookbook On a Budget

Dr. McAdams Easy Diet Plan | Delicious and Budget Friendly Recipes to Kickstart Your Body Transformation in Healthy Way!

By Lorely McAdams

Chapter 1 - Introduction

The lean and green diet has gained popularity all over the world, mainly because it allows to lose weight with short term results. However, one of its main features, which has made it a favorite among many people, is that it allows to have an affordable and easy to manage budget. Today more than ever it is important to take care of the health of our body and our finances.

Discover in the following pages how to start a lean and green diet, what it consists of and its main benefits.

What is the lean and green diet?

Lean and green diet is an approach based on a high protein intake and low sodium and carbohydrate intake, as well as avoiding the consumption of trans fats and sugars.

So, in this cookbook you will find the right portions of low carbohydrate but high protein foods, as well as probiotic cultures that will improve your intestinal health and the proposal of delicious snacks that you can enjoy between meals to keep you motivated during your diet. All of this while maintaining an affordable budget and a healthy diet to keep you in shape.

Benefits of the lean and green diet

- *This cookbook will help you stay on a budget. While the lean and green diet is affordable, it is not exactly low cost. However, with this cookbook you will be able to make delicious homemade food that is low in calories and sodium but high in protein.*
- *It allows you to lose weight with short-term results or maintain your ideal weight.*
- *Easy to follow. You will find an easy to follow meal plan, with simple options for your day to day life. The recipes are easy to prepare, as the program includes specific recipes and a list of food options.*
- *Prevents diabetes. One of the main causes of diabetes is the intake of sugary products, the lean and green diet avoids or eliminates them from your meal plan.*
- *Improves blood pressure. The lean and green diet is based on a low sodium intake which significantly improves blood pressure.*

So, keep on a budget and improve your diet with these delicious recipes, discover a healthy lifestyle without bankrupting yourself.

Chapter 2 -   Breakfast Recipes

1) Smoothie Bowl With Spinach Mango and Muesli

Preparation Time: 10 Minutes   **Cooking Time: 0 Minutes**   **Servings:1**

Ingredients:

- 150g Yogurt
- 30g Apple
- 30g Mango
- 30g Low carb muesli
- 10g Spinach
- 10g Chia seeds

Directions:

⇒ Soak the spinach leaves and let them drain.

⇒ Peel the mango and cut it into strips.

⇒ Remove apple core and cut it into pieces.

⇒ Put everything except the mango together with the yogurt in a blender and make a fine puree out of it.

⇒ Put the spinach smoothie in a bowl.

⇒ Add the muesli, chia seeds, and mango.

⇒ Serve the whole thing

Nutrition: Kcal: 362 Carbohydrates: 21g Protein: 12g Fat: 21g

2) Alkaline Blueberry Muffins

Preparation Time: 5 Minutes   **Cooking Time: 20 Minutes**   **Servings:3**

Ingredients:

- 1 Cup Coconut Milk
- 3/4 Cups Spelt Flour
- 3/4 Teff Flour
- ½ Cup Blueberries
- 1/3 Cup Agave
- 1/4 Cup Sea Moss Gel
- ½ Tsp. Sea Salt
- Grapeseed Oil

Directions:

⇒ Adjust the temperature of the oven to 365 degrees.

⇒ Grease 6 regular-size muffin cups with muffin liners.

⇒ In a bowl, mix together sea salt, sea moss, agave, coconut milk, and flour gel until they are properly blended.

⇒ Then crimp in blueberries.

⇒ Coat the muffin pan lightly with the grapeseed oil.

⇒ Pour in the muffin batter.

⇒ Bake for at least 30 minutes until it turns golden brown.

⇒ Serve.

Nutrition: Calories: 160 kcal Fat: 5g Carbs: 25g Proteins: 2g

3) Fried Egg With Bacon

Preparation Time: 5 Minutes   **Cooking Time: 10 Minutes**   **Servings:1**

Ingredients:

- 2 Eggs
- 30 Grams of bacon
- 2 Tbsp. olive oil
- Salt
- Pepper

Directions:

⇒ Heat oil in the pan and fry the bacon.

⇒ Reduce the heat and beat the eggs in the pan.

⇒ Cook the eggs and season with salt and pepper.

⇒ Serve the fried eggs hot with the bacon.

Nutrition: Kcal: 405 Carbohydrates: 1g Protein: 19g Fat: 38g

4) Crunchy Quinoa Meal

Preparation Time: 5 Minutes   **Cooking Time: 25 Minutes**   **Servings:2**

Ingredients:

- 3 Cups coconut milk
- 1 Cup rinsed quinoa
- 1/8 Tsp. Ground cinnamon
- 1 Cup raspberry
- ½ Cup chopped coconuts

Directions:

⇒ In a saucepan, pour milk and bring to a boil over moderate heat.

⇒ Add the quinoa to the milk, and then bring it to a boil once more.

⇒ You then let it simmer for at least 15 minutes on medium heat until the milk is reduced.

⇒ Stir in the cinnamon, then mix properly.

⇒ Cover it, then cook for 8 minutes until the milk is completely absorbed.

⇒ Add the raspberry and cook the meal for 30 seconds.

⇒ Serve and enjoy.

Nutrition: Calories: 271 kcal Fat: 3.7g Carbs: 54g Proteins: 6.5g

5) Banana Barley Porridge

Preparation Time: 15 Minutes   **Cooking Time: 5 Minutes**   **Servings:2**

Ingredients:

- 1 Cup divided unsweetened coconut milk
- 1 Small peeled and sliced banana
- ½ Cup barley
- 3 Drops liquid stevia
- 1/4 Cup chopped coconuts

Directions:

⇒ In a bowl, properly mix barley with half of the coconut milk and stevia.

⇒ Cover the mixing bowl, then refrigerate for about 6 hours.

⇒ In a saucepan, mix the barley mixture with coconut milk.

⇒ Cook for about 5 minutes on moderate heat.

⇒ Then top it with the chopped coconuts and the banana slices.

⇒ Serve.

Nutrition: Calories: 159 kcal Fat: 8.4g Carbs: 19.8g Proteins: 4.6g

6) Zucchini Muffins

Preparation Time: 10 Minutes   **Cooking Time: 25 Minutes**   **Servings: 16**

Ingredients:

- 1 Tbsp. Ground flaxseed
- 3 Tbsp. Alkaline water
- 1/4 Cup walnut butter
- 3 Medium over-ripe bananas
- 2 Small grated zucchinis
- ½ Cup coconut milk

- 1 Tsp. vanilla extract
- 2 Cups coconut flour
- 1 Tbsp. Baking powder
- 1 Tsp. Cinnamon
- 1/4 Tsp. Sea salt

Directions:

⇒ Tune the temperature of your oven to 375ºF.

⇒ Grease the muffin tray with the cooking spray.

⇒ In a bowl, mix the flaxseed with water.

⇒ In a glass bowl, mash the bananas, then stir in the remaining ingredients.

⇒ Properly mix and then divide the mixture into the muffin tray.

⇒ Bake it for 25 minutes.

⇒ Serve.

Nutrition: Calories: 127 kcal Fat: 6.6g Carbs: 13g Protein: 0.7g

7) Jackfruit Vegetable Fry

Preparation Time: 5 Minutes   **Cooking Time: 5 Minutes**   **Servings: 6**

Ingredients:

- 2 Finely chopped small onions
- 2 Cups finely chopped cherry tomatoes
- 1/8 Tsp. Ground turmeric
- 1 Tbsp. Olive oil
- 2 Seeded and chopped red bell peppers

- 3 Cups seeded and chopped firm jackfruit
- 1/8 Tsp. Cayenne pepper
- 2 Tbsp. Chopped fresh basil leaves
- Salt

Directions:

⇒ In a greased skillet, sauté the onions and bell peppers for about 5 minutes.

⇒ Add the tomatoes, then stir.

⇒ Cook for 2 minutes.

⇒ Then add the jackfruit, cayenne pepper, salt, and turmeric.

⇒ Cook for about 8 minutes.

⇒ Garnish the meal with basil leaves.

⇒ Serve warm.

Nutrition: Calories: 236 kcal Fat: 1.8g Carbs: 48.3g Protein: 7g

8) Zucchini Pancakes

Preparation Time: 15 Minutes   **Cooking Time: 8 Minutes**   **Servings:8**

Ingredients:

- 12 Tbsp. Alkaline water
- 6 Large grated zucchinis
- Sea salt
- 4 Tbsp. Ground Flax Seeds
- 2 Tsp. Olive oil
- 2 Finely chopped jalapeño peppers
- ½ Cup finely chopped scallions

Directions:

⇒ In a bowl, mix together water and the flax seeds, then set them aside.

⇒ Pour oil in a large non-stick skillet, then heat it on medium heat.

⇒ Add the black pepper, salt, and zucchini.

⇒ Cook for 3 minutes, then transfer the zucchini into a large bowl.

⇒ Add the flax seeds and the scallions mixture, then properly mix them.

⇒ Preheat a griddle, then grease it lightly with the cooking spray.

⇒ Pour 1/4 of the zucchini mixture into the griddle, then cook for 3 minutes.

⇒ Flip the side carefully, then cook for two more minutes.

⇒ Repeat the procedure with the remaining mixture in batches.

⇒ Serve.

Nutrition: Calories: 71 kcal Fat: 2.8g Carbs: 9.8g Protein: 3.7g

9) Porridge With Walnuts

Preparation Time: 5 Minutes   **Cooking Time: 10 Minutes**   **Servings:1**

Ingredients:

- 50g Raspberries
- 50g Blueberries
- 25g of Ground walnuts
- 20g of Crushed flaxseed
- 10g of Oatmeal
- 200ml Nut drink
- Agave syrup
- ½ Teaspoon cinnamon
- Salt

Directions:

⇒ Warm the nut drink in a small saucepan.

⇒ Add the walnuts, flaxseed, and oatmeal, stirring constantly.

⇒ Stir in the cinnamon and salt.

⇒ Simmer for 8 minutes.

⇒ Keep stirring everything.

⇒ Sweet the whole thing.

⇒ Put the porridge in a bowl.

⇒ Wash the berries and let them drain.

⇒ Add them to the porridge and serve everything.

Nutrition: Kcal: 378 Carbohydrates: 11g Protein: 18g Fat: 27g

10) Goat Cheese Zucchini and Kale Quiche

Preparation Time: 35 Minutes   **Cooking Time: 1 Hour 10 Minutes**   **Servings:4**

Ingredients:

- 4 Large eggs
- 8 Ounces fresh zucchini, sliced
- 10 Ounces kale
- 3 Garlic cloves (minced)
- 1 Cup of soy milk
- 1 Ounce Goat cheese

- 1 Cup grated parmesan
- 1 Cup shredded cheddar cheese
- 2 Teaspoons olive oil
- Salt and pepper, to taste

Directions:

⇒ Preheat the oven to 350°F.

⇒ Heat one teaspoon of olive oil in a saucepan over medium-high heat. Sauté garlic for 1 minute until flavored.

⇒ Add the zucchini and cook for another 5-7 minutes until soft.

⇒ Beat the eggs, and then add a little milk and Parmesan cheese.

⇒ Meanwhile, heat the remaining olive oil in another saucepan and add the kale. Cover and cook for 5 minutes until dry.

⇒ Slightly grease a baking dish with cooking spray and spread the kale leaves across the bottom. Add the zucchini and top with goat cheese.

⇒ Pour the egg, milk, and parmesan mixture evenly over the other ingredients. Top with cheddar cheese.

⇒ Bake for 50–60 minutes until golden brown. Check the center of the quiche. It should have a solid consistency.

⇒ Let it chill for a few minutes before serving.

Nutrition: Total Carbohydrates: 15g Dietary Fiber: 2g Net Carbs: 13g Protein: 19g Total Fat: 18g Calories: 290

11) Cream Cheese Egg Breakfast

Preparation Time: 5 Minutes   **Cooking Time: 5 Minutes**   **Servings:4**

Ingredients:

- 2 Eggs, beaten
- 1 Tablespoon butter

- 2 Tablespoons soft cream cheese with chives

Directions:

⇒ Melt the butter in a small skillet.

⇒ Add the eggs and cream cheese.

⇒ Stir and cook to desired doneness.

Nutrition: Calories: 341 Fat: 31g Protein: 15g Carbohydrate: 0g Dietary Fiber: 3g

12) Pumpkin Spice Quinoa

Preparation Time: 10 Minutes   **Cooking Time: 0 Minutes**   **Servings:2**

Ingredients:

- 1 Cup cooked quinoa
- 1 Cup unsweetened coconut milk
- One large mashed banana

- 1/4 Cup pumpkin puree
- 1 Tsp. Pumpkin spice
- 2 Tsp. Chia seeds

Directions:

⇒ In a container, mix all the ingredients.

⇒ Seal the lid, then shake the container properly to mix.

⇒ Refrigerate overnight.

⇒ Serve.

Nutrition: Calories: 212 kcal Fat: 11.9g Carbs: 31.7g Protein: 7.3g

13) Cheesy Spicy Bacon Bowls

Preparation Time: 10 Minutes   **Cooking Time: 22 Minutes**   **Servings: 12**

Ingredients:

- 6 Bacon Strips, pan-fried until cooked but still malleable
- 4 Eggs
- 60g Cheddar cheese
- 40g Cream cheese, grated
- 2 Jalapenos, sliced and seeds removed

- 2 Tablespoons coconut oil
- ¼ Teaspoon onion powder
- ¼ Teaspoon garlic powder
- Dash of salt and pepper

Directions:

⇒ Preheat oven to 375 degrees Fahrenheit

⇒ In a bowl, beat together eggs, cream cheese, jalapenos (minus six slices), coconut oil, onion powder, garlic powder, and salt and pepper.

⇒ Use the leftover bacon grease on a muffin tray, rubbing it into each insert, place bacon-wrapped inside the cavity of each insert.

⇒ Pour the beaten mixture halfway up each bacon bowl.

⇒ Garnish each bacon bowl with cheese and leftover jalapeno slices (placing one on top of each).

⇒ Leave in the oven for about 22 minutes or until the egg is thoroughly cooked and the cheese is bubbly.

⇒ Remove from oven and let cool until edible.

⇒ Enjoy!

Nutrition: Calories: 259 Fat: 24g Carbs: 1g Fiber: 0g Protein: 10g

14) Mushroom Quickie Scramble

Preparation Time: 10 Minutes   **Cooking Time: 10 Minutes**   **Servings: 4**

Ingredients:

- 3 Small-sized eggs, whisked
- 4 Pcs. Bella mushrooms
- ½ Cup of spinach
- ¼ Cup of red bell peppers

- 2 Deli ham slices
- 1 Tablespoon of ghee or coconut oil
- Salt and pepper to taste

Directions:

⇒ Chop the ham and veggies.

⇒ Put half a tablespoon of ghee or oil in a frying pan and heat it.

⇒ Sauté the ham and vegetables in a frying pan then set aside.

⇒ Get a new frying pan and heat the remaining butter.

⇒ Add the whisked eggs into the second pan while stirring continuously to avoid overcooking.

⇒ When the eggs are done, sprinkle with salt and pepper to taste.

⇒ Add the ham and veggies to the pan with the eggs.

⇒ Mix well.

⇒ Remove from burner and transfer to a plate.

Nutrition: Calories: 350 Total Fat: 29g Protein: 21g Total Carbs: 5g

15) Coconut Coffee and Ghee

Preparation Time: 10 Minutes   **Cooking Time: 10 Minutes**   **Servings:5**

Ingredients:

- ½ Tbsp. Of coconut oil
- ½ Tbsp. Of ghee
- 1 to 2 Cups of preferred coffee (or rooibos or black tea, if preferred)
- 1 Tbsp. Of coconut or almond milk

Directions:

⇒ Place the almond (or coconut) milk, coconut oil, ghee, and coffee in a blender (or milk frother).

⇒ Mix for around 10 seconds or until the coffee turns creamy and foamy.

⇒ Pour contents into a coffee cup.

⇒ Serve immediately and enjoy.

Nutrition: Calories: 150 Total Fat: 15g Protein: 0g Total Carbs: 0g Net Carbs: 0g

16) Tasty Breakfast Donuts

Preparation Time: 5 Minutes   **Cooking Time: 5 Minutes**   **Servings:4**

Ingredients:

- 43 Grams cream cheese
- 2 Eggs
- 2 Tablespoons almond flour
- 2 Tablespoons erythritol
- 1 ½ Tablespoons coconut flour
- ½ Teaspoon baking powder
- ½ Teaspoon vanilla extract
- 5 Drops stevia (liquid form)
- 2 Strips bacon, fried until crispy

Directions:

⇒ Rub coconut oil over the donut maker and turn it on.

⇒ Mix all ingredients except bacon in a blender or food processor until smooth (should take around 1 minute).

⇒ Pour the batter into the donut maker, leaving 1/10 in each round for rising.

⇒ Leave for 3 minutes before flipping each donut.

⇒ Leave for another 2 minutes or until a fork comes out clean when piercing them.

⇒ Take donuts out and let them cool.

⇒ Repeat steps 1-5 until all batter is used.

⇒ Crumble bacon into bits and use to top donuts.

Nutrition: Calories: 60 Fat: 5g Carbs: 1g Fiber: 0g Protein: 3g

17) Yummy Veggie Waffles

Preparation Time: 10 Minutes   **Cooking Time: 9 Minutes**   **Servings:3**

Ingredients:

- 3 Cups raw cauliflower, grated
- 1 Cup cheddar cheese
- 1 Cup mozzarella cheese
- ½ Cup parmesan
- 1/3 Cup chives, finely sliced
- 6 Eggs

- 1 Teaspoon garlic powder
- 1 Teaspoon onion powder
- ½ Teaspoon chili flakes
- Dash of salt and pepper

Directions:

⇒ Turn the waffle maker on.

⇒ In a bowl, mix all the listed ingredients very well until incorporated.

⇒ Once the waffle maker is hot, distribute the waffle mixture into the insert.

⇒ Let cook for about 9 minutes, flipping at 6 minutes.

⇒ Remove from the waffle maker and set aside.

⇒ Serve and enjoy!

Nutrition: Calories: 390 Fat: 28g Carbs: 6g Fiber: 2g Protein: 30g

18) Avocado Red Peppers Roasted Scrambled Eggs

Preparation Time: 10 Minutes   **Cooking Time: 12 Minutes**   **Servings:3**

Ingredients:

- ½ Tablespoon butter
- Eggs, 2
- ½ Roasted red pepper, about 1 ½ ounce

- ½ Small avocado, coarsely chopped, about 2 1/4 ounces
- Salt, to taste

Directions:

⇒ In a nonstick skillet, heat the butter over medium heat. Break the eggs into the pan and break the yolks with a spoon. Sprinkle with a little salt.

⇒ Stir and keep doing it until the eggs start to cook. Quickly add the bell peppers and avocado.

⇒ Cook and stir until the eggs suit your taste. Adjust the seasoning, if necessary.

Nutrition: Calories: 317 Fat: 26g Protein: 14g Dietary Fiber: 5g Net Carbs: 4g

19) Squash Hash

Preparation Time: 2 Minutes   **Cooking Time: 10 Minutes**   **Servings:2**

Ingredients:

- 1 Tsp. Onion powder
- ½ Cup finely chopped onion

- 2 Cups spaghetti squash
- ½ Tsp. Sea salt

Directions:

⇒ Using paper towels, squeeze extra moisture from spaghetti squash.

⇒ Place the squash into a bowl, then add the salt, onion, and onion powder.

⇒ Stir properly to mix them.

⇒ Spray a non-stick cooking skillet with cooking spray, then place it over moderate heat.

⇒ Add the spaghetti squash to the pan.

⇒ Cook the squash for about 5 minutes.

⇒ Flip the hash browns using a spatula.

⇒ Cook for 5 minutes until the desired crispness is reached.

⇒ Serve.

Nutrition: Calories: 44 kcal Fat: 0.6g Carbs: 9.7g Protein: 0.9g

20) Blueberry Cantaloupe Avocado

Preparation Time: 5 Minutes   **Cooking Time: 0 Minutes**   **Servings:2**

Ingredients:

- 1 Diced cantaloupe
- 2–3 Chopped avocados
- 1 Package of blueberries

- ¼ Cup olive oil
- 1/8 Cup balsamic vinegar

Directions:

⇒ Mix all ingredients.

Nutrition: Calories: 406 Protein: 9g Carbohydrate: 32g Fat: 5g

Chapter 3 -   Side Recipes

21) Vitamin C Smoothie Cubes

Preparation Time: 5 Minutes   **Cooking Time: 8 Hours to chill**   **Servings: 1**

Ingredients:

- 1/8 Large papaya
- 1/8 Mango
- 1/4 Cups chopped pineapple, fresh or frozen
- 1/8 Cup raw cauliflower florets, fresh or frozen
- 1/4 Large navel oranges, peeled and halved
- 1/4 Large orange bell pepper stemmed, seeded, and coarsely chopped

Directions:

⇒ Halve the papaya and mango, remove the pits, and scoop their soft flesh into a high-speed blender.

⇒ Add the pineapple, cauliflower, oranges, and bell pepper. Blend until smooth.

⇒ Evenly divide the puree between 2 (16-compartment) ice cube trays and place them on a level surface in your freezer. Freeze for at least 8 hours.

⇒ The cubes can be left in the ice cube trays until use or transferred to a freezer bag. The frozen cubes are good for about three weeks in a standard freezer or up to 6 months in a chest freezer.

Nutrition: Calories: 96 Fat: 1g Protein: 2g Carbohydrates: 24g Fiber: 4g

22) Bacon Spaghetti Squash Carbonara

Preparation Time: 20 Minutes   **Cooking Time: 40 Minutes**   **Servings: 4**

Ingredients:

- 1 Small spaghetti squash
- 6 Ounces bacon roughly chopped
- 1 Large tomato sliced
- 2 Chives chopped
- 1 Garlic clove minced
- 6 Ounces low-fat cottage cheese
- 1 Cup gouda cheese grated
- 2 Tablespoons olive oil
- Salt and pepper, to taste

Directions:

⇒ Preheat the oven to 350°F.

⇒ Cut the squash spaghetti in half, brush with some olive oil and bake for 20–30 minutes, skin side up. Remove from the oven and remove the core with a fork, to obtain the spaghetti.

⇒ Heat one tablespoon of olive oil in a skillet. Cook the bacon for about 1 minute until crispy.

⇒ Quickly wipe out the pan with paper towels.

⇒ Heat another tablespoon of oil and sauté the garlic, tomato, and chives for 2–3 minutes. Add the spaghetti and sauté for another 5 minutes, occasionally stirring to keep from burning.

⇒ Begin to add the cottage cheese, about two tablespoons at a time. If the sauce becomes thick, add about a cup of water. The sauce should be creamy but not too runny or thick. Allow cooking for another 3 minutes.

⇒ Serve immediately.

Nutrition: Calories: 305 Total Fat: 21g Net Carbs: 8g Protein: 18g

23) Maple Lemon Tempeh Cubes

Preparation Time: 10 Minutes **Cooking Time: 30 to 40 Minutes** **Servings:4**

Ingredients:

- 1 Packet Tempeh
- 2 to 3 Teaspoons coconut oil
- 3 Tablespoons lemon juice
- 2 Teaspoons maple syrup
- 1 to 2 Teaspoons Bragg's Liquid Aminos or low-sodium tamari or (optional)

- 2 Teaspoons water
- 1/4 Teaspoon dried basil
- 1/4 Teaspoon powdered garlic
- Black pepper, freshly ground, to taste

Directions:

⇒ Heat your oven to 400 ° C.

⇒ Cut your tempeh block into squares in bite form.

⇒ Heat coconut oil over medium to high heat in a non-stick skillet.

⇒ When melted and heated, add the tempeh and cook on one side for 2-4 minutes, or until the tempeh turns down into a golden-brown color.

⇒ Flip the tempeh bits, and cook for 2-4 minutes.

⇒ Mix the lemon juice, tamari, maple syrup, basil, water, garlic, and black pepper while the tempeh is browning.

⇒ Drop the mixture over tempeh, then swirl to cover the tempeh.

⇒ Sauté for 2-3 minutes, then turn the tempeh and sauté 1-2 minutes more.

⇒ The tempeh, on both sides, should be soft and orange.

Nutrition: Carbohydrates: 22 Fats: 17g Sugar: 5g Protein: 21g Fiber: 9g

24) Vanilla Buckwheat Porridge

Preparation Time: 5 Minutes **Cooking Time: 25 Minutes** **Servings:1**

Ingredients:

- One cup of water
- 1/4 Cup raw buckwheat grouts
- 1/4 Teaspoon ground cinnamon
- 1/4 Banana, sliced
- 1/16 Cup golden raisins
- 1/16 Cup dried currants
- 1/16 Cup sunflower seeds

- ½ Tablespoons chia seeds
- 1/4 Tablespoon hemp seeds
- 1/4 Tablespoon sesame seeds, toasted
- 1/8 Cup unsweetened nondairy milk
- 1/4 Tablespoon pure maple syrup
- 1/4 Teaspoon vanilla extract

Directions:

⇒ Boil the water in a pot. Stir in the buckwheat, cinnamon, and banana.

⇒ Cook the mixture. Mix it and wait for it to boil, then reduce the heat to medium-low.

⇒ Cover the pot and cook for 15 minutes, or until the buckwheat is tender.

⇒ Remove from the heat.

⇒ Stir in the raisins, currants, sunflower seeds, chia seeds, hemp seeds, sesame seeds, milk, maple syrup, and vanilla. Cover the pot. Wait for 10 minutes before serving.

⇒ Serve as it is or top as desired.

Nutrition: Calories: 353 Fat: 11g Protein: 10g Carbohydrates: 61g Fiber: 10g

25) High Protein Chicken Meatballs

Preparation Time: 5 Minutes   **Cooking Time: 25 Minutes**   **Servings:2**

Ingredients:

- 1 lb. Lean, ground chicken
- 3/4 Cup, rolled oats
- 2 Grated onions
- 2 Tsp. Ground allspice
- Salt and black pepper (dash)

Directions:

⇒ Heat a skillet (large) over medium heat, then grease using cooking spray.

⇒ Add in the onions (grated), chicken (lean, ground), oats (rolled), allspice (ground), and a dash of salt and black pepper in a large-sized bowl; stir well to incorporate.

⇒ Shape mixture into meatballs (small).

⇒ Place into the skillet (greased). Cook roughly for 5 minutes until golden brown on all sides.

⇒ Remove meatballs from heat, then serve immediately.

Nutrition: Calories: 519 Cal Protein: 57g Carbohydrates: 32g Fat: 15g

26) Tropical Greens Smoothie

Preparation Time: 5 Minutes   **Cooking Time: 0 Minutes**   **Servings:1**

Ingredients:

- One banana
- ½ Large navel orange, peeled and segmented
- ½ Cup frozen mango chunks
- 1 Cup frozen spinach
- One celery stalk, broken into pieces
- 1 Tablespoon cashew butter or almond butter
- ½ Tablespoon spiraling
- ½ Tablespoon ground flaxseed
- ½ Cup unsweetened nondairy milk
- Water, for thinning (optional)

Directions:

⇒ In a high-speed blender or food processor, combine the bananas, orange, mango, spinach, celery, cashew butter, spiraling (if using), flaxseed, and milk.

⇒ Blend until creamy, adding more milk or water to thin the smoothie if too thick. Serve immediately—it is best served fresh.

Nutrition: Calories: 391 Fat: 12g Protein: 13g Carbohydrates: 68g Fiber: 13g

27) Overnight Chocolate Chia Pudding

Preparation Time: 2 Minutes   **Cooking Time: Overnight to Chill**   **Servings:1**

Ingredients:

- 1/8 Cup chia seeds
- ½ Cup unsweetened nondairy milk
- One Tablespoon raw cocoa powder
- ½ Teaspoon vanilla extract
- ½ Teaspoon pure maple syrup

Directions:

⇒ Stir together the chia seeds, milk, cacao powder, vanilla, and maple syrup in a large bowl.

⇒ Divide between two (½-pint) covered glass jars or containers.

⇒ Refrigerate overnight.

⇒ Stir before serving.

Nutrition: Calories: 213 Fat: 10g Protein: 9g Carbohydrates: 20g Fiber: 15g

28) Zucchini Fritters

Preparation Time: 15 Minutes   **Cooking Time: 10 Minutes**   **Servings:4**

Ingredients:

- 1 ½ Pound of grated zucchini
- 1 Tsp. of salt
- 1/4 Cup of grated Parmesan
- 1/4 Cup of flour

- 2 Cloves of minced garlic
- 2 Tbsp. of olive oil
- 1 Large egg
- Freshly ground black pepper and kosher salt to taste

Directions:

⇒ Put the grated zucchini into a colander over the sink

⇒ Add your salt and toss it to mix properly, then leave it to settle for about 10 minutes.

⇒ Next, use a clean cheesecloth to drain the zucchini completely.

⇒ Combine drained zucchini, Parmesan, garlic, flour, and the beaten egg in a large bowl, mix, and season with pepper and salt.

⇒ Next, heat the olive oil in a skillet applying medium-high heat.

⇒ Use a tablespoon to scoop batter for each cake, put in the oil, and flatten using a spatula.

⇒ Allow to cook until the underside is nearly golden brown, then flip over to the other side and cook.

⇒ Your delicious zucchini fritters are ready to be served.

Nutrition: Total Fat: 12.0g Cholesterol: 101.9mg Sodium: 728.9mg Total Carbohydrate: 11.9g Dietary Fiber: 1.9g

Sugars: 4.6g Protein: 8.6g

29) Carrot Cake Oatmeal

Preparation Time: 10 Minutes   **Cooking Time: 15 Minutes**   **Servings:1**

Ingredients:

- 1/8 Cup pecans
- ½ Cup finely Shredded Carrot
- 1/4 Cup Old-fashioned Oats
- 5/8 Cups unsweetened Nondairy Milk
- ½ Tablespoon pure Maple Syrup

- ½ Teaspoon ground Cinnamon
- ½ Teaspoon ground Ginger
- 1/8 Teaspoon ground Nutmeg
- 1 Tablespoon chia seed

Directions:

⇒ Over medium-high heat in a skillet, toast the pecans for 3 to 4 minutes, often stirring, until browned and fragrant (watch closely, as they can burn quickly).

⇒ Pour the pecans onto a cutting board and coarsely chop them. Set aside.

⇒ In an 8-quart pot over medium-high heat, combine the carrot, oats, milk, maple syrup, cinnamon, ginger, and nutmeg.

⇒ When it is already boiling, reduce the heat to medium-low.

⇒ Cook everything uncovered for 10 minutes, stirring occasionally.

⇒ Stir in the chopped pecans and chia seeds. Serve immediately.

Nutrition: Calories: 307 Fat: 17g Protein: 7g Carbohydrates: 35g Fiber: 11g

30) Peanut Butter and Cacao Breakfast Quinoa

Preparation Time: 5 Minutes   **Cooking Time: 10 Minutes**   **Servings:1**

Ingredients:

- 1/3 Cup quinoa flakes
- ½ Cup unsweetened nondairy milk
- ½ Cup of water
- 1/8 Cup raw cacao powder
- 1 Tablespoon natural creamy peanut butter
- 1/8 Teaspoon ground cinnamon
- One banana, mashed
- Fresh berries of choice for serving
- Chopped nuts of choice for serving

Directions:

⇒ Using an 8-quart pot over medium-high heat, stir together the quinoa flakes, milk, water, cacao powder, peanut butter, and cinnamon.

⇒ Cook and stir it until the mixture begins to simmer. Turn the heat to medium-low and cook for 3 to 5 minutes, stirring frequently.

⇒ Stir in the bananas and cook until hot.

⇒ Serve topped with fresh berries, nuts, and a splash of milk.

Nutrition: Calories: 471 Fat: 16g Protein: 18g Carbohydrates: 69g Fiber: 16g

Chapter 4 -   Salads Recipes

31) Warm Chorizo Chickpea Salad

Preparation Time: 5 Minutes   **Cooking Time: 20 Minutes**   **Servings:6**

Ingredients:

- 1 Tablespoon extra-virgin olive oil
- 4 Chorizo links, sliced
- 1 Red onion, sliced
- 4 Roasted red bell peppers, chopped
- 1 Can chickpeas, drained
- 2 Cups cherry tomatoes
- 2 Tablespoons balsamic vinegar
- Salt and pepper to taste

Directions:

⇒ Heat the oil in a skillet and add the chorizo. Cook briefly just until fragrant, then add the onion, bell peppers, and chickpeas and cook for two additional minutes.

⇒ Transfer the mixture to a salad bowl, then add the tomatoes, vinegar, salt, and pepper.

⇒ Mix well and serve the salad right away.

Nutrition: Calories: 359 Fat: 18g Protein: 15g Carbohydrates: 21g

32) Broccoli Salad

Preparation Time: 5 Minutes   **Cooking Time: 0 Minutes**   **Servings:2**

Ingredients:

- 1 Head broccoli, chopped
- 2–3 Slices of fried bacon, crumbled
- 1 Diced green onion
- ½ Cup raisins or craisins
- ½–1 Cup of chopped pecans
- ¾ Cups sunflower seeds
- ½ Cup of pomegranate

Dressing:

- 1 Cup Organic Mayonnaise
- ¼ Cup Baking Stevia
- 2 Teaspoons White Vinegar

Directions:

⇒ Mix all ingredients together. Mix dressing and fold into the salad.

Nutrition: Calories: 239 Protein: 10g Carbohydrate: 33g Fat: 2g

33) Loaded Caesar Salad With Crunchy Chickpeas

Preparation Time: 5 Minutes   **Cooking Time: 20 Minutes**   **Servings: 6**

Ingredients:

For the chickpeas:

- 2 (15-ounce) cans chickpeas, drained and rinsed
- 2 Tablespoons extra-virgin olive oil
- 1 Teaspoon kosher salt
- 1 Teaspoon garlic powder
- 1 Teaspoon onion powder
- 1 Teaspoon dried oregano

For the dressing:

- ½ Cup Mayonnaise

- 2 Tablespoons Grated Parmesan Cheese
- 2 Tablespoons Freshly Squeezed Lemon Juice
- 1 Clove Garlic, Peeled and Smashed
- 1 Teaspoon Dijon Mustard
- ½ Tablespoon Worcestershire Sauce
- ½ Tablespoon Anchovy Paste

For the salad:

- 3 Heads romaine lettuce, cut into bite-size pieces

Directions:

⇒ To make the chickpeas:

⇒ Preheat the oven to 450°F. Line a baking sheet with parchment paper.

⇒ In a medium bowl, toss together the chickpeas, oil, salt, garlic powder, onion powder, and oregano. Scatter the coated chickpeas on the prepared baking sheet.

⇒ Roast for about 20 minutes, occasionally tossing until the chickpeas are golden and have a bit of crunch.

⇒ To make the dressing:

⇒ In a small bowl, whisk the mayonnaise, Parmesan, lemon juice, garlic, mustard, Worcestershire sauce, and anchovy paste until combined.

⇒ To make the salad:

⇒ In a large bowl, combine the lettuce and dressing. Toss to coat. Top with the roasted chickpeas and serve.

Nutrition: Calories: 367 Total fat: 22g Total carbs: 35g Cholesterol: 9mg Fiber: 13g Protein: 12g Sodium: 407mg

34) Taste of Normandy Salad

Preparation Time: 25 Minutes   **Cooking Time: 5 Minutes**   **Servings:4-6**

Ingredients:

For the walnuts:

- 2 Tablespoons butter
- ¼ Cup sugar or honey
- 1 Cup walnut pieces
- ½ Teaspoon kosher salt

For the dressing:

- 3 Tablespoons extra-virgin olive oil
- 1½ Tablespoons champagne vinegar

- 1½ Tablespoons Dijon mustard
- ¼ Teaspoon kosher salt

For the salad:

- 1 Head red leaf lettuce, torn into pieces
- 3 Heads endive, ends trimmed and leaves separated
- 2 Apples, cored and cut into thin wedges
- 1 (8-ounce) Camembert wheel, cut into thin wedges

Directions:

⇒ To make the walnuts:

⇒ In a skillet over medium-high heat, melt the butter. Stir in the sugar and cook until it dissolves. Add the walnuts and cook for about 5 minutes, stirring, until toasty—season with salt and transfer to a plate to cool.

⇒ To make the dressing:

⇒ In a large bowl, whisk the oil, vinegar, mustard, and salt until combined.

⇒ To make the salad:

⇒ Add the lettuce and endive to the bowl with the dressing and toss to coat. Transfer to a serving platter.

⇒ Decoratively arrange the apple and Camembert wedges over the lettuce and scatter the walnuts on top. Serve immediately.

Nutrition: Calories: 699 Total fat: 52g Total carbs: 44g Cholesterol: 60mg Fiber: 17g Protein: 23g Sodium: 1170mg

35) Coleslaw Worth a Second Helping

Preparation Time: 20 Minutes   **Cooking Time: 10 Minutes**   **Servings:6**

Ingredients:

- 5 Cups shredded cabbage
- 2 Carrots, shredded
- 1/3 Cup chopped fresh flat-leaf parsley
- ½ Cup mayonnaise

- ½ Cup sour cream
- 3 Tablespoons apple cider vinegar
- 1 Teaspoon kosher salt
- ½ Teaspoon celery seed

Directions:

⇒ In a large bowl, combine the cabbage, carrots, and parsley.

⇒ In a small bowl, whisk the mayonnaise, sour cream, vinegar, salt, and celery seed until smooth.

⇒ Pour the dressing over the vegetables and toss until coated. Transfer to a serving bowl and chill until ready to serve.

Nutrition: Calories: 192 Total fat: 18g Total carbs: 7g Cholesterol: 18mg Fiber: 3g Protein: 2g Sodium: 543mg

36) Barley and Lentil Salad

Preparation Time: 5 Minutes   **Cooking Time: 0 Minutes**   **Servings:2**

Ingredients:

- 1 Head romaine lettuce
- ¾ Cup cooked barley
- 2 Cups cooked lentils
- 1 Diced carrot
- ¼ Chopped red onion

- ¼ Cup olives
- ½ Chopped cucumber
- 3 Tablespoons olive oil
- 2 Tablespoons fresh lemon juice

Directions:

⇒ Mix all ingredients together. Add kosher salt and black pepper to taste.

Nutrition: Calories: 213 Protein: 21g Carbohydrate: 6g Fat: 9g

37) Blueberry Cantaloupe Avocado Salad

Preparation Time: 5 Minutes   **Cooking Time: 0 Minutes**   **Servings:2**

Ingredients:

- 1 Diced cantaloupe
- 2–3 Chopped avocados
- 1 Package of blueberries

- ¼ Cup olive oil
- 1/8 Cup balsamic vinegar

Directions:

⇒ Mix all ingredients.

Nutrition: Calories: 406 Protein: 9g Carbohydrate: 32g Fat: 5g

38) Wild Rice Prawn Salad

Preparation Time: 5 Minutes   **Cooking Time: 35 Minutes**   **Servings:6**

Ingredients:

- ¾ Cup wild rice
- 1¾ Cups chicken stock
- 1 Pound prawns
- Salt and pepper to taste

- 2 Tablespoons lemon juice
- 2 Tablespoons extra virgin olive oil
- 2 Cups arugula

Directions:

⇒ Combine the rice and chicken stock in a saucepan and cook until the liquid has been absorbed entirely.

⇒ Transfer the rice to a salad bowl.

⇒ Season the prawns with salt and pepper and drizzle them with lemon juice and oil.

⇒ Heat a grill pan over a medium flame.

⇒ Place the prawns on the hot pan and cook on each side for 2-3 minutes.

⇒ For the salad, combine the rice with arugula and prawns and mix well.

⇒ Serve the salad fresh.

Nutrition: Calories: 207 Fat: 4g Protein: 20.6g Carbohydrates: 17g

39) Beet Salad (from Israel)

Preparation Time: 5 Minutes   **Cooking Time: 0 Minutes**   **Servings:2**

Ingredients:

- 2–3 Fresh, raw beets grated or shredded in food processor
- 3 Tablespoons olive oil
- 2 Tablespoons balsamic vinegar
- ¼ Teaspoon salt

- 1/3 Teaspoon cumin
- Dash stevia powder or liquid
- Dash pepper

Directions:

⇒ Mix all ingredients together for the best raw beet salad.

Nutrition: Calories: 156 Protein: 8g Carbohydrate: 40g Fat: 5g

40) Greek Salad

Preparation Time: 15 Minutes   **Cooking Time: 15 Minutes**   **Servings:5**

Ingredients:

For the Dressing:

- ½ Teaspoon black pepper
- ¼ Teaspoon salt
- ½ Teaspoon oregano
- 1 Tablespoon garlic powder
- 2 Tablespoons Balsamic
- 1/3 Cup olive oil

For the Salad:

- ½ Cup sliced black olives

- ½ Cup chopped parsley, fresh
- 1 Small red onion, thin-sliced
- 1 Cup cherry tomatoes, sliced
- 1 Bell pepper, yellow, chunked
- 1 Cucumber, peeled, quartered, and sliced
- 4 Cups chopped romaine lettuce
- ½ Teaspoon salt
- 2 Tablespoons olive oil

Directions:

⇒ In a small bowl, blend all of the ingredients for the dressing and let this set in the refrigerator while you make the salad.

⇒ To assemble the salad, mix together all the ingredients in a large-sized bowl and toss the veggies gently but thoroughly to mix.

⇒ Serve the salad with the dressing in amounts as desired

Nutrition: Calories: 234 Fat: 16.1g Protein: 5g Carbs: 48g

41) Norwegian Niçoise Salad Smoked Salmon Cucumber Egg and Asparagus

Preparation Time: 20 Minutes   **Cooking Time: 5 Minutes**   **Servings:4**

Ingredients:

For the vinaigrette:

- 3 Tablespoons walnut oil
- 2 Tablespoons champagne vinegar
- 1 Tablespoon chopped fresh dill
- ½ Teaspoon kosher salt
- ¼ Teaspoon ground mustard
- Freshly ground black pepper

For the salad:

- Handful green beans, trimmed

- 1 (3- to 4-ounce) Package spring greens
- 12 Spears pickled asparagus
- 4 Large soft-boiled eggs, halved
- 8 Ounces smoked salmon, thinly sliced
- 1 Cucumber, thinly sliced
- 1 Lemon, quartered

Directions:

⇒ To make the dressing. In a small bowl, whisk the oil, vinegar, dill, salt, ground mustard, and a few grinds of pepper until emulsified. Set aside.

⇒ To make the salad. Start by blanching the green beans, bring a pot of salted water to a boil. Drop in the beans. Cook for 1 to 2 minutes until they turn bright green, then immediately drain and rinse under cold water. Set aside.

⇒ Divide the spring greens among four plates. Toss each serving with dressing to taste. Arrange three asparagus spears, one egg, 2 ounces of salmon, one-fourth of the cucumber slices, and a lemon wedge on each plate. Serve immediately.

Nutrition: Calories: 257 Total fat: 18g Total carbs: 6g Cholesterol: 199mg Fiber: 2g Protein: 19g Sodium: 603mg

42) Mediterranean Chickpea Salad

Preparation Time: 5 Minutes   **Cooking Time: 20 Minutes**   **Servings:6**

Ingredients:

- 1 Can chickpeas, drained
- 1 Fennel bulb, sliced
- 1 Red onion, sliced
- 1 Teaspoon dried basil
- 1 Teaspoon dried oregano

- 2 Tablespoons chopped parsley
- 4 Garlic cloves, minced
- 2 Tablespoons lemon juice
- 2 Tablespoons extra virgin olive oil
- Salt and pepper to taste

Directions:

⇒ Combine the chickpeas, fennel, red onion, herbs, garlic, lemon juice, and oil in a salad bowl.

⇒ Add salt and pepper and serve the salad fresh.

Nutrition: Calories: 200 Fat: 9g Protein: 4g Carbohydrates: 28g

43) Romaine Lettuce and Radicchios Mix

Preparation Time: 6 Minutes   **Cooking Time: 0 Minutes**   **Servings:4**

Ingredients:

- 2 Tablespoons olive oil
- A pinch of salt and black pepper
- 2 Spring onions, chopped
- 3 Tablespoons Dijon mustard

- Juice of 1 lime
- ½ Cup basil, chopped
- 4 Cups romaine lettuce heads, chopped
- 3 Radicchios, sliced

Directions:

⇒ In a salad bowl, mix the lettuce with the spring onions and the other ingredients, toss and serve.

Nutrition: Calories: 87 Fats: 2g Fiber: 1g Carbs: 1g Protein: 2g

44) Chicken Broccoli Salad With Avocado Dressing

Preparation Time: 5 Minutes   **Cooking Time: 40 Minutes**   **Servings:6**

Ingredients:

- 2 Chicken breasts
- 1 Pound broccoli, cut into florets
- 1 Avocado, peeled and pitted
- ½ Lemon, juiced

- 2 Garlic cloves
- ¼ Teaspoon chili powder
- ¼ Teaspoon cumin powder
- Salt and pepper to taste

Directions:

⇒ Cook the chicken in a large pot of salty water.

⇒ Drain and cut the chicken into small cubes—place in a salad bowl.

⇒ Add the broccoli and mix well.

⇒ Combine the avocado, lemon juice, garlic, chili powder, cumin powder, salt, and pepper in a blender. Pulse until smooth.

⇒ Spoon the dressing over the salad and mix well.

⇒ Serve the salad fresh.

Nutrition: Calories: 195 Fat: 11g Protein: 14g Carbohydrates: 3g

45) Zucchini Salmon Salad

Preparation Time: 5 Minutes   **Cooking Time: 10 Minutes**   **Servings:3**

Ingredients:

- 2 Salmon fillets
- 2 Tablespoons soy sauce
- 2 Zucchinis, sliced

- Salt and pepper to taste
- 2 Tablespoons extra virgin olive oil
- 2 Tablespoons sesame seeds

Directions:

⇒ Drizzle the salmon with soy sauce.

⇒ Heat a grill pan over a medium flame. Cook salmon on the grill on each side for 2-3 minutes.

⇒ Season the zucchini with salt and pepper and place it on the grill as well. Cook on each side until golden.

⇒ Place the zucchini, salmon, and the rest of the ingredients in a bowl.

⇒ Serve the salad fresh.

Nutrition: Calories: 224 Fat: 19g Protein: 18g Carbohydrates: 0g

Chapter 5 -   Soup and Stew Recipes

46) Mushroom & Jalapeño Stew

Preparation Time: 20 Minutes   **Cooking Time: 50 Minutes**   **Servings:4**

Ingredients:

- 2 Tsp. olive oil (1/8 condiment)
- 1 Cup leeks, chopped (½ green)
- 1 Garlic clove, minced (1/8 condiment)
- ½ Cup celery stalks, chopped (½ green)
- ½ Cup carrots, chopped (½ green)
- 1 Green bell pepper, chopped (½ green)
- 1 Jalapeño pepper, chopped (1/4green)
- 2 ½ Cups mushrooms, sliced (1 healthy fat)
- 1 ½ Cups vegetable stock (1 condiment)

- 2 Tomatoes, chopped (1green)
- 2 Thyme sprigs, chopped (1/4green)
- 1 Rosemary sprig, chopped (1/4green)
- 2 Bay leaves (1/4green)
- ½ Tsp. salt (1/8 condiment)
- 1/4 Tsp. ground black pepper (1/8 condiment)
- 2 Tbsp. vinegar (1/8 condiment)

Directions:

⇒ Set a pot over medium heat and warm oil.

⇒ Add in garlic and leeks and sauté until soft and translucent.

⇒ Add in the black pepper, celery, mushrooms, and carrots.

⇒ Cook as you stir for 12 minutes; stir in a splash of vegetable stock to ensure there is no sticking.

⇒ Stir in the rest of the ingredients.

⇒ Set heat to medium; allow to simmer for 25 to 35 minutes or until cooked through.

⇒ Divide into individual bowls and serve warm.

Nutrition: Calories: 65 Fats: 2.7g Protein: 2.7g

47) Easy Cauliflower Soup

Preparation Time: 5 Minutes   **Cooking Time: 15 Minutes**   **Servings:4**

Ingredients:

- 2 Tbsp. olive oil (1/4 condiment)
- 1 Tsp. garlic, minced (1/4 condiment)
- 1-pound cauliflower, cut into florets (1green)
- 1 Cup kale, chopped (½ green)
- 4 Cups vegetable broth (1 condiment)

- ½ Cup almond milk (½ healthy fat)
- ½ Tsp. salt (1/8 condiment)
- ½ Tsp. red pepper flakes (1/8 condiment)
- 1 Tbsp. fresh chopped parsley (1/4green)

Directions:

⇒ Set a pot over medium heat and warm the oil.

⇒ Add garlic and onions and sauté until browned and softened.

⇒ Place in vegetable broth, kale, and cauliflower; cook for 10 minutes until the mixture boils.

⇒ Stir in the pepper flakes, salt, and almond milk; reduce the heat and simmer the soup for 5 minutes.

⇒ Transfer the soup to an immersion blender and blend to achieve the desired consistency; top with parsley and serve immediately.

Nutrition: Calories: 172 Fats: 10.3g Protein: 8.1g

48) Tofu Stir Fry With Asparagus Stew

Preparation Time: 15 Minutes   **Cooking Time: 30 Minutes**   **Servings:4**

Ingredients:

- 1-pound Asparagus, cut off stems (1green)
- 2 Tbsp. olive oil (1/8 condiment)
- 2 Blocks tofu, pressed and cubed (1 lean)
- 2 Garlic cloves, minced (1/8 condiment)
- 1 Tsp. Cajun spice mix (1/8 condiment)

- 1 Tsp. mustard (1/8 condiment)
- 1 Bell pepper, chopped (1/4green)
- 1/4 Cup vegetable broth (1green)
- Salt and black pepper, to taste (1/8 condiment)

Directions:

⇒ Using a huge saucepan with lightly salted water, place in asparagus and cook until tender for 10 minutes; drain.

⇒ Set a wok over high heat and warm olive oil; stir in tofu cubes and cook for 6 minutes.

⇒ Place in garlic and cook for 30 seconds until soft.

⇒ Stir in the remaining ingredients, including reserved asparagus, and cook for four more minutes.

⇒ Divide among plates and serve.

Nutrition: Calories: 138 Fat: 8.9g Protein: 6.4g

49) Cream of Thyme Tomato Soup

Preparation Time: 5 Minutes   **Cooking Time: 20 Minutes**   **Servings:6**

Ingredients:

- 2 Tbsp. ghee (½ healthy fat)
- ½ Cup raw cashew nuts, diced (½ healthy fat)
- 2 (28 oz.) Cans tomatoes (1green)

- 1 Tsp. fresh thyme leaves + extra to garnish (1/4green)
- 1 ½ Cups water (½ healthy fat)
- Salt and black pepper to taste (1/8 condiment)

Directions:

⇒ Cook ghee in a pot over medium heat and sauté the onions for 4 minutes until softened.

⇒ Stir in the tomatoes, thyme, water, cashews, and season with salt and black pepper.

⇒ Cover and bring to simmer for 10 minutes until thoroughly cooked.

⇒ Open, turn the heat off, and puree the ingredients with an immersion blender.

⇒ Adjust to taste and stir in the heavy cream.

⇒ Spoon into soup bowls and serve.

Nutrition: Calories: 310 Fats: 27g Protein: 11g

50) Lime-Mint Soup

Preparation Time: 5 Minutes   **Cooking Time: 20 Minutes**   **Servings:4**

Ingredients:

- 4 Cups vegetable broth (1 condiment)
- 1/4 Cup fresh mint leaves (1/8 condiment)
- 1/4 Cup scallions (1/4green)

- 3 Garlic cloves, minced (1/8 condiment)
- 3 Tablespoons freshly squeezed lime juice (1/4 condiment)

Directions:

⇒ In a large stockpot, combine the broth, mint, scallions, garlic, and lime juice.

⇒ Bring to a boil over medium-high heat.

⇒ Cover, set heat to low, simmer for 15 minutes, and serve.

Nutrition: Fat: 2g Protein: 5g Calories: 214

Chapter 6 -   Vegan Recipes

51) Roasted Squash Puree

Preparation Time: 20 Minutes   **Cooking Time: 6 to 7 Hours**   **Servings: 8**

Ingredients:

- 1 (3-pound) Butternut squash, peeled, seeded, and cut into 1-inch pieces
- 3 (1-pound) Acorn squash, peeled, seeded, and cut into 1-inch pieces
- 2 Onions, chopped
- 3 Garlic cloves, minced
- 2 Tablespoons olive oil

- 1 Teaspoon dried marjoram leaves
- ½ Teaspoon salt
- 1/8 Teaspoon freshly ground black pepper

Directions:

⇒ In a 6-quart slow cooker, mix all of the ingredients.

⇒ Cover and cook on low for 6 to 7 hours or until the squash is tender when pierced with a fork.

⇒ Use a potato masher to mash the squash right in the slow cooker.

Nutrition: Calories: 175 Carbohydrates: 38g Sugar: 1g Fiber: 3g Fat: 4g Saturated Fat: 1g Protein: 3g Sodium: 149mg

52) Air Fryer Brussels Sprouts

Preparation Time: 5 Minutes   **Cooking Time: 10 Minutes**   **Servings: 5**

Ingredients:

- ¼ Tsp. salt
- 1 Tbsp. balsamic vinegar

- 1 Tbsp. olive oil
- C. Brussels sprouts

Directions:

⇒ Cut Brussels sprouts in half lengthwise. Toss with salt, vinegar, and olive oil till coated thoroughly.

⇒ Add coated sprouts to the air fryer, cooking 8-10 minutes at 400 degrees. Shake after 5 minutes of cooking.

⇒ Brussels sprouts are ready to devour when brown and crisp!

Nutrition: Calories: 118 Fat: 9g Protein: 11g Sugar: 1g

53) Thai Roasted Veggies

Preparation Time: 20 Minutes   **Cooking Time: 6 to 8 Hours**   **Servings:8**

Ingredients:

- 4 Large carrots, peeled and cut into chunks
- 2 Onions, peeled and sliced
- 6 Garlic cloves, peeled and sliced
- 2 Parsnips, peeled and sliced
- 2 Jalapeño peppers, minced

- ½ Cup Roasted Vegetable Broth
- 1/3 Cup canned coconut milk
- 3 Tablespoons lime juice
- 2 Tablespoons grated fresh ginger root
- 2 Teaspoons curry powder

Directions:

⇒ In a 6-quart slow cooker, mix the carrots, onions, garlic, parsnips, and jalapeño peppers.

⇒ In a small bowl, mix the vegetable broth, coconut milk, lime juice, ginger root, and curry powder until well blended. Pour this mixture into the slow cooker.

⇒ Cover and cook on low for 6 to 8 hours, do it until the vegetables are tender when pierced with a fork.

Nutrition: Calories: 69 Carbohydrates: 13g Sugar: 6g Fiber: 3g Fat: 3g Saturated Fat: 3g Protein: 1g Sodium: 95mg

54) Crispy Jalapeno Coins

Preparation Time: 10 Minutes   **Cooking Time: 10 Minutes**   **Servings:8-10**

Ingredients:

- 1 Egg
- 2-3 Tbsp. coconut flour
- 1 Sliced and seeded jalapeno
- Pinch of garlic powder

- Pinch of onion powder
- Pinch of Cajun seasoning (optional)
- Pinch of pepper and salt

Directions:

⇒ Ensure your air fryer is preheated to 400 degrees.

⇒ Mix together all dry ingredients.

⇒ Pat jalapeno slices dry. Dip coins into the egg wash and then into the dry mixture. Toss to thoroughly coat.

⇒ Add coated jalapeno slices to the air fryer in a singular layer. Spray with olive oil.

⇒ Cook just till crispy.

Nutrition: Calories: 128 Fat: 8g Protein: 7g Sugar: 0g

55) Crispy-Topped Baked Vegetables

Preparation Time: 10 Minutes   **Cooking Time: 40 Minutes**   **Servings:4**

Ingredients:

- 2 Tbsp. Olive oil
- 1 Onion, chopped
- 1 Celery stalk, chopped
- 2 Carrots, grated
- ½-pound Turnips, sliced
- 1 Cup vegetable broth

- 1 Tsp. Turmeric
- Sea salt and black pepper, to taste
- ½ Tsp. Liquid smoke
- 1 Cup Parmesan cheese, shredded
- 2 Tbsp. Fresh chives, chopped

Directions:

⇒ Set oven to 360°F and grease a baking dish with olive oil.

⇒ Set a skillet over medium heat and warm olive oil.

⇒ Sweat the onion until soft, and place in the turnips, carrots, and celery; and cook for 4 minutes.

⇒ Remove the vegetable mixture from the baking dish.

⇒ Combine vegetable broth with turmeric, pepper, liquid smoke, and salt.

⇒ Spread this mixture over the vegetables.

⇒ Sprinkle with Parmesan cheese and bake for about 30 minutes.

⇒ Garnish with chives to serve.

Nutrition: Calories: 242 Cal Fats: 16.3g Carbohydrates: 8.6g Protein: 16.3g

56) Jicama Fries

Preparation Time: 10 Minutes   **Cooking Time: 20 Minutes**   **Servings:8**

Ingredients:

- 1 Tbsp. Dried thyme
- ¾ C. Arrowroot flour

- ½ Large Jicama
- Eggs

Directions:

⇒ Sliced jicama into fries.

⇒ Whisk eggs together and pour over fries. Toss to coat.

⇒ Mix a pinch of salt, thyme, and arrowroot flour together. Toss egg-coated jicama into dry mixture, tossing to coat well.

⇒ Spray air fryer basket with olive oil and add fries— cook 20 minutes on the "CHIPS" setting. Toss halfway into the cooking process.

Nutrition: Calories: 211 Fat: 19g Protein: 9g Sugar: 1g

57) Spaghetti Squash Tots

Preparation Time: 5 Minutes   **Cooking Time: 15 Minutes**   **Servings:8-10**

Ingredients:

- ¼ Tsp. pepper
- ½ Tsp. salt
- 1 Thinly sliced scallion
- 1 Spaghetti squash

Directions:

⇒ Wash and cut the squash in half lengthwise. Scrap out the seeds.

⇒ With a fork, remove spaghetti meat by strands and throw out skins.

⇒ In a clean towel, toss in squash and wring out as much moisture as possible. Place in a bowl and with a knife, slice through meat a few times to cut up smaller.

⇒ Add pepper, salt, and scallions to squash and mix well.

⇒ Create "tot" shapes with your hands and place them in the air fryer. Spray with olive oil.

⇒ Cook 15 minutes at 350 degrees until golden and crispy!

Nutrition: Calories: 231 Fat: 18g Protein: 5g Sugar: 0g

58) Cheesy Cauliflower Fritters

Preparation Time: 5 Minutes   **Cooking Time: 14 Minutes**   **Servings:8**

Ingredients:

- ½ C. Chopped parsley
- 1 C. Italian breadcrumbs
- 1/3 C. Shredded mozzarella cheese
- 1/3 C. Shredded sharp cheddar cheese
- 1 Egg
- Minced garlic cloves
- Chopped scallions
- 1 Head of cauliflower

Directions:

⇒ Cut the cauliflower up into florets. Wash well and pat dry. Place into a food processor and pulse 20-30 seconds till it looks like rice.

⇒ Place the cauliflower rice in a bowl and mix with pepper, salt, egg, cheeses, breadcrumbs, garlic, and scallions.

⇒ With your hands, form 15 patties of the mixture, add more breadcrumbs if needed.

⇒ With olive oil, spritz patties, and place into your air fryer in a single layer.

⇒ Cook 14 minutes at 390 degrees, flip after 7 minutes.

Nutrition: Calories: 209 Fat: 17g Protein: 6g Sugar: 0.5g

59) Oat and Chia Porridge

Preparation Time: 5 Minutes   **Cooking Time: 5 Minutes**   **Servings:4**

Ingredients:

- 2 Tablespoons peanut butter
- ½ Teaspoons liquid Stevia
- 1 Tablespoon butter, melted
- 2 Cups milk
- ½ Cups oats
- 1 Cup chia seeds

Directions:

⇒ Preheat your air fryer to 390 degrees Fahrenheit.

⇒ Whisk the peanut butter, butter, milk, and Stevia in a bowl.

⇒ Stir in the oats and chia seeds.

⇒ Pour the mixture into an oven-proof bowl and place in the air fryer, and cook for 5-minutes.

Nutrition: Calories: 228 Total Fats: 11.4g Carbs: 10.2g Protein: 14.5g

60) Roasted Root Vegetables

Preparation Time: 20 Minutes　　　**Cooking Time: 6 to 8 Hours**　　　**Servings:8**

Ingredients:

- 6 Carrots, cut into 1-inch chunks
- 2 Yellow onions, each cut into 8 wedges
- 2 Sweet potatoes, peeled and cut into chunks
- 6 Yukon Gold potatoes, cut into chunks
- 8 Whole garlic cloves, peeled

- 4 Parsnips, peeled and cut into chunks
- 3 Tablespoons olive oil
- 1 Teaspoon dried thyme leaves
- ½ Teaspoon salt
- 1/8 Teaspoon freshly ground black pepper

Directions:

⇒ In a 6-quart slow cooker, mix all of the ingredients.

⇒ Cover and cook on low for 6 to 8 hours or until the vegetables are tender.

⇒ Serve and enjoy!

Nutrition:　Calories: 214 Carbohydrates: 40g Sugar: 7g Fiber: 6g Fat: 5g Saturated Fat: 1g Protein: 4g Sodium: 201mg

61) Hummus

Preparation Time: 10 Minutes　　　**Cooking Time: 10 Minutes**　　　**Servings:32**

Ingredients:

- 4 Cups of cooked garbanzo beans
- 1 Cup of water
- 1½ Tablespoons of lemon juice
- 2 Teaspoons of ground cumin
- 1 ½ Teaspoon of ground coriander

- 1 Teaspoon of finely chopped garlic
- ½ Teaspoon of salt
- 1/4 Teaspoon of fresh ground pepper
- Paprika for garnish

Directions:

⇒ On a food processor, place the garbanzo beans together with lemon juice, water, cumin, coriander, garlic, salt, and pepper and process it until it becomes smooth and creamy.

⇒ To achieve the desired consistency, add more water.

⇒ Then spoon out the hummus in a serving bowl.

⇒ Sprinkle your paprika and serve.

Nutrition:　Protein: 0.7g Carbohydrates: 2.5g Dietary Fiber: 0.6g Sugars: 0g Fat: 1.7g

62) Butter Glazed Carrots

Preparation Time: 20 Minutes　　　**Cooking Time: 15 Minutes**　　　**Servings:4**

Ingredients:

- 2 Cups Baby carrots
- 1 Tbsp. Brown sugar

- ½ Tbsp. Butter; melted
- A pinch of salt and black pepper

Directions:

⇒ Take a baking dish suitable to fit in your air fryer.

⇒ Toss carrots with sugar, butter, salt, and black pepper in that baking dish.

⇒ Place this dish in the air fryer basket and seal the fryer.

⇒ Cook the carrots for 10 minutes at 350°F on Air fryer mode.

⇒ Enjoy.

Nutrition:　Calories:151 Fat:2 Fiber: 4 Carbs: 14 Protein:4

63) Cinnamon Butternut Squash Fries

Preparation Time: 10 Minutes   **Cooking Time: 10 Minutes**   **Servings:2**

Ingredients:

- 1 Pinch of salt
- 1 Tbsp. powdered unprocessed sugar
- ½ Tsp. nutmeg
- ½ Tsp. cinnamon
- 1 Tbsp. coconut oil
- 0.5 Ounces pre-cut butternut squash fries

Directions:

⇒ In a plastic bag, pour in all ingredients. Cover fries with other components till coated and sugar is dissolved.

⇒ Spread coated fries into a single layer in the air fryer, cook 10 minutes at 390 degrees until crispy.

Nutrition: Calories: 175 Fat: 8g Protein: 1g Sugar: 5g

64) Carrot & Zucchini Muffins

Preparation Time: 5 Minutes   **Cooking Time: 14 Minutes**   **Servings:4**

Ingredients:

- 2 Tablespoons butter, melted
- ¼ Cup carrots, shredded
- ½ Cup zucchini, shredded
- 1 ½ Cups almond flour
- 1 Tablespoon liquid Stevia
- ½ Teaspoons baking powder
- Pinch of salt
- 2 Eggs
- 1 Tablespoon yogurt
- 1 Cup milk

Directions:

⇒ Preheat your air fryer to 350 degrees Fahrenheit.

⇒ Beat the eggs, yogurt, milk, salt, pepper, baking soda, and Stevia.

⇒ Whisk in the flour gradually.

⇒ Add zucchini and carrots.

⇒ Grease muffin tins with butter and pour the muffin batter into tins. Cook for 14-minutes and serve.

Nutrition: Calories:224 Total Fats:12.3 Carbs: 11.2g Protein:14.2g

65) Curried Cauliflower Florets

Preparation Time: 5 Minutes   **Cooking Time: 10 Minutes**   **Servings:4**

Ingredients:

- 1/4 Cup sultanas or golden raisins
- ¼ Teaspoon salt
- 1 Tablespoon curry powder
- 1 Cauliflower head, broken into small florets
- ¼ Cup pine nuts
- ½ Cup olive oil

Directions:

⇒ In a cup of boiling water, soak your sultanas to plump. Preheat your air fryer to 350 degrees Fahrenheit.

⇒ Add oil and pine nuts to the air fryer and toast for a minute or so.

⇒ In a bowl, toss the cauliflower and curry powder as well as salt, then add the mix to the air fryer mixing well.

⇒ Cook for 10-minutes. Drain the sultanas, toss with cauliflower, and serve.

Nutrition: Calories: 275 Total Fat: 11.3g Carbs: 8.6g Protein: 9.5g

66) Feta & Mushroom Frittata

Preparation Time: 15 Minutes   **Cooking Time: 30 Minutes**   **Servings:4**

Ingredients:

- 1 Red onion, thinly sliced
- 2 Cups button mushrooms, thinly sliced
- Salt to taste
- 1 Tablespoons feta cheese, crumbled

- 3 Medium eggs
- Non-stick cooking spray
- 2 Tablespoons olive oil

Directions:

⇒ Saute the onion and mushrooms in olive oil over medium heat until the vegetables are tender.

⇒ Remove the vegetables from the pan and drain them on a paper towel-lined plate.

⇒ In a mixing bowl, whisk eggs and salt. Coat all sides of the baking dish with cooking spray.

⇒ Preheat your air fryer to 325 degrees Fahrenheit. Pour the beaten eggs into the prepared baking dish and scatter the sautéed vegetables and crumble feta on top—bake in the air fryer for 30-minutes. Allow to cool slightly and serve!

Nutrition: Calories: 226 Total Fat: 9.3g Carbs:8.7g Protein: 12.6g

Chapter 7 -   Meat Recipes

67) Bacon and Garlic Pizzas

Preparation Time: 10 Minutes   **Cooking Time: 10 Minutes**   **Servings:4**

Ingredients:

- 32 oz. Dinner rolls, frozen
- ½ teaspoon Garlic cloves minced
- ½ Tsp. oregano dried
- ½ Tsp. garlic powder

- 1 Cup ketchup
- 2 Teaspoons Bacon slices, cooked and chopped
- 1 and ¼ Cups cheddar cheese, grated

Directions:

⇒ Place the rolls on a work surface and press them to obtain four ovals.

⇒ Spray each oval with cooking spray, transfer them to the air fryer and cook at 370°F for 2 minutes.

⇒ Spread the ketchup on each oval, divide the garlic, sprinkle with oregano and garlic powder, and garnish with bacon and cheese.

⇒ Return the pizzas to your hot air fryer and cook them at 370°F for another 8 minutes.

⇒ Serve hot for lunch.

Nutrition: Calories: 104 Fat: 9g Protein: 8.5g

68) Stuffed Meatballs

Preparation Time: 10 Minutes   **Cooking Time: 10 Minutes**   **Servings:4**

Ingredients:

- 1/3 Cup bread crumbs (1 healthy fat)
- 2 Tbsp. milk (½ condiment)
- 1 Tablespoon ketchup (1/4 condiment)
- 1 Egg (1 healthy fat)
- ½ Tsp. marjoram, dried (1/4 condiment)

- Salt and black pepper to the taste (1/8 condiment)
- 1-pound Lean beef, ground (1 lean)
- 20 Cheddar cheese cubes (½ healthy fat)
- 1 Tablespoon olive oil (1/8 condiment)

Directions:

⇒ In a bowl, mix the breadcrumbs with ketchup, milk, marjoram, salt, pepper, and egg and beat well.

⇒ Add the beef, mix and form 20 meatballs with this mixture.

⇒ Shape each meatball around a cube of cheese, sprinkle with oil and rub.

⇒ Place all the meatballs in your preheated air fryer and cook at 390°F for 10 minutes.

⇒ Serve them for lunch with a side of salad.

Nutrition: Calories: 112 Fat: 8.2g Protein: 7.7g

69) Low Carb Pork Dumplings With Dipping Sauce

Preparation Time: 30 Minutes   **Cooking Time: 20 Minutes**   **Servings:6**

Ingredients:

- 18 Dumpling wrappers (1 healthy fat)
- 1 Teaspoon olive oil (1/4 condiment)
- 4 Cups bok choy (chopped) (2 leans)
- 2 Tablespoons rice vinegar (½ condiment)
- 1 Tablespoon diced ginger (1/4 condiment)
- 1/4 Teaspoon crushed red pepper (½ green)

- 1 Tablespoon diced garlic (½ condiment)
- Lean ground pork ½ cup (2 leans)
- 2 Teaspoons Lite soy sauce (½ condiment)
- ½ Tsp. Honey (1/4 healthy fat)
- 1 Teaspoon Toasted sesame oil (1/4 condiment)
- Finely chopped scallions (1green)

Directions:

⇒ In a large skillet, heat the olive oil, add the bok choy, cook for 6 minutes and add the garlic, ginger and cook for one minute. Transfer this mixture to a paper towel and pat dry any excess oil

⇒ In a bowl, add the mixture of bok choy, red pepper, and lean ground pork and mix well.

⇒ Place dumplings wrap on a plate and add a spoon to fill half of the wrapper. With water, seal the edges and fold them.

⇒ Spray air fryer basket with oil, add dumplings into the air fryer basket and cook at 375°F for 12 minutes or until golden brown.

⇒ Meanwhile, to make the sauce, combine the sesame oil, rice vinegar, shallot, soy sauce, and honey in a mixing bowl.

⇒ Serve the dumplings with the sauce.

Nutrition: Calories: 140 Fat: 5g Protein: 12g

70) Gluten-Free Air Fryer Chicken Fried Brown Rice

Preparation Time: 10 Minutes   **Cooking Time: 20 Minutes**   **Servings:2**

Ingredients:

- 1 Cup Chicken Breast (1 lean)
- 1/4 Cup chopped White Onion (½ green)
- 1/4 Cup chopped Celery (½ green)

- 4 Cups Cooked brown rice (2 healthy fat)
- 1/4 Cup chopped Carrots (½ green)

Directions:

⇒ Place the foil on the air fryer basket, make sure to leave room for airflow, roll up on the sides

⇒ Spray the film with olive oil. Mix all the ingredients.

⇒ On top of the foil, add all the ingredients to the air fryer basket.

⇒ Give a splash of olive oil to the mixture.

⇒ Cook for five minutes at 390°F.

⇒ Open the air fryer and give the mixture a spin

⇒ Cook for another five minutes at 390°F.

⇒ Remove from the air fryer and serve hot.

Nutrition: Calories: 350 Fat: 6g Protein: 22g

71)Air Fryer Cheesy Pork Chops

Preparation Time: 5 Minutes   **Cooking Time: 8 Minutes**   **Servings:2**

Ingredients:

- 2 Lean pork chops
- Half teaspoon of Salt (1/4 condiment)
- ½ Tsp. Garlic powder (1/4 condiment)

- 4 Tbsp. Shredded cheese (1 healthy fat)
- Chopped cilantro (1green)

Directions:

⇒ Let the air fryer preheat to 350 degrees.

⇒ With garlic, coriander and salt, rub the pork chops. Put the air fryer on. Let it cook for four minutes. Turn them over and then cook for extra two minutes.

⇒ Drizzle the cheese on top and cook for another two minutes or until the cheese has melted.

⇒ Serve with salad.

Nutrition: Calories: 467 Protein: 61g Fat: 22g

72)Air Fryer Pork Chop & Broccoli

Preparation Time: 20 Minutes   **Cooking Time: 20 Minutes**   **Servings:2**

Ingredients:

- 2 Cups Broccoli florets (1green)
- 2 Pieces Bone-in pork chop (1 lean)
- ½ Tsp. Paprika (1/4 condiment)
- 2 Tbsp. Avocado oil (1 healthy fat)

- ½ Tsp. Garlic powder (1/4 condiment)
- ½ Tsp. Onion powder (1/4 condiment)
- Two cloves of crushed garlic (1/4 condiment)
- 1 Teaspoon of Salt divided (1/4 condiment)

Directions:

⇒ Let the air fryer preheat to 350 degrees. Spray the basket with cooking oil

⇒ Add an oil spoon, onion powder, half a teaspoon. of salt, garlic powder, and paprika in a bowl mix well, rub this spice mixture on the sides of the pork chop

⇒ Add the pork chops to the fryer basket and cook for five minutes

⇒ Meanwhile, add an oil teaspoon, garlic, a half teaspoon of salt, and broccoli in a bowl and coat them well

⇒ Turn the pork chop and add the broccoli, let it cook for another five minutes.

⇒ Remove from the air fryer and serve.

Nutrition: Calories: 483 Fat: 20g Protein: 23g

73) Mustard Glazed Air Fryer Pork Tenderloin

Preparation Time: 10 Minutes   **Cooking Time: 18 Minutes**   **Servings:4**

Ingredients:

- ¼ Cup Yellow mustard (½ green)
- One pork tenderloin (1 lean)
- ¼ Tsp. Salt (1/4 condiment)
- 3 Tbsp. Honey (½ healthy fat)
- 1/8 Tsp. Black pepper (1/4 condiment)
- 1 Tbsp. Minced garlic (1/4 condiment)
- 1 Tsp. Dried rosemary (1/4green)
- 1 Tsp. Italian seasoning (1/8 condiment)

Directions:

⇒ Using a knife, cut the top of the pork tenderloin. Add the garlic (minced) into the cuts. Then sprinkle with kosher salt and pepper.

⇒ In a bowl, add the honey, mustard, rosemary, and Italian seasoning mixture until well blended. Rub this mustard mix all over the pork.

⇒ Leave to marinate in the refrigerator for at least two hours.

⇒ Place the pork tenderloin in the basket of the air fryer. Cook for 18-20 minutes at 400°F. With an instant-read thermometer, verify that the internal temperature of the pig should be 145°F.

⇒ Remove from the air fryer and serve with a side of salad.

Nutrition: Calories: 390 Protein: 59g Fat: 11g

74) Air Fryer Pork Taquitos

Preparation Time: 10 Minutes   **Cooking Time: 20 Minutes**   **Servings:10**

Ingredients:

- 3 Cups of Pork tenderloin, cooked & shredded (2 leans)
- 2 and ½ cups, fat-free Shredded mozzarella (1 healthy fat)
- 10 Small tortillas (1 healthy fat)
- Salsa for dipping (1 condiment)
- Juice of a lime (1/4 condiment)

Directions:

⇒ Allow the air fryer to preheat to 380°F.

⇒ Add the lime juice to the pork and mix well

⇒ With a damp towel over the tortilla, microwave for ten seconds to soften it

⇒ Add the pork filling and cheese on top in a tortilla, roll the tortilla tightly.

⇒ Situate the tortillas on a greased baking sheet

⇒ Sprinkle oil on the tortillas. Bake for 7-10 minutes or until the tortillas are golden; turn them halfway.

⇒ Serve with salad.

Nutrition: Calories: 253 Fat: 18g Protein: 20g

75) Pork Rind Nachos

Preparation Time: 5 Minutes　　　　**Cooking Time: 5 Minutes**　　　　**Servings:2**

Ingredients:

- Tbsp. Of pork rinds (1 lean)
- 1/4 Cup shredded cooked chicken (½ lean)
- ½ Cup shredded Monterey jack cheese (1/4 healthy fat)
- 1/4 Cup sliced pickled jalapeños (1/4green)
- 1/4 Cup guacamole (1/4 healthy fat)
- 1/4 Cup full-fat sour cream (1/4 healthy fat)

Directions:

⇒ Place the pork rinds in a 6-inch round pan. Fill with grilled chicken and Monterey jack cheese. Place the pan in the basket with the air fryer.

⇒ Set the temperature to 370°F and set the timer for 5 minutes or until the cheese has melted.

⇒ Eat immediately with jalapeños, guacamole, and sour cream.

Nutrition:　　　　Calories: 295 Protein: 30g Fat: 27g

76) Air Fried Jamaican Jerk Pork

Preparation Time: 10 Minutes　　　　**Cooking Time: 20 Minutes**　　　　**Servings:4**

Ingredients:

- Pork, cut into three-inch pieces (1 lean)
- ¼ Cup Jerk paste (1/4 condiment)

Directions:

⇒ Rub the jerk dough on all the pork pieces.

⇒ Chill to marinate for 4 hours in the refrigerator.

⇒ Allow the air fryer to preheat to 390°F. Spray with olive oil

⇒ Before placing it in the air fryer, allow the meat to rest for 20 minutes at room temperature.

⇒ Cook for 20 minutes at 390°F in the air fryer, turn halfway.

⇒ Remove from the air fryer and let sit for ten minutes before slicing.

⇒ Serve with microgreens.

Nutrition:　　　　Calories: 234 Protein: 31g Fat: 9g

77) Beef Lunch Meatballs

Preparation Time: 10 Minutes　　　　**Cooking Time: 15 Minutes**　　　　**Servings:4**

Ingredients:

- ½ Pound beef, ground (½ lean)
- ½ Pound Italian sausage, chopped (½ lean)
- ½ Tsp. Garlic powder (1/4 condiment)
- ½ Tsp. Onion powder (1/4 condiment)
- Salt and black pepper to the taste (1/4 condiment)
- ½ Cup cheddar cheese, grated (½ healthy fat)
- Mashed potatoes for serving (½ healthy fat)

Directions:

⇒ In a bowl, mix the beef with the sausage, garlic powder, onion powder, salt, pepper, and cheese, mix well and form 16 meatballs with this mixture.

⇒ Place the meatballs in your air fryer and cook them at 370°F for 15 minutes.

⇒ Serve the meatballs with some mashed potatoes on the side.

Nutrition:　　　　Calories: 132 Fat: 6.7g Protein: 5.5g

78) Air Fryer Whole Wheat Crusted Pork Chops

Preparation Time: 10 Minutes   **Cooking Time: 12 Minutes**   **Servings:4**

Ingredients:

- 1 Cup whole-wheat breadcrumbs (½ healthy fat)
- ¼ Teaspoon salt (1/4 condiment)
- 2-4 Pieces pork chops (center cut and boneless) (2 leans)
- ½ Teaspoon Chili powder (1/4 condiment)
- 1 Tablespoon parmesan cheese (1/4 healthy fat)
- 1 ½ Teaspoons paprika (½ condiment)
- 1 Egg beaten (1 healthy fat)
- ½ Teaspoon Onion powder (1/4 condiment)
- ½ Teaspoon Granulated garlic (1/4 condiment)

Directions:

⇒ Allow the air fryer to preheat to 400°F.

⇒ Rub kosher salt on each side of the pork chops, let them rest

⇒ Add the beaten egg to a large bowl

⇒ Add the parmesan, breadcrumbs, garlic, pepper, paprika, chili powder, and onion powder to a bowl and mix well

⇒ Dip the pork chop in the egg and then in the breadcrumbs

⇒ Put it in the air fryer and spray it with oil.

⇒ Leave them to cook for 12 minutes at 400°F. Turn them upside down halfway through cooking. Cook for another six minutes.

⇒ Serve with salad.

Nutrition: Calories: 425 Fat: 20g Protein: 31g

79) Air Fried Philly Cheesesteak Taquitos

Preparation Time: 20 Minutes   **Cooking Time: 6-8 Hours**   **Servings:6**

Ingredients:

- 1 Package Dry Italian dressing mix (1 condiment)
- 1 Pack Super Soft Corn Tortillas (1 healthy fat)
- 2 Pieces green peppers chopped (½ green)
- 12 Cups lean beef steak strips (3 leans)
- 2 Cups Beef stock (1 condiment)
- 1 Cup Lettuce shredded (½ green)
- 10 Slices provolone cheese (1 healthy fat)
- 1 Onion, chopped

Directions:

⇒ In a slow cooker, add onion, beef, stock, pepper, and seasonings.

⇒ Cover, then cook at low heat for 6 or 8 hours.

⇒ Heat the tortillas for two minutes in the microwave.

⇒ Allow the air fryer to preheat to 350°F.

⇒ Remove the cheesesteak from the slow cooker, add 2-3 tablespoons of steak to the tortilla.

⇒ Add some cheese, roll the tortilla well, and place in a deep fryer basket.

⇒ Make all the tortillas you want.

⇒ Lightly brush with olive oil

⇒ Cook for 6-8 minutes.

⇒ Flip the tortillas over and brush more oil as needed.

⇒ Serve with chopped lettuce and enjoy.

Nutrition: Calories: 220 Protein: 21g Fat: 16g

80) Roasted Garlic Bacon and Potatoes

Preparation Time: 5 Minutes   **Cooking Time: 25 Minutes**   **Servings:4**

Ingredients:

- Medium-sized potatoes (1 healthy fat)
- 1 Strips of streaky bacon (1 lean)
- 2 tablespoon Sprigs of rosemary (1green)
- ½ Cloves of garlic unpeeled smashed, (½ condiment)
- 3 Tsp. of vegetable oil (½ condiment)

Directions:

⇒ Preheat Air fryer to 390°F.

⇒ Put the smashed garlic, bacon, potatoes, rosemary, and then the oil in a bowl. Stir thoroughly.v

⇒ Place into air fryer basket and roast until golden for about 25 minutes.

Nutrition: Calories: 114 Fat: 8.1g Protein: 6.2g

81) Peppery Roasted Potatoes With Smoked Bacon

Preparation Time: 15 Minutes   **Cooking Time: 11 Minutes**   **Servings:2**

Ingredients:

- 38g Small rashers smoked bacon (1 lean)
- 1/3 Tsp. garlic powder (1/4 condiment)
- 1 Tsp. sea salt (1/4 condiment)
- 1 Tsp. Paprika (1/4 condiment)
- 1/3 Tsp. ground black pepper (1/4 condiment)
- 1 Bell pepper (½ green)
- 1 Tsp. mustard (1/4 condiment)
- 2 Habanero peppers, halved (½ green)

Directions:

⇒ Simply toss all the ingredients in a mixing dish, then transfer them to your air fryer's basket.

⇒ Air-fry at 375°F for 10 minutes, serve warm.

Nutrition: Calories: 122 Fat: 9g Protein: 10g

Chapter 8 -   Snack Recipes

82) Grilled Avocado Capers Crostini

Preparation Time: 10 Minutes   **Cooking Time: 20 Minutes**   **Servings:2**

Ingredients:

- 1 Avocado thinly sliced
- 9 Ounces ripened cherry tomatoes
- 1.50 Ounces fresh bocconcini in water
- 2 Tsp. Balsamic glaze
- 8 Pieces Italian baguette
- ½ Cup basil leaves

Directions:

⇒ Preheat your oven to 375 degrees Fahrenheit

⇒ Arrange your baking sheet properly before spraying them on top with olive oil.

⇒ Cut and bake your baguette until golden brown. Rub your crostini with the cut side of garlic while they are still warm, and you can season them with pepper and salt.

⇒ Divide the basil leaves on each piece of bread and top them up with tomato halves, avocado slices, and bocconcini. Season it with pepper and salt.

⇒ Broil it for 4 minutes, and when the cheese starts to melt through, remove and drizzle balsamic glaze before serving.

Nutrition: Calories: 278 Fat: 10g Carbohydrates: 37g Proteins: 10g Sodium: 342mg Potassium: 277mg

83) Cheesy Garlic Sweet Potatoes

Preparation Time: 10 Minutes   **Cooking Time: 25 Minutes**   **Servings:4**

Ingredients:

- Sea salt
- ¼ Cup garlic butter melt
- ¾ Cup shredded mozzarella cheese
- ½ Cup of parmesan cheese freshly grated
- 4 Medium sized sweet potatoes
- 2 Tsp. freshly chopped parsley

Directions:

⇒ Heat the oven to 400 degrees Fahrenheit and brush the potatoes with garlic butter, and season each with pepper and salt. Arrange the cut side down on a greased baking sheet until the flesh is tender or they turn golden brown.

⇒ Remove them from the oven, flip the cut side up and top up with parsley and parmesan cheese.

⇒ Change the settings of your instant fryer oven to broil and on medium heat, add the cheese and melt it. Sprinkle salt and pepper to taste. Serve them warm.

Nutrition: Calories: 356 Fat: 9g Carbohydrates: 13g Proteins: 5g Potassium: 232mg Sodium: 252mg

84) Crispy Garlic Baked Potato Wedges

Preparation Time: 5 Minutes   **Cooking Time: 10 Minutes**   **Servings:3**

Ingredients:

- 3 Tsp. salt
- 1 Tsp. minced garlic
- 6 Large russet
- ¼ Cup olive oil

- 1 Tsp. Paprika
- 2/3 Finely grated parmesan cheese
- 2 Tsp. Freshly chopped parsley

Directions:

⇒ Preheat the oven to 350 degrees Fahrenheit and line the baking sheet with parchment paper.

⇒ Cut the potatoes into half-length and cut each half in half lengthways again. Make eight wedges.

⇒ In a small jug, combine garlic, oil, paprika, and salt and place your wedges in the baking sheets. Pour the oil mixture over the potatoes and toss them to ensure that they are evenly coated.

⇒ Arrange the potato wedges in a single layer on the baking tray and sprinkle salt and parmesan cheese if needed. Bake for 35 minutes and turn the wedges once half side is cooked.

⇒ Flip the other side until they are both golden brown.

⇒ Sprinkle parsley and the remaining parmesan before serving.

Nutrition: Calories: 324 Fat: 6g Carbs: 8g Proteins: 2g Sodium: 51mg Potassium: 120mg

85) Cheesy Mashed Sweet Potato Cakes

Preparation Time: 10 Minutes   **Cooking Time: 30 Minutes**   **Servings:4**

Ingredients:

- ¾ Cup bread crumbs
- 4 Cups mashed potatoes
- ½ Cup onions
- 2 Cup of grated mozzarella cheese
- ¼ Cup fresh grated parmesan cheese

- 2 Large garlic cloves finely chopped
- 1 Egg
- 2 Tsp. Finely chopped parsley
- Salt and pepper to taste

Directions:

⇒ Line your baking sheet with foil. Wash, peel and cut the sweet potatoes into six pieces. Arrange them inside the baking sheet and drizzle a small amount of oil on top before seasoning with salt and pepper.

⇒ Cover with a baking sheet and bake it for 45 minutes; once cooked, transfer them into a mixing bowl and mash them well with a potato masher.

⇒ Put the sweet potatoes in a bowl, add green onions, parmesan, mozzarella, garlic, egg, parsley, and bread crumbs. Mash and combine the mixture together using the masher.

⇒ Put the remaining ¼ cup of the breadcrumbs in place. Scoop a teaspoon of the mixture into your palm and form round patties around ½ an inch thick. Dredge your patties in the breadcrumbs to cover both sides and set them aside.

⇒ Heat a tablespoon of oil in a medium nonstick pan. When the oil is hot, begin to cook the patties in batches 4 or 5 per session and cook each side for 6 minutes until they turn golden brown. Use a spoon or spatula to flip them. Add oil to prevent burning.

Nutrition: Calories:126 Fat:6g Carbs: 15g Proteins 3g Sodium: 400mg

86) Sticky Chicken Thai Wings

Preparation Time: 10 Minutes   **Cooking Time: 30 Minutes**   **Servings:6**

Ingredients:

- 3 Pounds chicken wings removed
- 1 Tsp. sea salt to taste
- For the glaze:
- ¾ Cup Thai sweet chili sauce
- ¼ Cup soy sauce
- 4 Tsp. brown sugar

- 4 Tsp. rice wine vinegar
- 3 Tsp. fish sauce
- 2 Tsp. lime juice
- 1 Tsp. lemongrass minced
- 2 Tsp. sesame oil
- 1 Tsp. garlic minced

Directions:

⇒ Preheat the oven to 350 degrees Fahrenheit. Lightly spray your baking tray with the cooking spray and set it aside. To prepare the glaze, combine the ingredients in a small bowl and whisk them until they are well combined. Pour half of the mixture into a pan and reserve the rest.

⇒ Trim any excess skin off the wing edges and season it with pepper and salt. Add the wings to a baking tray and pour the sauce over the wings tossing them for the sauce to coat evenly. Arrange them in a single layer and bake them for 15 minutes.

⇒ While the wings are in the oven, bring your glaze to simmer in medium heat until there are visible bubbles.

⇒ Once the wings are cooked on one side, rotate each piece and bake for an extra 10 minutes. Baste them and return them into the oven to allow for more cooking until they are golden brown. Garnish with onion slices, cilantro, chili flakes, and sprinkle the remaining salt. Serve with some glaze as you desire.

Nutrition: Calories: 256 Fat: 16g Carbohydrates 19g Proteins: 20g Potassium: 213mg Sodium: 561mg

87) Caprese Stuffed Garlic Butter Portobellos

Preparation Time: 5 Minutes   **Cooking Time: 10 Minutes**   **Servings:6**

Ingredients:

For the garlic butter:
- 2 Tsp. of butter
- 2 Cloves garlic
- 1 Tsp. parsley finely chopped

For the mushrooms:
- 6 Large portobello mushrooms, washed and dried well with a paper towel
- 6 Mozzarella cheese balls thinly sliced

- 1 Cup grape tomatoes thinly sliced
- Fresh basil for garnishing

For the balsamic glaze:
- 2 Tsp. brown sugar
- ¼ Cup balsamic vinegar

Directions:

⇒ Preheat the oven to broil, setting on high heat. Arrange the oven shelf and place it in the right direction.

⇒ Combine the garlic butter ingredients in a small pan and melt until the garlic begins to be fragrant. Brush the bottoms of the mushroom and place them on the buttered section of the baking tray.

⇒ Flip and brush the remaining garlic over each cap. Fill each mushroom with tomatoes and mozzarella slices and grill until the cheese has melted. Drizzle the balsamic glaze and sprinkle some salt to taste.

⇒ If you are making the balsamic glaze from scratch, combine the sugar and vinegar in a small pan and reduce the heat to low. Allow it to simmer for 6 minutes or until the mixture has thickened well.

Nutrition: Calories: 101 Fat: 5g Carbohydrates: 12g Proteins: 2g Sodium: 58mg Potassium: 377mg

88) Veggie Fritters

Preparation Time: 10 Minutes   **Cooking Time: 10 Minutes**   **Servings:4**

Ingredients:

- 2 Garlic cloves, minced
- 2 Yellow onions, chopped
- 4 Scallions, chopped
- 2 Carrots, grated
- 2 Teaspoons cumin, ground
- ½ Teaspoon turmeric powder
- Salt and black pepper to the taste
- ¼ Teaspoon coriander, ground

- 2 Tablespoons parsley, chopped
- ¼ Teaspoon lemon juice
- ½ Cup almond flour
- 2 Beets, peeled and grated
- 2 Eggs, whisked
- ¼ Cup tapioca flour
- 3 Tablespoons olive oil

Directions:

⇒ In a bowl, combine the garlic with the onions, scallions, and the rest of the ingredients except the oil; stir well and shape medium fritters out of this mix.

⇒ Heat up a pan with the oil over medium-high heat, add the fritters, cook for 5 minutes on each side, arrange on a platter and serve.

Nutrition: Calories: 209 Fat: 11.2g Fiber: 3g Carbs: 4.4g Protein: 4.8g

89) Eggplant Dip

Preparation Time: 10 Minutes   **Cooking Time: 40 Minutes**   **Servings:4**

Ingredients:

- 1 Eggplant, poked with a fork
- 2 Tablespoons tahini paste
- 2 Tablespoons lemon juice
- 2 Garlic cloves, minced

- 1 Tablespoon olive oil
- Salt and black pepper to the taste
- 1 Tablespoon parsley, chopped

Directions:

⇒ Put the eggplant in a roasting pan, bake at 400°F for 40 minutes, cool down, peel, and transfer to your food processor.

⇒ Add the rest of the ingredients except the parsley, pulse well, divide into small bowls and serve as an appetizer with the parsley sprinkled on top.

Nutrition: Calories: 121 Fat: 4.3g Fiber: 1g Carbs: 1.4g Protein:4.3g

90) Coconut Shrimp

Preparation Time: 15 Minutes   **Cooking Time: 15 Minutes**   **Servings:6**

Ingredients:

- Salt and pepper
- 1-pound Jumbo shrimp peeled and deveined
- ½ Cup all-purpose flour

  For the batter:
- ½ Cup beer
- 1 Tsp. Baking powder

- ½ Cup all-purpose flour
- 1 Egg

  For the coating:
- 1 Cup panko bread crumbs
- 1 Cup shredded coconut

Directions:

⇒ Line the baking tray with parchment paper.

⇒ In a shallow bowl, add ½ cup flour for dredging, and in another bowl, whisk the batter ingredients. The batter should resemble a pancake consistency. If it is too thick, add a little mineral or beer whisking in between; in another bowl, mix together the shredded coconut and bread crumbs.

⇒ Dredge the shrimps in flour, shaking off any excess before dipping in the batter, and coat them with the bread crumb mixture. Lightly press the coconut into the shrimp.

⇒ Place them into the baking sheet and repeat the process until you have several.

⇒ In a Dutch oven skillet, heat vegetable oil until it is nice and hot, fry the frozen shrimp batches for 3 minutes per side. Drain them on a paper towel-lined plate.

⇒ Serve immediately with sweet chili sauce.

Nutrition: Calories: 409 Fat: 11g Carbohydrates: 46g Proteins: 30g Sodium: 767mg Potassium: 345mg

91) Salmon Sandwich With Avocado and Egg

Preparation Time: 15 Minutes   **Cooking Time: 10 Minutes**   **Servings:4**

Ingredients:

- 8 Ounces (250g) smoked salmon, thinly sliced
- 1 Medium (200g) ripe avocado, thinly sliced
- 4 Large poached eggs (about 60g each)

- 4 Slices whole wheat bread (about 30g each)
- 2 Cups (60g) arugula or baby rocket
- Salt and freshly ground black pepper

Directions:

⇒ Place one bread slice on a plate top with arugula, avocado, salmon, and poached egg—season with salt and pepper. Repeat the procedure for the remaining ingredients.

⇒ Serve and enjoy.

Nutrition: Calories: 310 Fat: 18.2g Carbohydrates: 16.4g Protein: 21.3g Sodium: 383mg

92) Tasty Onion and Cauliflower Dip

Preparation Time: 20 Minutes   **Cooking Time: 30 Minutes**   **Servings:24**

Ingredients:

- 1 and ½ Cups chicken stock
- 1 Cauliflower head, florets separated
- ¼ Cup mayonnaise
- ½ Cup yellow onion, chopped
- ¾ Cup cream cheese
- ½ Teaspoon chili powder
- ½ Teaspoon cumin, ground
- ½ Teaspoon garlic powder
- Salt and black pepper to the taste

Directions:

⇒ Put the stock in a pot, add cauliflower and onion, heat up over medium heat, and cook for 30 minutes.

⇒ Add chili powder, salt, pepper, cumin, and garlic powder and stir.

⇒ Also, add cream cheese and stir a bit until it melts.

⇒ Blend using an immersion blender and mix with the mayo.

⇒ Transfer to a bowl and keep in the fridge for 2 hours before you serve it.

⇒ Enjoy!

Nutrition: Calories: 40 kcal Protein: 1.23g Fat: 3.31g Carbohydrates: 1.66g Sodium: 72mg

93) Marinated Eggs

Preparation Time: 2 Hours and 10 Minutes   **Cooking Time: 7 Minutes**   **Servings:4**

Ingredients:

- 6 Eggs
- 1 and ¼ Cups of water
- ¼ Cup unsweetened rice vinegar
- 2 Tablespoons coconut aminos
- Salt and black pepper to the taste
- 2 Garlic cloves, minced
- 1 Teaspoon stevia
- 4 Ounces cream cheese
- 1 Tablespoon chives, chopped

Directions:

⇒ Put the eggs in a pot, add water to cover, bring to a boil over medium heat, cover and cook for 7 minutes.

⇒ Rinse eggs with cold water and leave them aside to cool down.

⇒ In a bowl, mix one cup of water with coconut aminos, vinegar, stevia, and garlic and whisk well.

⇒ Put the eggs in this mix, cover with a kitchen towel, and leave them aside for 2 hours, rotating from time to time.

⇒ Peel eggs, cut in halves, and put egg yolks in a bowl.

⇒ Add ¼ cup water, cream cheese, salt, pepper, and chives, and stir well.

⇒ Stuff egg whites with this mix and serve them.

⇒ Enjoy!

Nutrition: Calories: 289 kcal Protein: 15.86g Fat: 22.62g Carbohydrates: 4.52g Sodium: 288mg

94) Pumpkin Muffins

Preparation Time: 10 Minutes   **Cooking Time: 15 Minutes**   **Servings: 18**

Ingredients:

- ¼ Cup sunflower seed butter
- ¾ Cup pumpkin puree
- 2 Tablespoons flaxseed meal
- ¼ Cup coconut flour
- ½ Cup erythritol
- ½ Teaspoon nutmeg, ground
- 1 Teaspoon cinnamon, ground
- ½ Teaspoon baking soda
- 1 Egg
- ½ Teaspoon baking powder
- A pinch of salt

Directions:

⇒ In a bowl, mix butter with pumpkin puree and egg and blend well.

⇒ Add flaxseed meal, coconut flour, erythritol, baking soda, baking powder, nutmeg, cinnamon, and a pinch of salt and stir well.

⇒ Spoon this into a greased muffin pan, introduce in the oven at 350 degrees Fahrenheit and bake for 15 minutes.

⇒ Leave muffins to cool down and serve them as a snack.

⇒ Enjoy!

Nutrition: Calories: 65 kcal Protein: 2.82g Fat: 5.42g Carbohydrates: 2.27g Sodium: 57mg

95) Salmon Spinach and Cottage Cheese Sandwich

Preparation Time: 15 Minutes   **Cooking Time: 10 Minutes**   **Servings: 4**

Ingredients:

- 4 Ounces (125g) cottage cheese
- 1/4 Cup (15g) chives, chopped
- 1 Teaspoon (5g) capers
- ½ Teaspoon (2.5g) grated lemon rind
- 4 (2 oz. or 60g) Smoked salmon
- 2 Cups (60g) loose baby spinach
- 1 Medium (110g) red onion, sliced thinly
- 8 Slices rye bread (about 30g each)
- Kosher salt and freshly ground black pepper

Directions:

⇒ Preheat your griddle or Panini press.

⇒ Mix together cottage cheese, chives, capers, and lemon rind in a small bowl.

⇒ Spread and divide the cheese mixture on four bread slices. Top with spinach, onion slices, and smoked salmon.

⇒ Cover with remaining bread slices.

⇒ Grill the sandwiches until golden and grill marks form on both sides.

⇒ Transfer to a serving dish.

⇒ Serve and enjoy.

Nutrition: Calories: 261 Fat: 9.9g Carbohydrates: 22.9g Protein: 19.9g Sodium: 1226mg

96) Sausage and Cheese Dip

Preparation Time: 10 Minutes   **Cooking Time: 130 Minutes**   **Servings:28**

Ingredients:

- 8 Ounces cream cheese
- A pinch of salt and black pepper
- 16 Ounces sour cream
- 8 Ounces pepper jack cheese, chopped
- 15 Ounces canned tomatoes mixed with habaneros
- 1-pound Italian sausage, ground
- ¼ Cup green onions, chopped

Directions:

⇒ Heat up a pan over medium heat, add sausage, stir and cook until it browns.

⇒ Add tomatoes, mix, stir and cook for 4 minutes more.

⇒ Add a pinch of salt, pepper, and green onions, stir and cook for 4 minutes.

⇒ Spread the pepper jack cheese on the bottom of your slow cooker.

⇒ Add cream cheese, sausage mix, and sour cream, cover, and cook on High for 2 hours.

⇒ Uncover your slow cooker, stir dip, transfer to a bowl, and serve.

⇒ Enjoy!

Nutrition: Calories: 132 kcal Protein: 6.79g Fat: 9.58g Carbohydrates: 6.22g Sodium: 362mg

97) Pesto Crackers

Preparation Time: 10 Minutes   **Cooking Time: 17 Minutes**   **Servings:6**

Ingredients:

- ½ Teaspoon baking powder
- Salt and black pepper to the taste
- 1 and ¼ Cups almond flour
- ¼ Teaspoon basil dried one garlic clove, minced
- 2 Tablespoons basil pesto
- A pinch of cayenne pepper
- 3 Tablespoons ghee

Directions:

⇒ In a bowl, mix salt, pepper, baking powder, and almond flour.

⇒ Add garlic, cayenne, and basil and stir.

⇒ Add pesto and whisk.

⇒ Also, add ghee and mix your dough with your finger.

⇒ Spread this dough on a lined baking sheet, introduce in the oven at 325 degrees F and bake for 17 minutes.

⇒ Leave aside to cool down, cut your crackers, and serve them as a snack.

⇒ Enjoy!

Nutrition: Calories: 9 kcal Protein: 0.41g Fat: 0.14g Carbohydrates: 1.86g Sodium: 2mg

98) Bacon Cheeseburger

Preparation Time: 10 Minutes   **Cooking Time: 30 Minutes**   **Servings:4**

Ingredients:

- 1 lb. Lean ground beef
- 1/4 Cup chopped yellow onion
- 1 Clove garlic, minced
- 1 Tbsp. yellow mustard
- 1 Tbsp. Worcestershire sauce
- ½ Tsp. salt
- Cooking spray

- 4 Ultra-thin slices of cheddar cheese, cut into six equal-sized rectangular pieces
- 3 Pieces of turkey bacon, each cut into eight evenly-sized rectangular pieces
- 24 Dill pickle chips
- 4-6 Green leaf
- Lettuce leaves, torn into 24 small square-shaped pieces
- 12 Cherry tomatoes, sliced in half

Directions:

⇒ Pre-heat oven to 400°F.

⇒ Combine the garlic, salt, onion, Worcestershire sauce, and beef in a medium-sized bowl, and mix well.

⇒ Form the mixture into 24 small meatballs.

⇒ Put meatballs onto a foil-lined baking sheet and cook for 12-15 minutes.

⇒ Leave the oven on.

⇒ Top every meatball with a piece of cheese, then go back to the oven until cheese melts for about 2 to 3 minutes.

⇒ Let the meatballs cool.

⇒ To assemble bites, on a toothpick, put a cheese-covered meatball, a piece of bacon, a piece of lettuce, pickle chip, and a tomato half.

Nutrition: Fat: 14g Cholesterol: 41mg Carbohydrates: 30g Protein: 15g

Chapter 9 -   Dessert Recipes

99) Mini Lava Cakes

Preparation Time: 5 Minutes   **Cooking Time: 20 Minutes**   **Servings:3**

Ingredients:

- 1 Egg
- 4 Tbsp. sugar
- 2 Tbsp. olive oil
- 4 Tbsp. milk
- 4 Tbsp. flour

- 1 Tbsp. cocoa powder
- ½ Tbsp. baking powder
- ½ Tbsp. orange zest
- A pinch of salt

Directions:

⇒ Mix in egg with sugar, flour, salt, oil, milk, orange zest, baking powder, and cocoa powder, turn properly. Move it to oiled ramekins.

⇒ Put ramekins in the air fryer and cook at 320°F for 20 minutes.

⇒ Serve warm.

Nutrition: Calories: 329 Total Fat: 8.5g Total carbs: 12.4g

100) Ricotta Ramekins

Preparation Time: 10 Minutes   **Cooking Time: 1 Hour**   **Servings:4**

Ingredients:

- 6 Eggs, whisked
- 1 and ½ Pounds ricotta cheese, soft
- ½ Pound stevia

- 1 Teaspoon vanilla extract
- ½ Teaspoon baking powder
- Cooking spray

Directions:

⇒ In a bowl, mix the eggs with the ricotta and the other ingredients except for the cooking spray and whisk well.

⇒ Grease 4 ramekins with the cooking spray, pour the ricotta cream in each and bake at 360 degrees F for 1 hour.

⇒ Serve cold.

Nutrition: Calories: 180 Fat: 5.3 Fiber: 5.4 Carbs: 11.5 Protein: 4

101) Strawberry Sorbet

Preparation Time: 15 Minutes   **Cooking Time: 10 Minutes**   **Servings:6**

Ingredients:

- 1 Cup strawberries, chopped
- 1 Tablespoon of liquid honey

- 2 Tablespoons water
- 1 Tablespoon lemon juice

Directions:

⇒ Preheat the water and liquid honey until you get a homogenous liquid.

⇒ Blend the strawberries until smooth and combine them with the honey liquid and lemon juice.

⇒ Transfer the strawberry mixture to the ice cream maker and churn it for 20 minutes or until the sorbet is thick.

⇒ Scoop the cooked sorbet in the ice cream cups.

Nutrition: Calories: 30 Fat: 0.4g Fiber: 1.4g Carbs: 14.9g Protein: 0.9g

102) Crispy Apples

Preparation Time: 10 Minutes   **Cooking Time: 10 Minutes**   **Servings:4**

Ingredients:

- 2 Tbsp. cinnamon powder
- 5 Apples
- ½ Tbsp. nutmeg powder
- 1 Tbsp. maple syrup
- ½ Cup water

- 4 Tbsp. butter
- ¼ Cup flour
- ¾ Cup oats
- ¼ Cup brown sugar

Directions:

⇒ Get the apples in a pan, put in nutmeg, maple syrup, cinnamon, and water.

⇒ Mix in butter with flour, sugar, salt, and oat, turn, put a spoonful of the blend over apples, get into the air fryer and cook at 350°F for 10 minutes.

⇒ Serve while warm.

Nutrition: Calories: 387 Total Fat: 5.6g Total carbs: 12.4g

103) Cocoa Cookies

Preparation Time: 10 Minutes   **Cooking Time: 14 Minutes**   **Servings:12**

Ingredients:

- 6 oz. Coconut oil
- 6 Eggs
- 3 oz. Cocoa powder
- 2 Tbsp. vanilla

- ½ Tbsp. baking powder
- 4 oz. Cream cheese
- 5 Tbsp. sugar

Directions:

⇒ Mix the eggs with sugar, coconut oil, baking powder, cocoa powder, cream cheese, vanilla in a blender, then sway and turn using a mixer.

⇒ Get it into a lined baking dish and put it into the fryer at 320°F, and bake for 14 minutes.

⇒ Split cookie sheet into rectangles.

⇒ Serve.

Nutrition: Calories: 149 Total Fat: 2.4g Total carbs: 27.2g

104) Cinnamon Pears

Preparation Time: 2 Hours   **Cooking Time: 0 Minutes**   **Servings:6**

Ingredients:

- 2 Pears
- 1 Teaspoon ground cinnamon
- 1 Tablespoon Erythritol

- 1 Teaspoon liquid stevia
- 4 Teaspoons butter

Directions:

⇒ Cut the pears on the halves.

⇒ Then scoop the seeds from the pears with the help of the scooper.

⇒ In a shallow bowl, mix up together Erythritol and ground cinnamon.

⇒ Sprinkle every pear half with cinnamon mixture and drizzle with liquid stevia.

⇒ Then add butter and wrap in the foil.

⇒ Bake the pears for 25 minutes at 365°F.

⇒ Then remove the pears from the foil and transfer them to the serving plates.

Nutrition: Calories: 96 Fat: 4.4g Fiber: 1.4g Carbs: 3.9g Protein: 0.9g

105) Cherry Compote

Preparation Time: 2 Hours   **Cooking Time: 0 Minutes**   **Servings:6**

Ingredients:

- 2 Peaches, pitted, halved
- 1 Cup cherries, pitted
- ½ Cup grape juice
- ½ Cup strawberries

- 1 Tablespoon liquid honey
- 1 Teaspoon vanilla extract
- 1 Teaspoon ground cinnamon

Directions:

⇒ Add vanilla extract and ground cinnamon. Bring the liquid to a boil.

⇒ After this, put peaches, cherries, and strawberries in the hot grape juice and bring them to a boil.

⇒ Remove the mixture from heat, add liquid honey, and close the lid.

⇒ Let the compote rest for 20 minutes.

⇒ Carefully mix up the compote and transfer it to the serving plate.

Nutrition: Calories: 80 Fat: 0.4g Fiber: 2.4g Carbs: 19.9g Protein: 0.9g

106) Vanilla Apple Pie

Preparation Time: 15 Minutes   **Cooking Time: 50 Minutes**   **Servings:8**

Ingredients:

- 3 Apples, sliced
- ½ Teaspoon ground cinnamon
- 1 Teaspoon vanilla extract
- 1 Tablespoon Erythritol
- 7 oz. Yeast roll dough
- 1 Egg, beaten

Directions:

⇒ Roll up the dough and cut it into two parts.

⇒ Line a springform pan with baking paper.

⇒ Place the first dough part in the springform pan.

⇒ Then arrange the apples over the dough and sprinkle it with Erythritol, vanilla extract, and ground cinnamon.

⇒ Then cover the apples with the remaining dough and secure the edges of the pie with the help of the fork.

⇒ Make the small cuts on the surface of the pie.

⇒ Brush the pie with the beaten egg and bake it for 50 minutes at 375F.

⇒ Cool the cooked pie well, and then remove it from the springform pan.

⇒ Cut it on the servings.

Nutrition: Calories: 140 Fat: 3.4g Fiber: 3.4g Carbs: 23.9g Protein: 2.9g

107) Creamy Strawberries

Preparation Time: 15 Minutes   **Cooking Time: 10 Minutes**   **Servings:6**

Ingredients:

- 6 Tablespoons almond butter
- 1 Tablespoon Erythritol
- 1 Cup milk
- 1 Teaspoon vanilla extract
- 1 Cup strawberries, sliced

Directions:

⇒ Pour milk into a saucepan.

⇒ Add Erythritol, vanilla extract, and almond butter.

⇒ With the help of a hand mixer, mix up the liquid until smooth and bring it to a boil.

⇒ Then remove the mixture from the heat and let it cool.

⇒ The cooled mixture will be thick.

⇒ Put the strawberries in serving glasses and top with the thick almond butter dip.

Nutrition: Calories: 192 Fat: 14.4g Fiber: 3.4g Carbs: 10.9g Protein: 1.9g

108) *Special Brownies*

Preparation Time: 10 Minutes   **Cooking Time: 22 Minutes**   **Servings:4**

Ingredients:

- 1 Egg
- 1/3 Cup cocoa powder
- 1/3 Cup sugar
- 7 Tbsp. butter
- ½ Tbsp. vanilla extract

- ¼ Cup white flour
- ¼ Cup walnuts
- ½ Tbsp. baking powder
- 1 Tbsp. peanut butter
- A pinch of salt

Directions:

⇒ Warm pan with six butter tablespoons and the sugar over medium heat, turn, cook for 5 minutes, move to a bowl, put salt, egg, cocoa powder, vanilla extract, walnuts, baking powder, and flour, turn mix properly and into a pan.

⇒ Mix peanut butter with one butter tablespoon in a bowl, heat in the microwave for some seconds, turn properly, and sprinkle brownies blend over.

⇒ Put in the air fryer and bake at 320° F for 17 minutes.

⇒ Allow brownies to cool, cut.

⇒ Serve.

Nutrition: Calories: 438 Total Fat: 18g Total carbs: 16.5g

Chapter 10 - L & G McAdams Meal Plan – On a Budget

Day 1

20) Blueberry Cantaloupe Avocado | Calories 406

29) Carrot Cake Oatmeal | Calories 307

40) Greek Salad | Calories 234

48) Tofu Stir Fry With Asparagus Stew | Calories 138

69) Low Carb Pork Dumplings With Dipping Sauce | Calories 140

98) Bacon Cheeseburger | Calories

Total Calories 1225

Day 3

21) Vitamin C Smoothie Cubes | Calories 96

22) Bacon Spaghetti Squash Carbonara | Calories 305

46) Mushroom & Jalapeño Stew | Calories 65

66) Feta & Mushroom Frittata | Calories 226

74) Air Fryer Pork Taquitos | Calories 253

87) Caprese Stuffed Garlic Butter Portobellos | Calories 101

Total Calories 1046

Day 5

7) Jackfruit Vegetable Fry | Calories 236

23) Maple Lemon Tempeh Cubes | Calories

32) Broccoli Salad | Calories 239

67) Bacon and Garlic Pizzas | Calories 104

77) Beef Lunch Meatballs | Calories 132

85) Cheesy Mashed Sweet Potato Cakes | Calories 126

Total Calories 837

Day 7

18) Avocado Red Peppers Roasted Scrambled Eggs | Calories 317

30) Peanut Butter and Cacao Breakfast Quinoa | Calories 471

39) Beet Salad (from Israel) | Calories 156

57) Spaghetti Squash Tots | Calories 231

80) Roasted Garlic Bacon and Potatoes | Calories 114

96) Sausage and Cheese Dip | Calories 132

Total Calories 1421

Day 2

11) Cream Cheese Egg Breakfast | Calories 341

31) Warm Chorizo Chickpea Salad | Calories 359

43) Romaine Lettuce and Radicchios Mix | Calories 87

51) Roasted Squash Puree | Calories 175

81) Peppery Roasted Potatoes With Smoked Bacon | Calories 122

84) Crispy Garlic Baked Potato Wedges | Calories 324

Total Calories 1408

Day 4

1) Smoothie Bowl With Spinach Mango and Muesli | Calories 362

25) High Protein Chicken Meatballs | Calories 519

33) Loaded Caesar Salad With Crunchy Chickpeas | Calories 367

52) Air Fryer Brussels Sprouts | Calories 118

68) Stuffed Meatballs | Calories 112

99) Mini Lava Cakes | Calories 329

Total Calories 1807

Day 6

15) Coconut Coffee and Ghee | Calories 150

27) Overnight Chocolate Chia Pudding | Calories 213

37) Blueberry Cantaloupe Avocado Salad | Calories 406

60) Roasted Root Vegetables | Calories 214

70) Gluten-Free Air Fryer Chicken Fried Brown Rice | Calories 350

93) Marinated Eggs | Calories 289

Total Calories 1622

Chapter 11 - Conclusion

Warning, remember to consult with your medical professional before starting this diet, he/she knows what is best for you and what special requirements you may have.

I hope this cookbook has been useful and that you enjoy it as much as I did when I was writing it and testing it on myself.

In order to get the best results, I recommend you to accompany the diet with an exercise routine and trust in the process, I am sure you will see the results you expect by following these recipes.

I also recommend you to adopt this diet as part of your lifestyle, since it is a diet both in the beginning and in the maintenance of the results. That's right, you will be able to lose weight and stay in shape.

Adopting a healthy lifestyle increases your life expectancy, your quality of life and prevents diseases.

Best wishes,

Lorely McAdams

Lightning Source UK Ltd.
Milton Keynes UK
UKHW031113230821
389329UK00010B/909